WHAT'S WRONG WITH ME?

WHAT'S WRONG WITH ME?

LEARNING DISABILITIES AT HOME AND SCHOOL

REGINA CICCI

YORK
PRESS BALTIMORE

The book was manufactured in the United States of America.
Typography by The Type Shoppe, Inc.
Printing and binding by McNaughton & Gunn.
Cover Design by Joseph Dieter, Jr.

ISBN 0-912752-38-6

Library of Congress Cataloging-in-Publication Data

Cicci, Regina.
    What's wrong with me? : learning disabilities at home and school /
  Regina Cicci.
        p.   cm.
    Includes bibliographical references and index.
    ISBN 0-912752-38-6
    1. Learning disabled children--Education--United States.
  2. Learning disabled children--Education--Language arts.   I. Title.
  LC4705.C53   1993   95-40227
                                                                  CIP

CONTENTS

PREFACE

"What's wrong with me?" is a basic question children and adolescents have as they begin an evaluation process to find out if they have learning disabilities. They have tried as hard as they can and know they should be achieving better in school. They are puzzled and confused about their failures. Parents ask the same question, "What's wrong with me? How could I have provided more, read more, or helped more to prevent such school problems?" Some teachers also question "What's wrong with me?" as they feel unable to reach a child or adolescent who seems so bright and teachable.

Although there is much we do not understand about human learning and its disorders, making continued basic and applied research essential, there is a lot we do know. Individuals with learning disabilities have good ability to learn with many skills and talents to offer. The personal and financial effort and the energy that we invest in such children to help them learn and grow will be returned many times over by their contributions to their families and communities.

Some writers prefer the terms *learning differences* or *learning styles* to *learning disabilities*. I use the term *learning disabilities* because I believe that there is a problem when one cannot learn easily and must struggle to master basic skills. Changing names of conditions does not change the conditions. Individuals who do not learn easily can learn—if they have appropriate help.

As parents and professionals we continue our search to discover more about human learning and must help children understand their unique ways of acquiring knowledge. Parents' and teachers' observations have value before there is research to support them, but we must always remember that

vii

every characteristic seen in individuals with learning disabilities may be seen at one time or another in a developing child or in an adult.

The children and adolescents to be discussed have learning disabilities that many would consider mild to moderate. As I tell parents when they ask for such descriptive words as *mild*, *moderate*, or *severe*, these words are not really helpful descriptors for learning disabilities. All of us would agree that deafness, blindness, kinds of cerebral palsy, mental retardation, or degenerative neurological disease have a severe impact on a child's development. Compared to these conditions, a spoken language problem or reading disability may be regarded as mild. Yet if we use the word *mild* to describe a learning disability we are not considering the impact of the problem on particular children as they grow and learn. Even a mild learning disability can have a severe impact, not only on learning, but on cognitive and emotional growth.

Examples are used throughout the text to illustrate particular problems being discussed. These examples are from children and adolescents who have learning disabilities and are meant to be illustrative only. No one sign or symptom serves to diagnose any problem. When children are discussed by name, each has been given a fictitious name.

This is not a how-to book. Books and articles can provide information, stimulate thinking, and suggest possible courses to explore for teaching and other management. They do not replace diagnoses by competent professionals and instruction by talented teachers. An omission is that there is no chapter on disorders of mathematics. It is not that I regard these problems as unimportant, but rather that I cannot write about such problems with the same sense of confidence as I do about other problems affecting learning.

Chapter 1 is about getting ready for school or the years before first grade. Chapter 2 discusses diagnosis of learning disabilities in a general way. Spoken language disorders are explained in Chapter 3. Chapter 4 presents some ideas about reading and its disorders. Written expressive language disorders are the subject of Chapter 5. Chapter 6 covers issues related to learning that are not necessarily verbal, and Chapter 7 serves as a summary of the ideas introduced previously and offers suggestions especially for those who live and work with individuals with learning disabilities.

I must thank many individuals. Chief among them are Helmer R. Myklebust who first introduced the ideas and Doris J. Johnson who expanded them. Katrina de Hirsch and Jeannette Jefferson Jansky added in major ways to my thinking about the interactions of emotional and cognitive factors in learning.

The professional associations I have had during my years at University of Maryland Hospital have advanced my learning about otolaryngology, pediatrics, and child and adolescent psychiatry. Sharing patients, discussing their unique needs, and finding new ways to meet those needs broadened my understanding of human learning and behavior. Gratitude beyond measure is extended to physicians Theodore H. Kaiser, Raymond L. Clemmens, Alice Heisler, and especially the late Cyrus L. Blanchard; psychologists Mary Joan Albright, Stefanie Bergey, Aden A. Burka, and Thomas J. Kenny; and clinical social workers Victor Fitterman and John Gibbons. I thank Birdie Hack, a fine teacher of young children and volunteer for several projects, for suggestions and for listening. For contributing to the day-to-day pleasure of the job I am indebted to the audiologists and speech-language pathologists of the Audiology and Speech Service at the University of Maryland Hospital. And Charles Suter, Ph.D. offered significant encouragement and help. I also wish to acknowledge Douglas E. Mattox. M.D., Professor and Director, Otolaryngology-Head & Neck Surgery at University of Maryland School of Medicine and Mike F. Nola, Ph.D., Administrator in Otolaryngology-Head & Neck Surgery.

I appreciate the assistance and meticulous attention to detail in the editorial talent of Elinor Hartwig at York Press. Finally, I am grateful to the children; to the parents who have shared their children with me for a little while; and to the teachers who ask good questions and often provide the right answers.

Regina Cicci
Baltimore Maryland
July 1995

CHAPTER 1

GETTING READY FOR SCHOOL
The Preschool Years

Howard Gardner wrote, "Influences may be even more powerful in the early years than later. After all, such improbable bedfellows as Lenin and the Jesuits agreed: 'Give me a child until he is seven and I will give you the man.'"[1] From birth to first grade, children grow more and amass more knowledge than at any other period in their lives. If children fail to learn in critical areas during these years, or if they are deprived of stimulation and healthy interactions with adults, they may never catch up.

Children need the preschool years as a time of exploration and discovery—for general cognitive, language, emotional, and social development that form the undergirdings for the rest of their lives. Character, personality, values, and ideals as well basic knowledge begin to form. Young children search for patterns both nonverbally and verbally. Within this search, the new is related to what is already known, and a skill is practiced until it becomes automatic. This leads to a sense of comfort in mastery. With stimulation and comfortable responses, a young child achieves and learns to value the achievements.

Some children are hurried toward academic success with too great an emphasis placed on letters and numbers for school readiness. Such a practice can be harmful. We should not push children faster than they can manage neurodevelopmentally. All experiences foster learning, not just those activities that involve letters and numbers.

Both nature and nurture contribute to the person a young child becomes. From the genetic pool provided by the child's ancestors come inherited traits. Special talents, learning abilities and disabilities, characteristics such as eye color, body build, and a tendency toward acquiring certain diseases may be determined by these traits. If parents were poor students with difficulty learning, their child may have similar learning patterns.

Parents, by choice or chance, provide an environment in which their child will grow. Influenced by their personality structures, educational levels, and value systems they choose the persons, objects, and activities that form the world that their young child experiences. How a baby's needs are met, what responses are made to cries, how much talk is provided, what words, books, and objects are supplied, and what kinds of play are fostered or stifled, all influence development.

EARLY NONVERBAL LEARNING

Piaget[2] classified the earliest stage of cognitive development as sensory motor. An infant uses the senses of seeing, hearing, touching, tasting, and smelling combined with motor movements to learn about the world. This nonverbal cognition has been referred to as *inner language*[3] and includes all of what we know even before we have the words to think verbally about an experience or to talk about it. While a child is experiencing the personal world through sensory motor exploration, the beginnings of thought and the development of trust in other humans occur.

By exploring many kinds of objects, children develop nonverbal problem-solving abilities and a sense of control over the environment. When they perform an action, a consequence results. Young babies learn that if they pound the high-chair tray with a spoon or toy it will make a satisfyingly loud sound. If an object is hard, they strike with it; if it is soft, they pat it; if it makes a noise, they seek to repeat the sound. The baby is having an impact on the world and is learning what causes an object to drop, make a noise, or break.

The baby begins to learn about object permanence, which means that if an object drops from the high-chair tray, slips under a blanket, or falls out of the crib, it still exists. This is a gigantic discovery. As babies learn that objects still exist even if not seen, they also learn that when adults cannot be seen they continue to exist. During this time, babies learn that the nurturing figures or caregivers will come back when they go away. So along with learning that objects have permanence even when they can no longer be seen, human infants learn that other objects called Mommy and Daddy will return and meet their needs. They will relieve discomfort and provide pleasure. Babies learn to trust by knowing that adults are present, that they can be counted on, and that they will unconditionally provide nurture.[4, 5]

Before a year of age, babies find out much about the environment and the objects and people in it. They learn while in the high chair, crib, and playpen, and by crawling around the floor. Motor activity including exploration of toys and furniture; figuring out how things work; solving nonverbal problems; using large motor movements to climb and tumble and fall; and small motor movements to pick up small things—all of these influence children's understanding of the world, their place in it, and their effect on it.

A young child's world is tremendously expanded with the first step, around the time of the first birthday. There is so much more to learn once the child can walk. More objects can be reached, pushed, pulled, and broken. During this sensory motor period, curious children learn about the nonverbal domain as objects are experienced through, and appreciated by, the senses. Experiences can be organized and classified, and objects and events can be controlled by interactions with them.

HEARING AND EARLY LANGUAGE LEARNING
Sounds and Early Speech and Early Speech Comprehension

Simultaneously, as nonverbal experiences occur, babies respond to sounds. Infants' early responses to sound are primarily reflexive, as when newborns startle to a loud sound. Early in life, however, babies show consistent responses to many kinds of sound. They respond differently to their mother's voices and other women's voices. Their responses include arousal, body movements orienting toward the source of sound, facial grimacing, and initiation or cessation of an act such as crying or sucking.[6] Babies in newborn nurseries perceive small differences in speech sounds.[7] They are able to discriminate between such similar syllables as "pah" and "bah," where the *p* is voiceless and the *b* is voiced. And they localize sound; they locate it by turning to its source.

They begin to discriminate among different sounds and to attach meaning to them. The opening of a door, the ring of a telephone, the sound of a car in the driveway, the turn of a key in a lock all have meanings and incite responses. Babies quickly realize that certain sets of sounds represent specific experiences, and thus, they begin to understand speech. During the first year of life, they understand some words and phrases, will wave bye-bye, make pat-a-cake, and reach toward a familiar person when told to go to *Mommy* or *Daddy*. Increasingly, they learn to associate words with objects, actions, and experiences. They begin to discover that these objects and experiences can be represented by words.

Beginning Speech Production

The acquisition of speech is a remarkable feature of our being human and is easy to take for granted. Through cries, cooing, and other vocal noises, a baby communicates with the mother. These sounds become differentiated and let the caregiver know if the baby is satisfied, hungry, or hurting. Quite by accident, babies make sounds as they play with the mechanisms for speech—the lips, teeth, tongue, hard and soft palates, and vocal folds. If they make the same movements again, they can repeat the sounds. This vocal play gives them pleasure. Then, as parents or other caregivers imitate what the baby does in vocal play, he or she wants to repeat it and get a response from an adult. In this process of discovery, babies produce many sounds in early babbling that occur in languages other than the one they will learn as their own. As some of the sounds are reinforced, they remain in the array of sounds that babies produce, while other disappear. With their production of sounds and attempts to communicate, babies begin to show the human drive to be like other humans through interactive play with sounds—the beginnings of speech.

Some young children, even before they say the first word may use a speech sound to suggest different meanings. For example they may say "a" to represent the word *that*. They may use a downward inflection with the "a!" as a strong statement meaning "I want that!" or "I want no other but that!" or use a questioning inflection in the "a?" to mean "What is that? Tell me, and tell me right now." This is a fascinating stage and leaves observant first-time parents or novice observers of speech development in awe of what can be communicated directly by children before they use real words. This purposeful communication is different from earlier cries that were involuntary and indicated hunger or discomfort.

First Word Combinations

When young children have mastered some single words, they begin to combine them. At first they are bumped together to represent thoughts and ideas. These combinations are pre-sentences and can have different meanings depending on the situation. Children may begin to use a noun with another word for communicating various ideas, such as "car broke," "car dirty," "eat cookie," or "want juice." "Daddy shoe" said by a two-year-old child may mean, "Daddy, where is my shoe?" or "Daddy, I want my shoe" or "That is Daddy's shoe" or "Daddy, my shoe is lost, dirty, under the bed, or being chewed by the dog." Gradually words are added and toddlers put words in an order that conveys meaning.

While listening to children during this period of development, we hear them combine words in novel ways, in ways that they have not heard said by anyone. This use of grammar that is not imitated but created by the child, with errors he or she can never have heard from an adult's speech, supports Chomsky's notion of universal grammar[8] and Pinker's of language acquisition as an instinct.[9] Pinker writes that as spiders weave webs because they have spider brains, humans use language because they have human brains. It is as though each human child is programmed to discover his or her own language system.

Expanding Word Combinations

As children combine words, they may correctly say "I ran" or "I ate" or "I went," but as they become more consciously aware of the rule of adding -*ed* for past tense they may go through a period of saying " I runned" or "I eated" or "I goed," or as a 5-year-old boy bitterly complained. "She fighted me and she bited me!" Another young child was not pleased with his drawing of a line that was not straight. He said with disgust "I crookeded it!" Such errors illustrate how young children develop awareness and sophistication about the rules of grammar and how words are used.

We do not teach children directly that in English an adjective precedes a noun, while in other languages the adjective may follow the noun. Children who acquire language easily don't need to be taught about the order of words in sentences, that we say *big house* not *house big*. They also learn that adjectives are arranged in order before a noun. They learn to use such structures as "I can run" and "Can I run?" appropriately. They learn that "a boy chases a dog" and "a dog chases a boy" are not the same. They learn that subjects must agree with verbs. "A boy jumps," but "Boys jump." They begin to use transition words such as *then* and *last*. The appropriate use of syntax for the language to which children are exposed begins as soon as they put two words together, and by the time they start to school they know an amazing amount about grammar. They have many of the grammatical structures they will use throughout their lives.

Extending Word Meanings

Although syntax may be well developed by school age, vocabulary continues to enlarge throughout our lives. We can always learn a new word or have new associations to words first learned in preschool years.

As preschool children develop, they learn multiple meanings of words. For example, they discover that there is a color called *blue* that can refer to blue car, blue eyes, blue sky, that something can come from *out of the blue*, and that one who is sad might *feel blue*.

Words can be used as actions and as names of things, and sometimes both. You *drink* milk but milk is *a drink*. A *circle* is a round shape, but the word also expresses an action, as in *circle the answer*. A *match* is something a child must never play with, but *match* also means to find another one just like a target. Knowing that words can be used in different ways occurs early in preschool years. A 29-month-old girl walked around thoughtfully saying "I pet the cat. My cat is a pet. My cat is a pet. I pet the cat." She was expressing both puzzlement and interest in the beginning recognition of words as different parts of speech, even when they are said the same way.

Children also learn the meaning of function words. Function words, or connective words, such as conjunctions and prepositions can best be understood in context, or in relation to other words. Children acquire the meaning of these words as the words are embedded in the syntax of the language. For instance, *and*, *but*, *to*, *on* and words that express the negative such as *not*, have little meaning by themselves; they have meaning within a sentence. The experience or event for the word *on* varies with the context. Standing *on* a table, a box, or the floor is a different experience from "putting me on" or "being on a roll." The word, spoken or written, is the same, but the experience is different. Other function words suggest how actions and events occur over time such as *first* and *then*.

Words and concepts related to time, space, quantity, and distance are learned as individual words but also as part of grammar. "Wait a minute." "Hurry! We'll be late." "Maybe later." "You can do it after your nap." "Take just one." "You can have two pieces." "Eat just a few peas." "Do you want more milk?" "We'll cut it in half so you can share it." "That is too big." "You are getting so big, your shirt is too little."

Later, children learn that words may have unclear meanings. "Maybe we'll go to the mall" does not mean "for sure." A word such as *near* can mean an inch away, in the same house, or the same city. Children experience both clarity and confusion in the process of learning their language, just as in all learning.

The Importance of Early Verbal Play and Reinforcement

Babies may be programmed to develop language, but language development also requires reinforcement from caring adults. It is because the infant relates to humans that he or she wants to share the unique human act of speech. In the recent past, when babies were kept in large institutions where they were cared for physically, but were not verbally stimulated or played with, they did not develop normally in any way, including aquiring language. From time to time we read about children who are cruelly deprived of stimulation, being tied to chairs or locked in closets. They not only fail to develop language but may not show what we consider intelligence. A recent case that has been widely reported is that of a child referred to as "Genie."[10]

The Power of Early Speech

Young children understand and produce language by acquiring the symbols or words of their language. They learn that words are strung together in a certain order, and that there is an almost magical quality about the power of speech. Speech can control others, solve problems, request help, and offer assistance. Once preschool children learn words, they have a tool that they can use to communicate, manipulate, and satisfy others as well as themselves.

LEARNING THROUGH PLAY

After basic sensory motor exploration, an essential part of a preschool child's life is play. Through play, new learning is practiced, intelligence developed, and personality formed. It is exciting to watch children at play, because their actions demonstrate what they think and feel. Children learn about objects, including toys, by exploring. They see, hear, touch, taste, and smell. At first they explore by chance. Then they begin to manipulate objects in a more purposeful way.

Curiosity satisfied by exploration lets children learn about materials and what can be done with them. Clay can be rolled, pushed, pounded, flattened, made into a snake-like form, a ball, or a pancake. Sand and water can fit in some containers, such as a cup but will spill through others, such as a funnel or a strainer. It can be great fun to pile blocks up and even greater fun to knock them down. If a toy car is pushed, it will bump into a barrier such as a table leg or Daddy's foot, and if a car is driven to the very edge of a table, it will fall off. Crayons make wonderful marks on paper, and these marks and scribbles draw praise. Thus, children begin to create products during their play.

Symbolic or Pretend Play

Another form of symbolic functioning, in addition to words, is symbolic play or pretending. Children pretend that an object is something other than what it really is. They develop representation in play as well as in language. At about the time they begin to combine words they may use a stick to represent a horn, or a block to stand for a car, a teapot, or a birthday cake. One eighteen month-old-child walked around shaking a kaleidoscope over various objects saying "aw-aw" pretending it was a shaker of salt (the "aw" sound being the child's approximation of *salt*).

Children pretend with objects, but they also pretend by assuming roles. They develop a sense of "as-if," behaving as if they are in other situations as they pretend to read a book or newspaper, sweep the floor, or drive a car. They assume roles as cook or mommy or train engineer or controller of airplanes, spaceships, or weapons. Sometimes parents may be horrified as they see some of their habits being acted out by a child of two or three years.

Young children can play out scary events and happy ones. When preschool children return from the doctor, they may take their blocks and toys and repeatedly play being at the doctor's. After a birthday party, they may pretend to have a party, complete with a block being used as a cake with candles to be blown out. Through their play they recapture both discomforts and pleasures.

A child's understanding of what is real versus what is make-believe develops gradually over the preschool years. Aden Burka, a clinical psychologist and father, gives the example of reading a story to his 3 1/2-year-old daughter.[11] In the story there is a wicked wolf who tries to scare some ducks. At the end of the story, his daughter asked her father to put the book outside her door. He talked with her about the story's not being real, and she understood. She informed him that she knew the story was not real, but asked that he put the book outside the door anyway. When he asked why, she responded, "Just in case you're wrong." Fantasy and make-believe were not yet quite separated from reality.

Preferred Objects for Play and Learning

Preschool children like blocks, sand, water, dolls, cars and trucks and trains, small representations of adult objects, dress-up clothes, pots and pans, crayons and paper, and books. They are curious and not bored by repetitive play as they constantly try out new ways to play with an object. As they practice, they develop mastery.

Children learn most by playing with toys that can be used in many ways and permit discovery and imagination. Some, such as building blocks, allow children to develop fantasy. Block construction can extend to middle childhood years, while a battery-operated single-function toy may be relegated to the trash heap.

As children grow, they will become interested in games with rules, such as board games, card games, computer games, and athletic activities; however, in the preschool years they learn by exploring, solving problems, constructing imaginative objects, and pretending. They practice motor skills and learn a sense of control over objects and events. Play allows experimentation and also enables a child to express feelings by playing them out when words are not yet available.

FURTHER READINESS FOR SCHOOL

Learning to play and to use language begin the preparation for school. Learning letters and numbers at 18 months or being taught to read at age 3 is not necessary. Some children do teach themselves to read at an early age and demand to have letters and words that they see on cereal boxes, street signs, and grocer's shelves pronounced for them. But by the end of second grade, such children do not necessarily read better than those who learn to crack the code of reading in first grade.

Young children need to acquire a wide background of experiences and knowledge of vocabulary and concepts. They gain vitally important knowledge to support later reading, writing, and arithmetic learning, even if specific letters and numbers are not learned early.

Phonological Development Related to Pre-Reading

Children enjoy playing with speech and speech sounds. Some love rhymes and rhythmic presentation of material. They may begin to rhyme words on their own and regard this as fun. As they become more skilled in using language, they become aware of fine differences in the way words sound. Most children quickly and easily learn how minor differences change the meaning of a combination of speech sounds. Thus, *bat* does not mean the same as *bad*, nor *big* the same as *bug*. Young children may begin to recognize how words sound alike and how a beginning or ending sound can be changed to make a different word. *Man* can change to *fan*, and *fan* to *fat*. Attending to these differences in speech affects a child's understanding of the meanings of words and also prepares a child for a later step in language development—to learn to superimpose print on the sounds of speech in order to read.

Other Reading Readiness

Children who are ready to learn to read in first grade are ready because of the knowledge gained in the areas just discussed. Some preschoolers will ask names of letters and show interest in them. As parents read to them, children may notice that, as words sound the same to the ear, they also look the same in print.

The ability to name letters is a predictor of those children who read at the end of second grade.[12, 13, 14] However, the capacity to name letters reflects a complex combination of knowledge that a child has acquired both about sounds of speech and visual representations of letters. Children should not be pushed to learn letter names and sounds before they are ready. Parents and nursery school teachers need to be careful about insisting that children participate in reading readiness activities if they cannot find them satisfying, which generally means comfortably mastered. Requiring children to learn letter names and sounds can make those who are not ready for such tasks turn away from print. Such emotional reactions will then need to be dealt with before serious attempts can be made to teach reading.

One 5-year-old girl began to push away any papers with letters on them. That she had the concept of "letterness" was evident—she pushed away only materials with letters and words, not other kinds of papers, including those with numbers. She was fully cooperative and showed joy in play and even in paper work as long as the papers had no letters. She was moved to a kindergarten that was flexible and encouraged general development. Neither at home nor school was any focus placed on learning letters. Indeed, for a few weeks she was not shown any print at all, but stories continued to be read to her. At close to 6 years of age, she was encouraged to draw pictures and gradually to tell a tutor what to write about the pictures. Then she was shown books with easy stories. She began to see reading as an activity at which she could be successful. By the beginning of second grade she was reading well. These changes, easily made, required understanding parents, flexible school personnel, and a gifted teacher who was willing to move quite slowly in proving to the child that she could learn to read and that she no longer had to be afraid of letters.

Children should not be forced to acquire auditory skills—or those skills that are referred to as phonological awareness—too soon. Forcing them to try before they are ready is doomed to fail and to extinguish a child's desire to learn. With that caution, some suggestions are made in Chapter 4 for activities to develop phonological awareness as a prerequisite to reading. They can be used with preschool children who are interested and ready.

Exposure to letter sounds and their names in print can be presented as play. Using alphabet books can be fun, and many wonderful ones are available. Illustrations are often exciting, beautiful, and informative. Children enjoy looking at such books repeatedly, and in doing so, may learn letter names and sounds with little effort.

Along with acquiring language and learning about objects, young children also learn how to relate to others. They develop a sense of trust and begin to appreciate how valuable one person is to others. They learn appropriate ways to behave with peers, family members, and others. They learn to take turns, ask for help, assist others by doing small chores, and become social beings.

WHEN THINGS GO WRONG

In early life, the brain and the rest of the central nervous system continue to develop as infants and young children learn continually from their experiences. Some children will learn more easily than others. Parents, particularly with a first child, may not know how to judge if their child's progress is normal. The section that follows deals with developmental problems and may help parents consider how their child compares with others, and it provides suggestions about consulting professionals.

Motor and Sensory Deficits

Problems with motor functioning are generally noticed early by parents, particularly if the baby is not a first child. Professionals observe such problems in the first hours of life for the broad group of disorders regarded as cerebral palsy. Reaching motor milestones of sitting, crawling, and walking help us see if babies are developing motor skills as expected. More subtle motor problems may emerge later.

Children with sensory impairments can be identified early. Hearing screening is carried out with many high-risk newborns before they leave hospital nurseries. Children with severe hearing impairment do not respond normally to environmental sounds. For example, they may not startle to a loud noise. Or they might respond to very loud sounds but be unresponsive to voices unless looking at the speaker's face. Milder problems with hearing in preschool years can arise because of ear infections, and these mild hearing losses may affect the child's language development.[15]

Babies with normal vision begin looking all around them. At a very early age when placed on their stomachs they lift their heads to see the fascinating world. Babies with severe visual disturbance can be identified early, but mild problems may not be noticed until later in preschool years. If there is any question about a young child's language, learning, or about development, professionals should assess hearing, vision, and if necessary, motor skills.

Temperamental Differences

Babies are born with different temperaments. From birth, some are calm and easy while others are tense and difficult to soothe. Thomas and Chess reported early work on temperament in infants.[16] Mothers need to know that some babies are difficult and it is not their fault. It is just the way the baby is. Most babies are responsive to cuddling and can be soothed by a parent's calming voice, but others become stiff and reject being held. A child-health professional may need to be consulted about problems in this area, especially when mothers find it hard to adapt to difficult babies.

Global Lags in Development

Different problems are noted at different times because of a particular developmental milestone and its age of expectation. Pediatricians, because of their experiences, can diagnose motor delays and detect signs of early problems with sensory functioning. Some babies are delayed in all areas of development, do not meet motor milestones at expected times, and, although they can see and hear, do not understand verbal and nonverbal cues well, and are delayed in starting to talk. Such children may be mentally retarded, cognitively limited, mentally challenged, or whatever current term one chooses to apply. Their learning difficulties relate to their cognitive functioning.

Uneven Development

Some children have uneven development. They may excel in verbal skills but lag behind for visual-motor ones, or they may be adept at visual-spatial-motor activities and show a language delay. Children with uneven development in preschool years are often those who will have learning disabilities at school age. But parents need to be aware that throughout childhood there are wide ranges of normal behavior. For example, children between the ages of 18 months and 3 years may show marked differences of language comprehension and production. One 2-year-old child may use only single words while another may speak in paragraphs, but six months later these two toddlers may show the same language patterns. Because of such ranges in average or normal development, child experts often recommend that parents "wait and see." But when parents have concerns, they need to have their questions answered. There are now public programs throughout the country for children, from birth to age 3, who have developmental problems. Such programs are found in public schools and ideally involve cooperation between health and education resources.

There can be delays in receiving special services. Children are being denied services because their problems are not regarded as severe enough to warrant supplemental help, but the preschool years are times when maximum stimulation geared to each child's needs is essential. If public services are not made available, parents may need to seek private resources which can include speech and language intervention for verbal problems and physical and occupational therapy for motor difficulties.

Language Comprehension Problems

As difficult as life might be for the child who has a speech or expressive language disorder, the child with deficient receptive language has even greater problems. Receptive language disorders are problems with understanding language, with attaching meaning to what is heard. Young children with such problems may have difficulty being soothed by words and understanding explanations of discipline. They may be confused about words used at play and with new vocabulary and verbal concepts, or they may have trouble following oral directions or interpreting questions. In addition, they may be overwhelmed by too much talking and be unable to sort out meaningful parts of messages. Although exposing most children to a rich input of language is desirable, too much talking can create confusion for the child who fails to comprehend language.

As an example, here are the responses of a 5-year-old child with a receptive language disorder when asked some questions:

What is a pencil?	"write it"
What is a fork?	"time for dinner"
What do we hear with?	"a radio"
What do we use our eyes for?	"brown"
What does ice become when it melts?	"gets all sticky"

The child provided answers, but did not understand the questions fully.

Some children with severe communication disorders are hyperactive. In some instances, a receptive language disorder can cause overactive behavior. With little understanding of the language they hear, children may be overly active in order to maintain adult attention; others may not be still long enough to take in the language around them and will require structure of their world until they can structure themselves.

Oral Expressive Language Problems

When preschool children cannot easily communicate with speech that is understood by others, they will attempt to communicate in any way they can. Such attempts may take the form of hitting or having a tantrum. Language helps very young children control their thinking and behaving. With inadequate language development, they may become disorganized, confused, and difficult to manage; in addition they will have trouble communicating.

Dysfluencies, repetitions in speech, or stuttering. As children begin to use sentences, they may repeat words or the beginnings of words or phrases. These dysfluencies occur as part of normal language development in some children, but not in others. Although this is probably a stage of normal development, parents should discuss their questions with their pediatrician and with a speech-language pathologist or speech therapist if concerns persist. The responses to such queries may be reassurances only, but management techniques may also be suggested.

Problems with speech production or articulation. A child may have a problem with articulation or pronouncing the sounds of speech. Children learn to say sounds such as *p, b, m, t, d,* and *n* early. Normally, children are later in acquiring the sounds of *r, th* and *s.*

It is generally agreed that articulation or pronunciation of speech sounds follows a progression. Vowels and *m, b, p, k, g, w, h, n, t, d* emerge at 1 to 2 years. A child masters these previous sounds and tries *f, v, th, s, z,* and some *r* and *l* blends at 3 to 4 years. He or she masters the previous sounds and *f* and *v* at about 4 to 5 years and *l, r, th,* and *l* and *r* blends at 5 to 6 years. All speech sounds are mastered by most children by about 7 1/2 years including *s, sh, ch, j,* and voiced and voiceless *th.*

Parents become so accustomed to hearing their children's speech that they may not notice that others do not understand what the child says. Even with articulation errors 3- and 4-year-old children can be understood by adults who are accustomed to the speech of developing children. When children are about 4 years of age their speech should be understood by adults who do not know them well.

When articulation is evaluated, it is essential to consider not only defective sounds of speech but to obtain a measure of how well the child can be understood—a measure of intelligibility. Some children can imitate nearly all speech sounds correctly, alone or in words, but have unintelligible speech when they put words together in phrases or sentences. Speech must be evaluated by considering single sounds in isolation and in words, but it is essential to evaluate if the child can be understood when he or she talks in sentences. If a child has speech that cannot be understood when speaking spontaneously, intervention is necessary.

Expressive syntax problems. When children first begin to combine words, they do not necessarily follow adult rules of grammar, but they quickly learn about the grammar of their language. By the age of about 4 years they have mastered many of the complexities of the grammar system. About this time, they may make mistakes in grammar but they have internalized many rules. If a child is not using correct grammar most of the time by age four, there may be reason for concern.

Particular attention needs to be paid to the word order (*come here* not *here come*), subject-verb agreement (*the boy walks* not *boy walk* and *boys walk* not *boyzez walks*), the presence of the function words or the little words such as *is* (*the kid is looking at the plant*, not *the kid looking at plant*), or *are* (*they are walking to school* not *they walking*), and the use of conjunctions such as *and* and *but*, and prepositions such as *to* or *in* (*he goes to the doctor* not *he go doctor* or *leaves go in the bag* not *leaves go bag*). "Mommy car" may be acceptable when a 2-year-old child wants to ride in a car, but this same construction at age 4 could suggest a problem.

Word retrieval problems. Another difficulty that occurs often in children with language impairment is a word-finding problem. The desired word is in the child's vocabulary, but cannot be recalled quickly for use. This problem with retrieval is most commonly seen when a specific word is needed. For example, the most specific words that we use are persons' names, so names may cause children particular difficulty. Color words are also specific. When *red* is called for, *blue* is not acceptable. Once when I was working with a group of 4-year-old language impaired children, a child wanted to demonstrate how well he had learned the colors. I showed him a swatch of red and he said "ketchup," for yellow he said "butter," and for green, "grass." He had learned associations, but could not yet retrieve the specific color words. Many preschool children with expressive language disorders have a difficult time with color names. If children have such retrieval problems in their preschool years, they may have difficulty quickly recalling names and sounds of printed letters later on.

COMMON MYTHS ABOUT EARLY LANGUAGE AND SPEECH PROBLEMS

Some common myths about early development should be put to rest. The following statements may be true some of the time, but for the most part are false.

*   *Wait! He or she will outgrow the problem.* We cannot be sure of this. Some will. Many won't. Children often benefit from immediate inter-

vention. Parents can profit from suggestions for home management that encourage the development of communication.

- *He or she is too young to be tested.* This is never true. Hearing can be tested in infants; language comprehension, play behavior, and social interaction can be assessed even if the child is not yet talking.
- *He or she is not talking so there cannot be a speech evaluation.* But we can evaluate language comprehension and pre-speech behavior. Suggestions can be made for helping to initiate speech, or the youngster may benefit from a parent-child or other early intervention program.
- *The problem is that all needs are anticipated, so there is no need to talk.* Actually, to communicate through language appears to be a fundamental human drive. It is as natural for a child to talk as it is to walk if the child is in a nurturing and stimulating environment.
- *He or she is imitating an older brother with poor speech.* A child is not likely to choose to imitate a defective speech model when correct models are present.
- *He's a boy. Boys are later to speak than girls.* Some studies do indicate that girls speak earlier than boys, but this does not mean by many months. If parents have concerns, preschool boys as well as girls should be seen for professional consultation.
- *He or she is just stubborn. The child could do it if he or she wanted to.* The seeming stubbornness may come from a child's failure with verbal communication and the frustration that results from such failure.
- *He or she is deprived or disadvantaged.* Deprivation, neglect, and abuse are always considered when children live in chaotic homes or when there is failure to thrive. Neglect or abuse can cause problems with all development including learning language and speech. However, children in such situations do need intervention and referral to appropriate educational resources while the other problems are being managed. It is important that dialect speech patterns, bilingualism, and cultural differences not be confused with disadvantage and deprivation.
- *He or she is retarded and that accounts for the speech delay.* Maybe—but severe hearing impairment is still sometimes mistaken for retardation, so it is important to assess hearing in speech-delayed children. Also, there may be a discrepancy between mental ability and the understanding and use of language. Early specific help in language and speech may help mentally retarded children use their cognitive potentials in maximal ways.
- *He or she is emotionally disturbed, which causes the speech problem.* This may be true, but an assessment of speech and language functioning can be important to assist in an overall management plan. Emotional problems and language problems can co-occur. Also, documentation of

language use can be helpful in later years when growth is being evaluated.

- *It's just a developmental problem.* This statement is used in so many ways that it has little value, and it can be harmful if it delays treatment. Developmental problems do not necessarily go away without any help, and you cannot count on a child's outgrowing a developmental problem. When a child has a developmental disorder, it does not imply that he or she will get better or outgrow the problem with no intervention.

- *Wait until he or she gets to school.* Early problems need immediate attention for optimal learning. Weak motor skills can be helped by physical or occupational therapy. Speech and language can be improved through a structured program, along with suggestions to parents for stimulating speech and language at home. Services for young children are available in public schools, but parents may need assistance to gain access to them.

- *He or she is immature.* This is not a helpful statement for parents. Immature in what way? Socially? Emotionally? Behaviorally? Linguistically? Spatially? Perceptually? Does this statement imply that maturity will appear without any intervention? Parents need to be sure what the words mean.

WHEN PARENTS SHOULD SEEK PROFESSIONAL CONSULTATION

If parents have concerns about their children's development they should seek help. The pediatrician is usually the first person to consult about a young child. Because developing a standard of what is normal and what is not takes experience with many babies and children, parents of young children are wise to have a pediatrician, family doctor, or nurse practitioner to whom they can turn. Such health-care professionals recognize normal development, and they are experienced in suggesting management at different stages of growth. Wonderful, agreeable babies do turn into terrors around the age of two, and at various times as they grow, children surprise parents with unusual behaviors and interests. Those who spend their lives working with children know how to interview them. They know what is outside the range of acceptability and can be helpful to both children and to their parents. They can reassure parents, suggest ways of encouraging development, tell whether additional professional consultations are necessary, and most of the time, they can refer the parents and child to appropriate community resources.

A common complaint is that pediatricians do not identify language and learning problems. But ask parents if they have ever discussed the language or learning problem with their pediatrician, and they often say that these are not medical problems, so of course are not discussed with the doctor. Even if they are not experts in language disorders, behavioral differences, or social–emotional difficulties in young children, primary health care providers can refer parents to appropriate community resources.

Children with learning problems who regularly see one primary health provider, even when they are well, are better off than those who see a doctor only when they are sick. Knowing a family's expectations and values allows professionals to be of immediate help if parents have concerns. Health care and recommendations are more consistent when a child is seen by the same individual or group over time.

Well-child visits are brief. Many pediatricians will arrange extended appointments, but parents must first express their concerns. Pediatricians and pediatric nurse practitioners know early development well and understand that parents need to ask questions. They recognize that this particular child is the most important child in the whole world for this set of parents. They are respectful of parents' questions. Most of the time they enjoy children and appreciate parents. But many do specialize and not all are expert in the many developmental disorders of young children; therefore, when parents feel they are not getting enough help from the doctor or nurse practitioner, they should ask for a referral to a professional who specializes in their area of concern. Under managed care in the health professions, limitations in making referrals may be imposed on primary-care providers. Parents may need to consider what is best for their child by way of consultation, rather than whether or not a service is covered by health insurance. Because a condition is not covered by health insurance does not mean the condition does not exist, and if a service for children is not paid for by health insurance it does not mean the service is unnecessary for a particular child. Often it is worth the financial investment to learn if a child is developing typically in understanding, in talking, or in learning, and, if not, what can be done to help.

A speech–language pathologist is the appropriate person to consult if there is suspicion of a speech or language delay. Physical therapists can be of help with problems in motor development. Occupational therapists may also offer assistance for some fine motor skills that precede handwriting. Early childhood specialists are on school teams. Public school systems now have programs for children experiencing developmental difficulties in the years from birth to age three. Services do exist, but parents may need to be resourceful to find them.

WHICH CHILDREN SHOULD BE DISCUSSED WITH THE PEDIATRICIAN AND/OR REFERRED FOR FURTHER ASSESSMENT?

- Children who are delayed in meeting such motor milestones as sitting at about six to eight months or walking by 12 to 16 months.

- Children who do not respond visually to objects and people in the environment.
- Children, who from birth, or at any age, show deviations in their responses to sound. They may not respond at all; they may respond inconsistently; or they may be hypersensitive to sound.
- Babies who show little vocal play in the early months of life. They should coo, babble, and show a wide variation of play with speech sounds.
- Babies who do not like to be held or who tense their bodies when held.
- Children who push adults away, who seem to have no interest in people.
- Children who are never still and seem never to be satisfied.
- Children with recurrent middle ear disease.
- Children who have no real words at age 2.
- Children who are not combining words by age 3.
- Children at 4 years of age whose speech cannot be understood most of the time by strangers.
- Children who "don't listen" or who have trouble following directions when compared with age-mates. We must be particularly aware of those who seem to follow directions only "when they want to." Such children may have basic problems with language comprehension but can at times interpret parts of the message.
- Children whose use of vocabulary is deficient when compared with peers.
- Children who repeat, or echo, everything they hear but with little understanding. Such children may recite the Pledge of Allegiance and know many TV commercials, may be able to read words in print, but cannot follow simple oral directions or understand words they read.
- Children who have difficulty in formulating sentences after about 4 years of age. They may omit words, leave off word endings, or confuse word order.
- Children who, when attempting to tell about something important, cannot retrieve specific words for use. They may give an associated response (for example, saying *fork* for *knife*), excessively use general terms (such as *stuff* and *thing*), give the function of the object (such as *pounding thing* for hammer), or mix up sounds (such as saying "rabby bunnit" for *bunny rabbit*). Or they might shrug their shoulders and walk away from communication situations.
- Children who talk spontaneously but do not respond in a give-and-take conversational way, respond to questions, or follow conversation when direct responses are expected.
- Children who never want to have stories read to them.
- Children who reject all puzzles, small blocks, and crayons or markers.

- Children of any age whose parents are concerned about their development of motor skills, hearing and vision, language, speech, learning, or about their relating to other children in age-appropriate ways.

WHAT CAN PARENTS AND OTHER ADULTS DO?

The following suggestions are for parents, day-care providers, teachers, nannies, and baby-sitters in their work with young children.

General Recommendations

- Use repetition. Repetition is needed for learning by all children, but especially for children who do not learn easily. Through practice, skills become automatic. Children who have problems may take longer to master a task or may show no interest initially, and so must be encouraged in small steps.
- Provide a rich environment. Have objects available that encourage exploration through the senses—things to see, hear, touch, smell, and taste.
- Avoid overstimulation, having too much going on at one time such as talking or loud music. Everyone, even a young child, needs quiet time.
- As a parent or playful adult, be careful of dangerous practices such as throwing babies up in the air, holding them upside down, shaking them, or yanking them by their arms. These activities can be harmful to young children even if the intent is playful.
- Encourage hiding things and finding them. For example, cover a toy with a blanket and encourage the child to look for it under the blanket. This gives practice in the notion that objects have a permanence, that out-of-sight does not mean the objects no longer exist.
- Encourage imitation. Use pat-a-cake, body movements, facial grimaces, and games of "you do what I do."
- Encourage imitation of speech sounds. If the baby makes a sound, parents should repeat it immediately. This parental imitation of a baby's speech sounds encourages him or her to make more speech sounds.
- Encourage your child to notice things—to find all round things or square things, red things, hard things, soft things. You cannot and should not stop a developing preschooler from being curious, from noticing things, from exploring, from finding out how things work. Children with learning problems often need help in noticing how things look, sound, and move. They may also require help in learning how to play—to use objects, to recognize cause and effect, and to pretend.
- Stop any activity before your child becomes tired.
- Provide tools and materials that can be used in multiple ways to encourage fantasy and imagination. One-purpose toys do not allow for such learning.

- Allow exploration, but teach new skills. Children cannot be creative until certain skills are present. The ability to roll clay, move a pencil, cut with scissors, or hold a brush are necessary before a child can go further in imaginative ways. Some learning disabled children may never learn if allowed to progress at their own rate. They need intervention and help to learn what is easily mastered by most children.
- If a child shows no interest in objects, put them away for two weeks or a month, but do get them out again. When tasks are hard, there is a human tendency to avoid them. Children acquire this pattern at a young age. Exploring the world of the senses and exploring play with language are essential parts of growth and of building a foundation for later learning in school. A child who was never interested in Dr. Seuss at a young age may love the books later, either to be read aloud by parents, or to read on his or her own. The same is true of blocks. The child who was not interested in small plastic building blocks at age 4 may be mesmerized by them later. Continue to re-introduce activities that have at first been refused.
- Children need organization and consistent schedules so they can begin to learn the value and importance of organization. Without organization there is chaos.
- From early on, teach clean up. Show that appropriate containers hold objects and provide appropriate shelves for books and toys. This helps children begin to develop organization skills.
- As a child becomes part of a group in day-care or nursery school, be sure he or she understands the language used—not in imitation, not because gestures or pictures are used, not because it is time for juice and cookies—but because of a real understanding of vocabulary, commands, and instructions.
- Many children who have trouble learning are very bright, attractive youngsters from advantaged homes. Care must be taken that these problems are not denied because "*such* children do not have learning problems."
- Take time to have fun with young children. If you have a single-parent household or if both parents work outside the home, there is a tendency to take time only for essentials. Spend some time—if only 10 minutes a day—for activities that are a pleasure for both you and your child. Unlike older children, preschoolers have a sense of egocentrism, of believing themselves to be the center of the universe, so they demand attention.

Stimulating Speech and Language

- When children show articulation problems and do not say sounds correctly, consult with a speech-language pathologist. There are different kinds of problems with articulation. Some errors with saying sounds are appropriate for a particular stage of development. When a 3-year-old child says all sounds correctly, except for /r/ as "wabbit" for *rabbit*, we are not concerned. But if a 3-year-old has many incorrectly produced sounds, then speech therapy may be necessary. Preschool children require speech therapy if they show deviations in production of speech sounds—if they do not correctly say sounds expected for their developmental age.

- Be sure the speech-language pathologist comments on intelligibility of speech—how well the child is understood. Speech is communication. It has little value if it is not understood by others. It is important that the speech pathologist who works with preschool children is experienced with children of this age.

- If your child has marked problems with speech production, teach him or her stock phrases such as "Help me," "I want - - -," "please," "I hurt my - - -," "Give me - - -," so he or she can communicate needs in ways that can be understood.

- Talk about what you are doing while you are engaged with your child in such activities as eating, bathing, and playing. Continuing to feed in language means that your child will develop understanding of vocabulary even before he or she can say the words. You must continue to stimulate language even if the child does not use speech in return.

- Work to establish the idea of imitation if your child does not readily imitate. Establishing imitation of non-speech activities is an important prerequisite for children who cannot yet imitate speech. Activities could include some of the following.

    These imitations can be without words; encourage actions.

    > Put your hands up.
    > Put your hands down.
    > Bend over.
    > Bend to one side.
    > Bend to the other side.
    > Clap hands.
    > Shut your eyes.

    Then later, again without words:

    > Open your mouth.
    > Close your mouth.

    Still later, encourage imitation of a sound such as saying, "ah":

    Then you can repeat it several times. "Ah.""Ah.""Ah." and ask the child to imitate.

    The "ah" can then be combined with a consonant to form "bah," "mah," etc.

- Time the presentation of language. Say a word or words along with the relevant experience. Say "juice" while pouring juice, "open" as a carton (or bag or the mouth) is opened.
- Reduce the length of what is said to the young child as in "time to eat," "time for bed," "put toys away" rather than using a lengthy sentence.
- Say "no" without long explanations to young children who may have difficulty understanding language.
- Use private time with a child as an opportunity for language development.
- Provide many repetitions of names of things that can be pointed to such as body parts (including *elbow*, *neck*, and *knee* after *eyes*, *nose*, *mouth*), common objects (toys, furniture, eating utensils), and parts of objects (*sleeve* of shirt, *laces* on shoes, *button* on coat, *handle* of cup).
- Teach verbs to be associated with such actions as eating, bathing, play-time, and other daily activities (*eat*, *drink*, *chew*; *swallow*, *cough*, *sneeze*, *yawn*; *splash*, *spill*; *roll*, *hit*, *pat*, *throw*).
- Expand words that are used consistently. A child who says "cookie" can be encouraged to say *big cookie*, *broken cookie*, *all-gone cookie*. Additional expansions could include: *cookie*, *please*, *juice*, *please*. A child who consistently says "ouch" (or "ow") when sick or hurt could be encouraged to say *tummy ouch*, *finger ouch*, *knee ouch*.
- Use correct verb forms to talk about something that will happen and after it is over that it *happened* (We *will walk* to the store. We *are walking*. We *walked*).
- Teach words for feelings at appropriate times (*happy*, and *sad*, but also *angry* or *mad*, *disappointed*, *scared*, *worried*, *excited*, *tired*, etc.) With basic words available to inform parents and teachers of needs, a child's frustration can be reduced a bit. Having words tied to both negative and positive feelings can replace striking out or whining or a high activity level of excitement that can lead to tears.
- Teach the language of manners, discipline, turn-taking, and seeking help.
- Teach common sensory adjectives (as *hot–cold*, *big–little*, *hard–soft*, *rough–smooth*, etc.).
- Begin work on matching answers to question words (including: *who*? *what*? *how many*? *where*? *why*?). When the question word *who* is used, the answer must be the name of a person; *where* requires a location. The goal is to establish the idea that a certain question word requires a certain kind of response. For example, when an event is occurring you could ask,
    "Who is at the door? Daddy is at the door."
    "Who will go in the car? Mommy will go in the car"
    "Who woke up? Michael woke up."
    "Who fell down? Timmy fell down."
Or you could ask:

"Where is the ball? The ball is on the chair."
"Where is the ball? The ball is on the table."
"Where is the ball? The ball is on the floor."
"Where is the ball? The ball is under the chair."

- Vary the questions for the type of response required: single word, phrase, or sentence. Don't ask all questions requiring *yes* or *no* or one-word replies once children have mastered the single-word stage.
- Provide models of word combinations. Expand what the child has said. If the child says "Cat" say "Big cat," "White cat," "Cat says meow," "Cat is soft," "Pat the cat." If the word said is *car* one can say, "Big car," "Daddy's car," "Mommy's car," "Ride in the car," "New car," "The car is new," "Car broken," "Fix the car." If there is a delay in combining two words, many, many models of two words need to be presented with imitation encouraged.
- Be sure your child understands language before you expect him or her to carry out a request or command.
- Teach meanings of *first* and *last* visually (*first* thing in line, *first* picture in a row) with objects and pictures the child can see, and auditorily (*first* name, *first* word in sentence or story) as the child listens.
- Do not try to teach or correct language when the child is in the midst of communicating, when he or she is telling something of importance. During these times, communication is more important than correctness.

Categorization and Classification

- Develop the notion that things go together, fit in groups, and can be classified.
- Sort laundry (big socks-little socks, Daddy's shirt-Michael's shirt).
- Sort groceries (to shelf, refrigerator, freezer)
- From early on, teach that blocks go in a bag, books on a shelf, and cars in a box.
- Sort objects into groups of the same colors.
- Sort objects according to shape.
- Sort objects according to function—things to eat, things to drink, things to wear, things for play, things for work.
- Once facility is developed with objects you can use pictures for sorting.

Pretend Play

- Encourage and foster pretend play. Children develop a sense of "as-if" and behave as if things were something else. Children seem to pretend first with objects (a block can be a car, an airplane, a sandwich, a birthday cake) and then place themselves in roles by pretending they are mommy or daddy or other adult. They can act out scary events and happy ones.

- Provide dolls that represent people—babies, adults, boys and girls, of your own race and other races.
- Provide housekeeping toys such as a tea set, pots and pans, brooms, lawn mowers, and toy furniture.
- Give them cars, trucks, and airplanes. Provide toy furniture, gas stations, airports, fire houses, and garages and/or encourage them to use blocks to construct such buildings.
- Have dress-up clothes available. Hats of various occupations are generally available, store easily, and can be used for pretending.

Other Play

- Provide safe places for play.
- Provide a place where it is acceptable to make a mess.
- Provide places for sand and water play with containers to fill and spill. Help children notice that water or sand that fits in one container may be too much to fit in another one.
- Make available chalk, paints, pencils, markers, finger paints, and a surface that can be used playfully without harming the child, objects, or floor covering.
- Practice motor activities. Some children will need help to learn to jump, run, and skip—motor skills that other children acquire easily. Words can be associated with the actions.
- Practice activities with a ball—rolling and bouncing it. This encourages waiting and anticipating, as well as language learning.
- Help children notice that when they perform a certain act, something else happens. For example, when a toy car is pushed across a table, it will fall off the edge; when a bell is moved, it will produce a sound; when too much liquid is poured into a container, it will spill; when a glass is dropped, it will break, but when a ball is dropped, it will bounce.
- Provide practice with big motor movements that leave a visible mark. Marks can be made in the sandbox, in a baking tray filled with sand or salt, by using a brush with water on a chalkboard, by moving finger over a dirty chalkboard, by using fingers in finger paint or shaving cream. The motor movement combined with a mark that is seen helps establish visual-motor associations.
- As the child shows interest in crayons, teach correct grasp. Pencil grasp becomes a habit quickly so learning to hold a pencil or crayon early is important.
- Provide blocks, at first large sturdy cardboard ones, then large plastic ones, moving to smaller plastic or wooden ones when the child discriminates between what may go in the mouth and what should not. Blocks can be used to stack, knock down, build up again, and to construct walls,

bridges, trains, garages, and houses.

- Present wooden or plastic jigsaw puzzles, gradually introducing ones with more pieces.
- Develop matching skills—visually at first. Provide opportunities for children to find a picture or shape that is just the same as a target or designated one. They could be asked to match geometric forms of circles, triangles, and squares of different colors and then the same colors; to match same colored shapes; to match a number of objects (such as a number of different dogs); to find objects that are all a particular color (with the color being presented visually, not with its name alone); to match pre-letter forms (the various horizontal, vertical, and diagonal lines as well as circular forms that will later form letters). Finally, letters and numerals can be used for matching.
- Once children can match, encourage them to discriminate or to find the one from an array that is different. For instance, they could see a triangle, a square, a triangle, and a triangle arranged in a row. They could then be asked to choose the one that does not belong with the others. Colors, and later, letters and numbers can be used. Discrimination, or picking out one that does not belong with a group or set, is an important preschool skill.
- Once visual discrimination skills are established, provide practice with words that children hear. Any time children must listen, auditory memory becomes a factor. Once said, a sound, word, or sentence is off in time. In contrast visual materials can stay in front of children as long as they want them there—until a decision is made about them. When they listen, the sound or word is immediately gone. For listening, children can be presented with a word. Then other words can be said with their being encouraged to indicate every time the same word is heard. For example, children could hear "dog" and then be asked to indicate by raising a hand, dropping a pellet into a container, or pushing a button, every time the word "dog" is presented in a group of words such as: "dog, cat, lion, dog, tiger, cow, horse, dog." Such activities can prepare preschool children for later listening for words that rhyme and those that begin or end with specified sounds.
- Provide visual memory practice—to remember when an object is no longer present, how it looked, where it was—to begin developing imagery.

Using Pictures

- Be careful when using pictures. Be sure your child understands that a picture represents, or stands for, an object. Some children with delays in language may not know that pictures represent real objects. Real objects should be used first. Later photographed objects, from commercial materials or from magazines, could be used. Finally, line drawings may be presented.

Preparing for Print

"Children who are not spoken to by live and responsive adults will not learn to speak properly. Children who are not answered will stop asking questions....And children who are not told stories and who are not read to will have few reasons for wanting to learn to read."[17]

- At home, read aloud to children from picture books, at times talking about the pictures rather than reading the printed words that accompany the story.
- Have your child point to pictured objects and parts of objects.
- Ask questions. Expect responses. Children can point to pictures before they can say the word or words.
- Ask your child to predict what he or she thinks will happen.
- Have him or her help turn the pages.
- Once your child is ready to listen, having both the language to understand and the attention span to appreciate the story as written, you can read the story as the author has written it, rather than talking about pictures.
- It is important that children learn the sense of a story, that it is organized, that it starts and moves along until it reaches a conclusion. They learn that there is a predictability to stories. This sense of completion is important for learning. Children begin to learn how stories are structured by having stories read to them.
- You can read to infants, as you hold them, from the newspaper or any print material you happen to be reading. The baby gets to spend time in a positive relationship with you, and you can get some reading done.
- Reading to a child early establishes the notion that there is magic between the covers of a book, and that it will be wonderful to someday learn to read.
- Help children develop a sense that there is a purpose in reading printed materials. Call attention to print as you read directions to put things together, learn to program a VCR, read recipes for cooking, read for information, and read for pleasure. Reading is not just sitting down with a book.
- Teach common nursery rhymes, for example, "Jack and Jill," "Three Little Kittens," and "Humpty-Dumpty." These rhymes are a part of our culture.
- Rhythmic reading from Dr. Seuss books can be entertaining and can establish a sense of rhyme and rhythm.
- Do not become annoyed with the seemingly endless repetitions children want in having a favorite book read. The repetition allows them to pre-

dict what comes next in stories. Children enjoy the familiarity. They may need time to develop the notion that the story always comes out the same way.

- Read books with rhymes while having your child sit beside you. Help him or her notice the association between the printed and spoken words. Words that sound the same, as in rhymes, often look the same in print
- Talk about words. Point out words on pages of text so that children begin to have a sense of print representing speech.
- If your child does not like to sit still to be read to, use rhythmic rhymes accompanied by motor activities. Sing songs before sleep. Keep trying to hold attention for brief moments to look at books, hear captions under pictures, or listen to rhymes.
- Say names of letters on alphabet blocks and magnetic letters.
- Provide these activities with a sense of fun. Do not insist that children name letters or in any way "perform."

Playing with Speech Sounds

- Encourage attention to rhyme during play.
- Carry out rhythmic games with made-up rhymes.
- Say rhyming words while splashing in the bathtub, driving in the car, eating, getting ready for bed. Encourage the child to tell words that rhyme.
- Introduce words—real and nonsense—that start with the same sounds.
- Continue such activities, even if your child does not enjoy them, for brief periods of time. They need to hear such words, and with repetition, they will begin to try to carry out the word games.
- See Chapter 4 for other suggestions to encourage these activities referred to as *phonological awareness* or *auditory processing*.

Numbers

- Count objects, beginning with body parts (one mouth, two eyes, five fingers, ten fingers).
- Count other objects.
- Teach concepts about number. Beginning with *two*, help children understand that two things are labeled with the word "two." Be sure that many objects are presented so they get the idea of what it means when we speak of "two." Continue with other numbers.
- Be sure that an array of objects is not always arranged in the same way to represent the number. For instance, three things should be shown in many different positions, not just in a horizontal line. Children need to learn that no matter what the position, three things are labeled as *three*. Counting without any idea of what the numbers represent has little value.

- Number books can be used for counting and establishing the concept of number. Many different books should be shared with the child so that he or she does not believe that *four* always refers to the four flowers in a certain number and picture book.
- Repetitively count objects around the house (socks, shoes, spoons, books, cups, shirts, etc.) beginning with two, then three and increasing as concept and counting are mastered. Use phrases such as *let's count* and *how many?* appropriately.
- Teach words related to space and quantity and time such as *big, little, small, large, more, less, fewer, wide, narrow, as many as, another one, first, last, middle, before, after, most, least*. Also teach the comparative form of words using -er (such as *bigger than, smaller than*). The comparative form of words is often difficult for children with language problems to understand.

SUMMARY

Programs for preschool children have varied from time to time. In previous generations, only the poor were thought to need preschool programs; whereas in other eras, only the wealthy had access to such programs. Maria Montessori began her work with poor children in the slums of Italy, but later, as her schools developed they were used by those who could pay fees for private education. During the Depression of the 1930s, in the United States, young children of those on relief sometimes had child care with preschool education in settlement houses. Later, nursery schools were for the affluent, until the 1960s when Headstart was begun to help prepare underprivileged children for school. Currently, many children have access to preschool education, and for children with educationally handicapping conditions, special programs are offered by public schools.

During the preschool years, young children—at home, in day care, or in nursery school—experience the world first through sensory motor exploration. They learn that acts produce consequences, that they have power to control objects and events, that experiences can be organized and classified, that objects are related to other objects in space, and that a visible mark is left behind from some visual–motor activities. They also learn to understand and use language. They learn that questions can be asked and that others will answer. They learn to use language to communicate and to control others, to solve problems, to ask for help, to offer assistance, and to think with words. Finally, the preschool years are a time for learning how to interact with others. Children learn that others can be counted on and have feelings to be respected. They begin to appreciate that things work out better if they take turns and play fair, and they learn that they can seek help, and it will be forthcoming.

When children progress comfortably through the preschool years they learn to persist in reaching goals. One of the most wonderful examples of persistence that we ever witness, is the baby just beginning to stand up and balance and take the first few steps. There are hundreds of tries, hundreds of falls, but the baby keeps on trying. In some way, at this young age, the baby knows that this act can be mastered. It is this same persistence that we must foster in children who confront learning difficulties in their early years.

CHAPTER 2

WHAT DO THE LABELS MEAN?
Beginning an Evaluation

Some evaluation should precede any specialized intervention when a learning disability is suspected in a child or adolescent. Having an assessment before treatment begins conserves financial and emotional resources for families. A diagnostic evaluation is a process, and that process defines the specific nature of the problem and offers suggestions for management.

Parents know their children better than anyone else. They live with them in their worst moments and their best. They may suspect that their child has a learning disability for various reasons. It is not unusual for learning disabilities to be noticed first during a time of change, such as when youngsters move from elementary to middle school or from middle school to high school. As demands increase, learning difficulties become more apparent.

Parents use a variety of approaches when their son or daughter has trouble in school. Some of them may restrict privileges in an attempt to encourage a child to try harder. Others may help with homework, hire a tutor, insist the child repeat a grade, or shift the child to a religious school because they believe there will be greater discipline. A number of approaches may be tried and then when parents are at their wits' end, they may seek a diagnostic workup. It is far better for the child, as well as for the parents, to begin with a determination of what is wrong rather than to delay this step until all other attempts have failed.

WHAT IS A LEARNING DISABILITY?

The term *learning disabilities* refers to a group of disorders affecting learning. Many children carry the label (estimates range from 5 to 40 percent of school populations). Not all of these children *do* have learning disabilities, but many bright children do fail to learn to the level of their potential because of learning disabilities.

Learning disabilities were described later than many other learning handicaps such as blindness, deafness, cerebral palsy, and mental retardation. As referrals to special education grew, definitions and formulas emerged for classifying a child to receive special education services. The definitions were never specific enough to be used as they have been. Some school systems applied quite rigid definitions, consequently, services to deserving children have been denied, while others used broad definitions to include children who had other handicapping conditions.

Now with reductions in funding, increasingly strict eligibility requirements, the push toward a least restrictive environment, and inclusion, many learning disabled children are in regular classes presenting as problems, puzzles, or challenges to regular classroom teachers. Increasingly the general educator is required to manage and teach children with a wide variety of learning potentials and learning problems.

The term *learning disabilities* may not be the best, the clearest, or the most accurate but it is the one accepted by professional organizations and by the federal and most state governments. In 1987, following a symposium sponsored by the U.S. Interagency Committee on Learning Disabilities and the Foundation for Children with Learning Disabilities, the following revised definition was recommended to Congress:

> Learning disabilities is a generic term that refers to a heterogeneous group of disorders manifested by significant difficulties in the acquisition and use of listening, speaking, reading, writing, reasoning, or mathematical abilities, or of social skills. These disorders are intrinsic to the individual and presumed to be due to central nervous system dysfunction. Even though a learning disability may occur concomitantly with other handicapping conditions (e.g., sensory impairment, mental retardation, social and emotional disturbance), with socioenvironmental influences (e.g., cultural differences, insufficient or inappropriate instruction, psychogenic factors), and especially attention deficit disorder, all of which may cause learning problems, a learning disability is not the direct result of those conditions or influences.[1]

Most definitions of learning disabilities make some reference to exclusion, or what learning disabilities are not. Children who show cognitive limitations or are mentally retarded have problems with learning, may learn at a slower rate, and may have a ceiling on what can be learned. Such children have learning problems but not learning disabilities. Children who are blind or severely visually impaired have problems acquiring information that a sighted person manages easily, and they must learn in different ways. Deaf or severely hearing impaired children may not learn language through the ear as a hearing person does but must learn to take in language and develop communication through residual hearing and speechreading (lipreading) or through the language of sign. Children or adolescents who are severely emotionally disturbed may have problems learning and/or interacting with others. Some are so withdrawn that they cannot profit from instruction, while others act out to such an extent that management in a classroom becomes difficult and perhaps impossible. Children from chaotic homes cannot marshal resources to prepare for school. Neglect and abuse occur too often. Some children, with their families, are homeless, while others spend minimal time in school because their parents are migrant workers. Bilingual children may be exposed to a language other than English in their homes while being expected to understand, read, and write English in school. All of these conditions can have mild or severe effects on children and their learning, but are not regarded as learning disabilities. The learning failures evolve from other sources.

PROCESSING IN LEARNING

Some educators write about processing and processing problems in children and adolescents with learning disabilities. Some of these processes include interpretation, memory, retrieval, organization, and expression. The processing of information is complex, and problems with any of these areas can interfere with successful learning.

Perception is interpretation of information that is received by the senses—what is heard and seen, for example. A sound may indicate a telephone, doorbell, beeper, or computer error. A picture is seen to stand for an object or experience. A facial expression is recognized as representing an emotion.

Sometimes a person can have normal vision and hearing but be unable to attach meaning to what is seen or heard. This is a rare condition called *agnosia*. In visual agnosia, a person has normal vision in some respects but has trouble associating the visual image with meaning. In dramatic form, this can be seen in an occasional adult patient who has suffered a stroke and is unable to recognize faces of familiar people—even a spouse. In auditory agnosia, the person can hear but cannot associate the sound with meaning. When a bell is heard, for example, the person may not know if it is from a telephone or other sound producing object.[2] Milder forms of auditory and visual perceptual disturbances are seen in some children with learning disabilities.[3]

Memory can be thought of as information entering the mind and being placed in storage. We have memories for different kinds of experiences—for events or episodes, for visual–spatial material, for spoken language, and for content that is familiar or is novel.

Retrieval means getting information from storage in the brain. Sometimes information exists in a person's head but cannot be recalled quickly. A problem with retrieval is referred to as a *word–finding problem* or *dysnomia*. A problem with word retrieval can occur in those with no language disorder at times of fatigue or stress, and word–finding problems increase with age.

Organization involves taking the bits of retrieved information and arranging them in some sensible way. When fragments are retrieved with poor organization, there is little that can be remembered or shared meaningfully. Disorganization can affect notebooks, desks, rooms at home, projects, or written work for tests or homework assignments. Often a lack of organization does not bother disorganized people.

Expression is the act of presenting messages through speech, writing, sign language, visual or performing arts, music, or execution of a play on the football field or basketball court. Whether or not faulty expression matters depends on the significance of the action at a given time. In general, in our society, being unable to express ourselves in speech or writing is a problem. On the other hand, being unable to ski or play a musical instrument is not a problem unless we are in a group where skiing is important or we belong to a family of musicians where each member is expected to perform.[4]

AREAS OF ACHIEVEMENT TO BE ASSESSED

During an assessment, broad areas of learning are studied including spoken language, reading, written expressive language, mathematics, and nonverbal learning. *Spoken language* is generally assessed by speech–language pathologists. For most of us, language enters the system through hearing, is processed through various cognitive mechanisms, and is expressed through speech. Later-developing reading and written expression are extensions of the basic oral linguistic functions.

In evaluating spoken language, the focus is on what an individual understands as well as on what can be expressed orally. Consideration is given to how information is retrieved, how it is organized in syntactic structure, and how it is formulated for units longer than sentences in extended discourse. Also evaluated is whether or not language is used in ways appropriate for various situations. Children with no language problems learn the rules of language with little effort; those with varying handicapping conditions do not.

In addition to oral language, when students experience difficulty in school their *reading* must be assessed. In order to read, children must relate printed letters (text) to the sounds of speech. The inability to link print to speech can result in a learning disability in the area of decoding for reading. To read, an individual must look at print and decode it. The reader can either pronounce the word aloud or silently or go directly from print to meaning.

The basic measure of beginning to read is reading individual words. If an individual cannot read words, there is no text to comprehend. Some students can read the words, yet they fail to understand what they read; some of these children show problems with comprehension of spoken language as well. Others comprehend spoken language, at least as it can be measured, but have trouble with comprehending text.

It is essential in all instances of school failure to assess *written expressive language*. Areas of handwriting, spelling, and written formulation need to be analyzed. Adequate writing is required to take notes in class, complete written examinations, write papers, summarize findings in experiments, observations, or medical charts, prepare professional reports, and often, to apply for a job.

In *mathematics* we need to consider computation and application. Application is using numerical or quantitative knowledge to solve real-life problems. Handwriting can also be a problem in mathematics, as when numbers are not legible or are not lined up correctly. Some children can manage basic arithmetic but experience difficulty when multiple steps are required to solve problems, or when advanced logical reasoning is needed.

Problems with *nonverbal learning*, including visual spatial functioning as well as interpretation of social cues, must not be overlooked. We are called on continually to make visual-spatial judgments. To get along with others, we need to be able to judge what a person means when we observe such nonverbal communication as facial expression, body posture, and tone of voice. Deficits in these nonverbal skills may have a greater impact on adult life than a reading and spelling problem, so learning disabilities in the nonverbal domain must also receive consideration in testing.

SCREENING AND PREPARATION FOR TESTING.

Screening refers to the first level of testing or observation to determine if there are problems that require further and more comprehensive study. Screening measures are general. They are not the same as, and not meant to be the same as, diagnostic testing.

A first level of screening for learning disabilities may be a teacher's comments about classroom behavior. This may be followed by observation from a learning specialist who notes how the child interacts with others, maintains attention on the assigned task, and in general compares with peers. Perhaps a team will review notes regarding teachers' concerns, study all past achievement testing, and determine if further testing is necessary. If the team members feel that the child or adolescent is working to capacity or is learning as well as can be expected, they may conclude that no further testing is necessary. If parents are still concerned, or if they want special education assistance, they can appeal this decision. Or they can have testing completed outside of school.

ACHIEVEMENT TESTING

Standardized tests of achievement are used throughout the lives of children. *Achievement* and *intelligence*, specifically achievement and intelligence testing, are often confused. *Intelligence* is what is in a person's head as a capacity, ability, or potential to achieve. *Achievement* is what has been learned in various areas as a result of teaching or through incidental learning. Some achievement tests are administered to groups of children in school, while others are given individually as part of diagnostic study.

Scores on Standardized Tests

Standardized tests are developed by having test items, believed to measure a specific area or skill, administered to a large group of individuals who share characteristics of age, sex, social class, and primary or first language use. How individuals in the large group score on the tests sets a standard, allowing a test to be regarded as standardized. A student's score on a test is meaningful only if he or she shares characteristics with the group on whom the test was developed. A test standardized on inner city children in the United States is inappropriate for a child in rural Mexico. A measure of listening designed for 6-year-old children will not provide meaningful information about a 12-year-old child.

Age and grade equivalents are one way of comparing how a child is functioning, measured against a guideline, but it may be more helpful to have the raw scores converted to standard scores. *Raw scores* are the number of correct responses on a test or task. It is impossible to compare raw scores from different tests. For example, the total number of items for one test might be 46 and for another test, 20. If a child achieved a raw score of 20 on each test, for one test the score would be perfect, but for the other would show fewer than half the items correct. If the raw scores are converted to a common scale, such as a *standard score*, it is easier to compare test results. For many educational tests, the scale used for standard scores has 100 as average, with about half the population scoring above and half below 100. There is a range in the middle where most people fall, perhaps between standard scores of 90 and 109 or between 85 and 115. The standard scores of the achievement tests can then be compared with results of IQ testing, which uses the same kind of scale. The scores from the achievement tests and the IQ tests should be similar. If a girl has scores of 100 on an IQ test and 92 on a reading test, she would be regarded as reading within the range of expectation for her IQ. If another girl has an IQ of 100, but standard scores on reading tests of 75, everyone would agree that there is a reading problem of some kind.

Another way that scores are reported is by *percentiles*. The average is 50. This means that 50 percent of those taking the test or showing the behavior would be above, and 50 percent below, the 50th percentile. An individual who scores at the 50th percentile is average; one who scores at the 80th percentile is above average, and at the 20th percentile below average. Test results may also be expressed in *stanines*. These are units expressed from 1 to 9 with the 4th, 5th, and 6th stanines regarded as average.

These measurements and numbers are only important as they contribute to understanding about a child's functioning. They should not be off-putting for parents. Parents need to ask questions if they do not understand what the numbers mean. Those of us who use tests, discuss results, and write reports need to be sure those who receive the results understand the numbers we report.

Teachers are accustomed to dealing with scores on standardized tests; for the most part, parents are not. Parents often bring pages of computer-generated test scores to me with no idea what the numbers represent. It is essential that numbers are understood by parents and others who are expected to use the information. Having a piece of paper with numbers on it means nothing if the person holding the paper does not understand the numbers.

Discrepancy

After scores are obtained from group or individual tests, the question then is, are the individual's scores discrepant when compared with ability, age, and/or grade? If the child performs as expected there is no discrepancy.

To show a discrepancy with ability, we must have a measure of intelligence to compare with the scores from the achievement test (such as a reading test). How or for what purpose the discrepancy information will be used may determine what test should be used to measure ability or intelligence. If a child is being excluded from special supplemental help because there is not enough of a discrepancy, then an individual IQ test administered by a competent examiner may be essential. If a certain level of IQ is necessary to attend a particular school or if parents believe their child is brighter than the teachers or team members believe, then, of course, individual testing may also be important. Some group tests provide an IQ equivalent or *student ability index* reported as SAI. Sometimes these tests are adequate, and individually administered IQ tests are not necessary. If a child is struggling with reading but does not show a discrepancy between ability and achievement, he or she does not meet criteria for classification as learning disabled and thus may be unable to receive special education or any specialized reading instruction. This does not mean the child has no reading problem and needs no special teaching. Such a child does need to be taught to read.

A discrepancy between an achievement test score and what is expected for age or grade is easier to document. Scores from the achievement tests are compared with the child's grade and age. Test scores must always be considered as falling within a range. Just as there is a range for what is regarded as average in individuals' weight, height, or blood pressure, there is a range of average expectation in achievement scores for age and grade. For example, all children in the fourth month of third grade do not achieve grade equivalents on a reading test that are at grade 3.4. In any typical third grade classroom, there will be a range of reading skills. A few children will be reading several years above their grade. A few will read two years below their grade, but most of the third graders will read at about a third-grade level, or second-grade level, or fourth-grade level. This range of reading is considered normal. Children within this range of normal would not be considered as having a disability. However, children need to be able to read the books other children in their grade are reading. If they cannot, they need to be taught, so they can manage school requirements for reading.

How much of a discrepancy is significant between achievement and expectation? This varies from place to place. Sometimes complex formulas are used, or the discrepancy may be regarded as significant if the individual scores two years below grade placement. Although there may be general agreement that a 4th-grader achieving at a second-grade level has a learning disability, using two years below grade as a yardstick is completely inappropriate for a child in first or second grade. Making a child wait until he or she scores two years below grade level is cruel and can cause emotional reactions and poor self image that take a long time to repair. It should be noted that using discrepancy formulas to classify children as having or not having learning disabilities is being called into question by researchers.

Uses and Limitations of Test Scores

Scores on standardized tests are useful. Such tests show where a particular child stands in relation to the original group on whom the test was standardized, and they can document change. However, these tests do have limitations. A standardized test may not have enough items to assess a particular skill or concept. For example, a few letters may be presented to be named or their sounds given. Although a score can be recorded for the responses provided, it does not tell us if the child knows all upper and lower case letters, or the sounds of all the consonants and short vowels. Tests to measure a learning behavior that concerns us may not exist, and a given test may not measure what it purports to measure. Because tests have limitations and because there are not tests for all areas we wish to measure, observations of a child at home and school are invaluable.

Of course, even the best tests do not simulate real life. The best vocabulary test does not measure colloquial expressions a teenager needs to know to be part of a peer group. The best standardized test of reading comprehension does not simulate reading a chapter, a short story, or a novel, and preparing it for study. Writing sentences or a creative story about a picture does not require the same skills as writing a report. Therefore, in addition to any test we administer, we must also consider the daily work in the classroom and how the child or teenager is able to function with peers and at home.

Group versus Individual Testing

Some tests, such as the achievement tests at the end of a school year, are given to children in groups, while others are administered individually. Group tests provide information for comparing the student taking the test with his or her classmates. But from group test results, it is not known if attention was completely focused on the task at hand. Children may daydream or fail to work as quickly and accurately as possible. Some may have problems marking the answers. If they must locate an answer and then blacken in a circle, they may become confused and lose their place. When children perform poorly on a group test, we do not know if they did not know the answers or did not mark them correctly.

If a test is administered individually, an observer can have some sense of whether or not the student is actively involved. Notes are made about the child's level of comfort, anxiety, freedom from distractibility, and extent of participation. For each test item, the individual being tested is expected to make a response. Watching individual children during administration of achievement tests, particularly when they are working independently, such as in marking answers for arithmetic problems or silently reading for comprehension, can be important. Some mark answers at random, but at a reasonable rate as though they are figuring out the math problem or reading text, when they are not engaged in the task at all. These observations are taken into account along with the scores on tests.

Children may behave differently for tests given on any particular day. A child may have a cold, be worried about a sick pet, or parents' squabbles, or may experience anxiety specifically related to taking tests. Such observations are difficult when a child is tested as part of a group.

ADDITIONAL EVALUATION

To obtain a complete picture of both an individual and his or her learning, evaluation in addition to achievement is often necessary. One approach to diagnosing children with learning disabilities and/or emotional difficulties uses an interdisciplinary team. Each of the professionals on the team puts his or her area of specialty in the foreground while always maintaining awareness of other areas of development. Professionals who have worked in such programs over a number of years can attest to their value in understanding the complex problems that a child or adolescent might have. A comprehensive assessment includes a complete history along with evaluation of the child's health, intelligence, emotional development, structure and function of the family, and finally, of his or her learning.

A child or adolescent may behave differently with each professional, which increases the interdisciplinary group's understanding of the individual. A child who is anxious about school may show this anxiety to an educational specialist but manage to hide it during a family interview. One with attentional difficulties may be able to control activity level except when put under the pressure of school-like tasks. During the evaluation process, a reluctant or shy child may gain confidence and begin to share thoughts and feelings he or she would never have dreamed of sharing with the first professional seen. Team members compile history information, review past records and previous testing, consider current test findings, develop a diagnostic statement of the problem, and propose a set of recommendations.

An advantage to using a team from outside the school is that such a team faces no requirement to fit within certain guidelines established by a public school system. For example, the number of spaces available for children with special needs in a certain school will not influence the diagnosis or recommendation of an outside team. They tend to look at basic processes, rather than current fads or teaching approaches used in particular schools. The team has only one goal, to suggest what is best for a child and family that can be provided in reasonable, practical, and financially possible ways.

Health insurance may or may not pay for parts of interdisciplinary evaluations of suspected learning disabilities. If finances are a problem in a family with a child showing learning problems, a comprehensive educational evaluation—an evaluation of the child's language and learning rather than a full evaluation by a team of several members—may provide the highest yield for the lowest cost. Such an evaluation focuses directly on the child's learning strengths and deficits.

Diagnostic services are available through public school systems without charge to families. (Parents may wish to begin with an evaluation within the school, but if they are denied complete evaluations or do not receive answers to their questions they may wish to enlist services outside the school.) Families with children in parochial or independent schools do qualify for services from their local public school systems, although parents may need to provide transportation to the site of services.

Health Status

When a child shows problems learning, we look first to physical causes, because some illnesses can impede learning. Health-care providers examine the child or adolescent, make sure immunizations are up to date, look into such areas as proper nutrition and adequate sleep, and question any drug or alcohol use. They also review general areas of behavior and consider how well the child or adolescent is managing a current developmental stage. It is important that parents carefully select reputable, experienced physicians or other health care professionals and then trust their recommendations about possible sensory impairments. Newspaper advice columnists, television personalities, and tabloid reporters often provide misleading information about common childhood problems.

Sensory Function. Sensation means that the signal from the senses of hearing, seeing, touching, smelling, or feeling reaches the brain. Persons with limited sight or hearing have differences at the level of signals reaching the brain. Vision and hearing need to be checked to rule out any possible interference to learning by a visual or hearing impairment. Surprisingly, there continue to be children with vision and hearing problems who are not identified in preschool years.

Vision should always be checked if there is any question about the child's ability to interpret visual material. A medical doctor specializing in the function and diseases of the eyes is an *ophthalmologist*. Ophthalmologists treat all kinds of eye problems, prescribe medication and eyeglasses, admit patients to hospitals, and perform surgery. They generally keep current about new developments and are aware of fads that emerge from time to time. Other eye care professionals are *optometrists*. They evaluate eye function and make prescriptions for some medications and for eyeglasses. They have specialized training but are not medical doctors. A person who fits eyeglasses, following prescriptions of an ophthalmologist or optometrist is an *optician*.

Well-advertised and expensive programs may offer cures for various learning disabilities through visual activities or exercises, but results are questionable. Most of the time, in order to learn to read, we must be taught to read words; to perform exercises unrelated to reading and writing generally does not improve reading and writing. Confusing visually similar letters in print or reversing letters and numbers when writing (which are sometimes seen in young children with learning difficulties) are not problems with the mechanism of sight. Instead, they suggest problems with visual perception and memory.

When a young child has speech delays or an older child experiences problems learning, it is essential that *hearing* is tested. Early hearing loss may affect both speech development and later learning. The medical doctor who is a specialist in functions of the ear, and diseases and problems of the ear, nose, and throat is called an *otolaryngologist* or may be referred to as an *ENT physician*. An otolaryngologist whose sub-specialty is the ear is an *otologist*. Otolarnyngologists diagnose diseases, prescribe medication, and perform surgery. They are also the medical specialists who understand hearing loss and the function of hearing aids.

Although hearing may be screened in a general pediatric office, complete audiologic assessment is essential if there is any question of hearing loss. Comprehensive hearing tests, or *audiologic evaluations*, are performed by *audiologists*. Audiologists practice in hospitals, clinics, public school systems, and in private practice.

In general, audiologists ask: Is hearing normal? If not, is the loss mild, moderate, or severe? Is the individual a candidate for a hearing aid? If so, what aid would best help this person with this particular hearing loss? If it is a hearing loss that can be treated medically or surgically, or if there is a question of complex problems, referral is made to an otologist or otolaryngologist for medical management.

Attention

To learn, we must focus attention on that which is to be learned. Some children who have difficulties with attention have trouble learning, yet others who seem never to pay attention, learn well. At times, children with attentional problems show these problems most when confronted with tasks that tax their skills. If they have difficulty writing, they may show inattention most during a period when writing is required. Although some children do have problems sustaining attention for nearly every kind of activity, many children with attention deficit disorders have varying attention spans for different activities, different times of day, and differing levels of fatigue.

Children with learning disabilities who have problems with attention and concentration may be easily distracted and show impulsive responses and actions. Some of them are motorically overactive, while others have trouble paying attention but do not show excessive activity. When an evaluation of attentional problems with or without hyperactivity is needed, a health-care professional such as a pediatrician, family practice physician, nurse practitioner, psychiatrist, or pediatric neurologist may provide it.

Psychological Assessment

Intelligence testing. After a child's health status is determined, we need to know about the child's ability to learn. This ability is referred to as *capacity*, *potential*, *expectation*, *cognition*, *intelligence*, or *IQ*. Measures of ability are provided by group tests or by individually administered tests.

Group intelligence tests are administered in schools. They involve paper and pencil and are included in children's cumulative records. Such tests have value in giving general indications about ability but must not replace an individually administered test when serious questions arise about one's ability to learn.

Intelligence tests, administered by psychologists, measure different abilities from those measured by group paper-and-pencil tests. Among the commonly used measures of intelligence are the Wechsler series including: the Wechsler Preschool and Primary Scale of Intelligence (WPPSI)[5] for young children, the Wechsler Intelligence Scale for Children-III (WISC-III formerly the WISCR)[6] and the Wechsler Adult Intelligence Scale—Revised (WAISR).[7] These tests assess functioning in verbal and performance areas. For the verbal scale, an individual is asked questions and he or she provides oral responses. For the performance scale, there is an opportunity to interpret puzzles, identify missing parts of pictured objects, arrange pictures in order to tell a story, to remember and copy a code, and use a pencil for mazes. The importance of measuring nonverbal as well as verbal abilities is that individuals are able to demonstrate problem solving with and without verbal responses. Psychologists may elect to use other measures of intelligence as well. The value of any of these tests is only as great as the skill of the examiner who uses it.

Typically, the score from the IQ test is used as part of a battery of tests to determine if a child has a learning disability. Some kind of formula is used to establish if the child is learning in a way that would be predicted on the basis of tested ability. If there is a discrepancy between capacity (intelligence) and learning (achievement), such discrepancy forms part of the definition of the learning disability.

A different concept of intelligence has been proposed by Howard Gardner.[8] In his view, there are discrete intelligences that include linguistic, musical, logical-mathematical, spatial, bodily-kinesthetic, and inter- and intrapersonal. This formulation allows for a broader way of considering human behavior and may help both parents and teachers focus on the multiplicity of areas involved in a child's development. A child or adolescent who is deficient in one area may be quite competent in another.

Evaluating emotional status. In addition to intelligence, we often need to know more about a child's emotional development. How do children or adolescents feel about themselves and their places in their world? To find out, a psychologist may use a set of tests, called *projective measures*. For these tests, the individual is shown some neutral stimulus such as a picture or an inkblot and is asked to tell about it. Or the person may be presented with a partial sentence and asked to complete it. The person being tested projects, or reads into, the inkblot, picture, or sentence part, thoughts and feelings that he or she might have about various people, situations, and experiences. Additional projective measures may include asking children to draw their family or familiar objects. In the hands of a skilled clinician, such tests can provide indications of how children feel about themselves and their roles in relationship to others, including family members and peers.

Projective tests do not measure objective reality. Instead, they reveal an individual's perception of various events or circumstances. Shown a picture of a child or animal, young children may tell stories about the child or animal being afraid. They may have fears that they are reluctant to talk about, but they find it comfortable to discuss the fears as they project them onto a pictured child or animal.

Parents should understand, when results from projective tests are discussed, in person or in a report, that what their child has said is his or her interpretation about people and events. Children's thoughts and ideas filter through their levels of maturity, their experiences, and their fantasies. When parents listen open-mindedly to discussions about projective test results, they may learn important things about their children and how they regard themselves.

For most psychological tests, the child or adolescent is not required to read or write, or solve many written math problems. Intelligence tests do not test all the processes or skills needed for learning in school. To know about reading, one must test reading. To know about how an individual writes, specific writing samples must be obtained.

In some communities *neuropsychologists* do testing that suggests what part of the brain may be working differently to cause problems in performance. They use some of the same measures as clinical or school psychologists and some additional ones as well. Some psychologists and neuropsychologists measure areas of achievement, but others do not.

Family Assessment

A family interview is part of the comprehensive evaluation of a child's functioning. It is used to learn how children function at home, how they fit into the family, and how they are regarded by the family members. Children begin to develop their sense of self and of their place in the world as reflections of how their parents regard them and respond to them. It is useful to understand how much parents know about how their children function in school and with peers, about what they are learning, and about who their friends are. Some parents know more about how their children think and feel than do others.

A child's learning can be influenced by how he or she is expected to learn. If too much is expected, a child may feel overwhelmed and as though he or she were a disappointment to the parents. But expecting too little may also be harmful. One 11-year-old boy was praised for how well he had performed on certain tests. When told he would want to share that information with his parents, he said, "Oh they will never believe it. They think I function at about a 3-year level." He did not believe his parents expected very much from him, and he did not regard himself as capable of achieving to the level of his ability. If little is expected, a child may have no adequate models for achievement. Seeing adults as models who respect school and learning is essential so that growing children can place value on school success and the consequences of achievement.

Children begin to develop images of themselves as learners from their parents, but they quickly become harsh self critics. By early school age, those children experiencing learning difficulty may already regard themselves as school failures. They know they are not measuring up to their own expectations.

STRENGTHS AND DEFICITS

In evaluation, a learner's strengths are as important to consider as weaknesses. Analyzing only weak areas does not provide an adequate understanding of how a child processes information and learns. If a child cannot read, but performs well in math, for example, it is important to know that. If a child does poorly in math, but is an excellent reader, this is also important to know. When a child shows poor reading comprehension, but scores quite well with printed word problems in math, we need to explore reasons for this difference, since language comprehension is involved with both tasks. If a child performs better in one area, can we use it to develop the other? We need to use the child's strengths to improve weak areas. How skills should be taught is influenced by the individual's strengths.

We often hear that learning disabled individuals compensate for their weaknesses. The term *compensation* is used in different ways. For this discussion, compensation refers to a skill that replaces a deficient skill. For instance, using a typewriter or word processor compensates for or replaces bad handwriting. A good secretary helps an individual compensate for poor spelling. My preference is for teaching the skill rather than compensating for it. To say an 8-year-old boy should never use a pencil but should have a word processor is, to me, absurd. He is too young for us to make such a recommendation; with good teaching he may learn to use a pencil. To say a child with a reading disability should have all printed material read to her when she is in the third grade shows no respect for the child's capacity to learn. She may enjoy some recorded books, but she should be taught to read. This is not to say compensatory measures should never be used. Students with very slow reading rate, even when they can decode well, can be helped immeasurably by being read to or having access to taped books when they must master great amounts of print material. But they need to continue practicing reading so the skill will become more automatic. Many people with bad handwriting will function better with a word processor than writing by hand; but this does not mean we should refrain from teaching a child how to write.

SHARING DIAGNOSTIC INFORMATION

Good educational assessments provide tentative diagnoses and offer a set of hypotheses about how a child should be taught. Ideally diagnostic teaching is provided at the time, or shortly after the assessment. In diagnostic or trial teaching, various approaches are tried with modifications in both the material used and how a child is expected to respond. Thus, recommendations from testing can be evaluated over a short period to determine what is likely to be effective for long-term teaching. If diagnostic teaching is not feasible, the educational diagnostician interprets findings and makes suggestions that seem sensible on the basis of behaviors and responses to diagnostic tests. There should always be some built-in program of reassessment to determine if recommendations are effective.

Children and adolescents who have learning disabilities need to have advocates to help with the implementation of recommendations. Parents are the primary advocates, but teachers are as well. In elementary school, the main teacher is the one who understands best about a child's learning and can help the other teachers understand how the learning disability can affect multiple areas of functioning. Art, music, physical education, and computer are regarded as "specials" and are welcomed by most students. They are often the first classes into which learning disabled students are mainstreamed. If these classes are areas where learning disabled students shine, they can be a salvation for them; but they are often classes that cause the greatest difficulty. Children may have auditory perceptual difficulties in responding to music, for example. They may have trouble being as still as necessary between particular activities. Clumsy children may be figures of fun in gym class or may have auditory memory problems so that they are always out of step with what they are supposed to be doing. Those with visual spatial problems can have a difficult time in gym class, art, and shop classes. These "specials" can provide as great a range of difficulty for children as can reading and arithmetic.

When students move into middle school and above, they have a number of different teachers who are skilled in their subject areas but may not have much formal education regarding developmental issues and disorders. Their empathy with learning disabled students varies tremendously. Learning disabled students in middle and secondary school need an advocate within the school who understands the problems and their impact on learning. This person could be a resource room teacher of learning disabilities, a vice principal, guidance counselor, or chair of the school diagnostic team. Sharing information, unfortunately, often means merely that test scores are added to a student's cumulative record with no interpretation and no direction for the classroom teacher. Such practices cannot be called assessments. Recommendations are often written on a child's Individual Educational Plan (or IEP), and their writing becomes so automatic that they may have little meaning for a parent reading them or as directions for teaching an individual learner. How skills will be taught, including how they will be presented, how they will be practiced, and how learning will be measured, should be part of meaningful recommendations.

In an evaluation, useful recommendations, as free from jargon as possible, need to be made about how to present materials to facilitate learning. In a reasonable time, if the recommendations are followed but are not successful, then the teaching procedures need reassessment. A modification of teaching approach, or different ways of introducing and reinforcing material, may be needed. Sometimes small changes in the way a teacher introduces material or how a child practices a skill can make big differences in rate of and retention for learning.

Making predictions about human behavior is fraught with uncertainty. Multiple events can occur to impede or facilitate learning. Any of us who has worked in the field of learning disabilities or special education for a long time has seen individuals in school and/or vocational settings for whom we would never have predicted success on the basis of earlier performance or test results. There is a quality of perseverance in some individuals that is amazing, especially when they see peers exerting little effort with much better results. We have also seen individuals with good ability and good skills who never seem to achieve personal or job success or satisfaction.

Early on, we need to begin discussing with children or adolescents and their families what the particular kind of learning disability may be, and what possible impact it may have at home and school. We must also help students understand that there are prerequisite skills necessary for certain jobs and professions. Television advertisements and public service announcements often tell young people that all they need to do is try, and they can achieve success at any level, or reach any goal. Such messages are misleading and can result in terrible discouragement and disappointment when maximum effort is exerted but failure occurs. Just wanting something desperately and working hard are not necessarily enough. I could wish more than anything to be an excellent athlete, try as hard as I could, and I would still fail. Certain talents are necessary to be an athlete, musician, ballerina, or student before intense instruction and practice are put forth. A certain level of ability is necessary for any career, and use of conventional spoken language and adequate reading for many.

Diagnostic studies should precede educational planning for children and adolescents with suspected learning disabilities, and are financially and emotionally wise investments. However, if a child cannot speak well enough, read well enough, do mathematics well enough, or write well enough to meet the demands of the classroom, no test is needed to say there is a problem with learning. What to do about the problems needs to be the focus of any evaluation.

ADVICE FOR PARENTS REQUESTING TESTING

- Begin discussion with your child's teacher when you suspect a problem.
- Determine if you and the teacher have similar concerns.
- If behavior is different at home and school, search for causes of the difference.
- If you wish to have testing done through the school system, make your request in writing. Be sure to date your request and include your full name, address, and telephone number for a reply. Do not rely on a telephone request to begin the assessment process.
- Know the qualifications of the professionals whose help you seek when you are pursuing services outside of school (as well as in school).
- Keep your child informed as you take him or her to different professionals. Explain the reasons for consulting the different people.
- Ask your child's or teenager's opinions so you know what he or she thinks about professionals who are consulted and about appointments.
- Be clear about what you want and what your questions are when you call to make an appointment.
- Beware of any educational treatment or procedure that promises cures or states it is always successful.
- Be sure you understand the test results. Ask questions until you do understand. If necessary, make another appointment. Part of any consultation is that you understand words used in the evaluation of your child and the stated opinion of the consultant.
- Get a written report from the consultant, whether within or outside the school.
- Do not be afraid of a label. A label is merely a name. We name things so we are able to talk about them, to agree on what they mean. Saying a child has a learning disability of a specific kind should allow everyone involved, including parents and teachers, to discuss the child more easily. Labels are not harmful; they are just words, and they can be helpful.
- Do not be afraid that your child will learn that there is "something wrong." You can be sure your child already knows he or she has a problem with learning. If a child worries but does not talk about the worry, parents may never know some of the horrible fantasies he or she might

have. The most frequent one when children have trouble in school is that they are dumb, stupid, or "a retard." This fantasy is far worse than a child's understanding that he or she has good ability to learn, but has some specific problems—problems that will respond to help.

- Do not tell your child that he or she will play games when being tested. The child will be doing hard work. You can ask the person doing the testing if he or she has suggestions about what to tell the child. This will differ depending on the age of the child. Teenagers need to have the answers from testing as much as their parents do. Young children can be cajoled into cooperating; adolescents can refuse. Some professionals refuse to see reluctant children. I prefer seeing them, even if for an abbreviated appointment, to demystify the setting and show them the kinds of activities that we will do. Explaining and then asking them to complete just one task often can result in cooperation and the child or teen has a sense of pride in accomplishing a hard or frightening task.
- Telling young children about the testing only the night before, or even in the morning, may be a good idea so they will not worry excessively. However, the appointment should not be kept a secret until arriving in the testing office.
- Sometimes appointments for testing are scheduled when other important events are happening in the child's life. Parents must be sensitive to this. If a child's team is playing in a tournament, if he or she is to receive an award, or if there is some other special event, requesting an alternative appointment time is important. A routine event such as team practice or a dance lesson may need to be missed. Some coaches and instructors build in a sense of responsibility about never missing a practice or class. If children or teenagers need to miss practice, it should be without penalty to them.
- Parents should receive reports of all testing that is done. Keep these reports. If later testing is necessary, do not give up your copies of the reports. Have copies made but keep yours for your own file. From the first screening or testing, keep all records. They become important to document long-standing problems (often needed to qualify for special provisions when taking standardized tests as adults). They also serve as records of growth. The child, adolescent, or young adult will have some objective record to understand more fully the nature of the learning difficulty.
- Young people need to know of any difficulties that may have a genetic component (and that might occur later in their own children).
- Divorced parents should each maintain copies of their children's records if they both continue to be involved with their children.

TO TEACHERS

- Consider possible referral for testing when you notice a difference between a child's ability and performance, such as when a cooperative child does not perform as well as it seems he or she should.
- Seek further testing if the child is inconsistent, some days showing development well above expectations and other days well below. Such inconsistencies represent partial learning. Until a skill is really learned, it is not consistent.
- Become suspicious when the rate at which a student learns is much slower than that of his or her peers.
- Consider requesting special assessment if a student seems uncomfortable with him or herself, if there is no pleasure in accomplishments or undue distress with failure.
- Ask the student's opinion about what he or she thinks is wrong. From a young age, children are often astute in describing why they think they are not doing well. They may be more responsive if you frame your questions as a desire to know on your part, not a punitive "why did you...?" or "why didn't you...?" Young children may say they are afraid to respond in a group, while others say it is "no fun when you're not called on." Teenagers may really not understand concepts taught in science or social studies. What they say can be invaluable.
- Within your school system you need to follow specified policy and procedures, and this differs from place to place and often from school to school in a district.
- Share your observations about students with consultants. Any consultant values observations from the teacher or teachers who spend the most time with a student.
- Observation notes can be handwritten. The reason for seeking this information is not to increase your work but to understand better how you see a child and to learn of any questions you, as a child's teacher, might have.
- Read reports of assessments. Next to the parents, the most important person to read the educational reports is the teacher. Suggestions that might be helpful for teaching may be included in the reports or explanations may be offered that explain unusual behaviors.
- Respect confidentiality of the student and family not only in getting written permission to discuss a child but also in oral discussions with others at the school.
- Check to be sure that the student described in the report is the one you see in the classroom. If he or she was hyperactive in the test setting, but is never overly active in school, or if reading in the classroom is far below your expectation but the test scores are high, these differences need to be explained.

- Become familiar with tests used in your district. Know how a child or adolescent is expected to respond. The name of a test does not always give a good indication of what is measured. (For instance, a spelling test may require the speller to hear a word and then write it, or it may have the child look at several words and select the one that is spelled correctly. Both are labeled as spelling tests; and yet they make different demands on the speller.)
- Be sure you understand terminology used in reports. New terms are included in reports all the time. They often mean something different than what we would expect them to mean. (For example, the term *auditory processing* may refer to a task administered experimentally by an audiologist or psychologist, to a task of segmenting words heard into syllables, or to a task of sequencing sounds within words.)

SUMMARY

Learning disabled children and adolescents deserve the best that is available diagnostically and that leads to the best and most effective teaching approaches we know. Wendell Johnson wrote, one cannot "read reading, write writing, or speak speaking, except...as one reads about something, writes about something, or speaks about something."[9] We need to heed these words in reporting our test findings. Children need to have skills, but our assessment needs to include some observation about how willing and able they are to speak about, read about, and write about the universe around them.

CHAPTER 3

WORDS AND THINGS
Spoken Language

"If you understand and appreciate my language, you must understand and appreciate me. My language is me," said a young man as he completed his psychotherapy.[1] Language is made up of words, and words are symbols. A symbol is a sign that stands for or represents an object, action, or event but is not a part of that object, action, or event. Some representations of an object may be closely tied to that object. For example, a photograph is a representation of an object that looks like the object; a color photograph looks more like the object than one that is black and white. A drawing of an object can look exactly like the object or only resemble it slightly, but it can be interpreted as the object.

Spoken words are at a greater distance from the experience than a picture or drawing, and marks or letters on paper made to represent spoken words are at an even greater distance. Words can be written in manuscript or cursive, upper or lower case letters, typed or written by hand, but once read, printed words serve as representations of spoken words, which are, in turn, representations of actual objects or events. Day to day, from the time we wake until the time we sleep, we use words, arranged in a conventional order, automatically and with little conscious thought.

Language, with all it variations and intricacies, makes us human. Animals have ways of communicating but none can convey ideas, about the seen and unseen, and actions that are happening now, happened yesterday, and will happen tomorrow. The acquisition of language is a natural process for most children. Language is so natural and easy to acquire that it is referred to as an instinct.[2]

THE LANGUAGE TO BE LEARNED

A language is described by its phonology, morphology, syntax, semantics, and pragmatics. Most languages are represented in print by an orthography.

Phonology refers to the sound structure of a language, with a phoneme being considered here as a speech sound, a small unit that changes one word to another word. We hear words like *big* or *bag* or *bug* as whole words. A change in a phoneme, in this case the vowel, changes meaning. For words like *big*, *bit*, *bin*, or *bid*, the final phoneme—a consonant—changes, forming a different word. The understanding and early production of speech reflects the beginning of a developing child's phonological system. Later when children learn to read, they map print onto this phonology, or the sounds of speech. Before they can carry out this mapping of print onto speech, they must achieve some conscious level of phonological awareness, of understanding that spoken words have parts. [3,4,5,6]

Syntax refers to the grammar of language, the way words are arranged conventionally to convey meaning. The order of words can make a statement or ask a question. For instance, we say, "The kite is red" to make a statement about the kite or ask, "Is the kite red?" when we wish to know its color. The term *grammar*, as it is used here, does not refer to what children must learn in school as parts of speech, their definitions, and their relationships. Grammar, or the way sentences are structured, is an abstract notion. It is something that is inside our heads like a scaffold on which we can hang words. Grammar is a universal of the world's languages; all languages have a way of putting words in order according to a system of rules. Children learn—some would say discover or invent—these rules quickly. If they are regular language learners, they understand grammar and use complex sentences that they will later read in text.

Morphology is another part of a language system. A *morpheme* is the smallest unit of meaning. Morphemes can stand alone or be bound to other morphemes. A word such as *books* is made up of two morphemes. One is *book* and the other is the *s* at the end of the word that marks the word *books* as being more than one, or plural. Children learn that endings to show plurals may be pronounced as /s/, /z/, or /uz/ (as in *cats*, *dogs*, and *buses*) depending on which sound precedes the ending. These morphological changes are referred to as inflectional, and they are used in a fairly regular way.

Other morphemes are derivational and are not as consistent. In English, for example, how we change verbs to nouns varies. When we change the verb *employ* to a noun, the result is *employment*, but the resulting noun for allow is allow*ance*. Knowledge of morphemes is important for comprehension of language and for speech production and is essential later for reading and writing.

Semantics refers to meaning and involves vocabulary but also figurative language, sentences, and extended discourse. Vygotsky wrote, "A word without meaning is an empty sound."[7] A linguistic community depends on the shared meanings of words, because without such shared meaning there is no communication.

Pragmatics is the use of language in a social context—how language is used for interaction with others. Included are the ways in which language and behavior are modified depending on the situation. How formality and politeness are understood and expressed depend on pragmatics. Later, we learn when to request and when to demand, when to expand a point and when to keep quiet, and how to refrain from putting the proverbial "foot in one's mouth."

It is assumed that when children start to school their language system is well developed and they are ready to study the *orthography* of the language—to learn to read and spell. They learn how print stands for the language that they speak.

ORAL RECEPTIVE LANGUAGE

Children learn to associate words with experiences early in life. They learn the complexities of words, the realities they represent, and their flexibility. They understand grammatic structures and appreciate word usage and how words function in sentences. They understand regular and irregular forms of words and respond to variations in word endings. They appreciate humor. They come to understand multiple word meanings, figurative language, literary references, proverbs, and clichés. Furthermore, they discover that melody and emotional tone are conveyed by non-speech parts of verbal messages.

Children and adults generally understand more than they say and have greater vocabularies than they use expressively. Developing children understand speech before they talk. Language comprehension continues to grow; it does not stop when school stops.

When children have trouble learning, we first ask how well they understand language. Receptive language serves as the bridge between what individuals know and how they express to others that they do know. Language understanding cannot be judged easily from casual conversation, because assumptions are often made that children and adolescents understand when, indeed, they do not. It is not unusual for adolescents and young adults to first become aware of receptive language problems in themselves as related to reading comprehension in literature or in the physical, biological, or social sciences. Appreciating how interpretation of spoken language relates to reading comprehension is important for both children and adults.

Standardized tests to measure receptive language are available, but there may never be adequate tests to tell us all we would like to know about an individual's language understanding. For instance, it is not difficult to develop tests for preschool children, because there is wide agreement about what a 3-year-old child should know. All children of that age in the same culture and socioeconomic status share similar experiences. Then as children grow into adolescence and adulthood their interests, school successes or failures, goals, and levels of education determine what language they need to function satisfactorily. Vocabulary requirements differ depending on a person's vocations and avocations. Complexity of syntax needed can also vary.

To understand what an individual understands, we need to focus on particular parts of language. We can then select tests, devise tasks, or systematically observe various elements to answer questions about receptive language function.

Single Words

Children demonstrate understanding of single words of various parts of speech by showing they can associate the word they hear with an object, picture, or action. Certain words, including some nouns and action verbs are *concrete*. They are closely tied to sensory experiences of being heard, seen, touched, smelled, or tasted. An individual can associate a word such as *table*, *apple*, or *book* with an object or picture. Action verbs such as *running, jumping, skipping, reading, falling, eating*, and *writing* are related to the actions. Some adjectives relate to sensory experiences. Visual ones can include color, size, and shape; ones that are heard can be *loud* or *soft* sounds; or ones felt can have *rough* or *smooth* textures. Adjectives are used flexibly. Although *soft* can refer to sound it also refers to how a pillow feels. A person can be *short* or *tall*, and a rod or stick can be *short* but is *long* not *tall*.

Many words and concepts are removed from concrete sensory experiences and are regarded as *abstract*. They are more difficult to describe, to teach, or to learn. The further the distance from concrete sensory experiences, the more abstract are the words. It is not as easy to appreciate a shared experience for abstract nouns such as *hope, justice*, or *patriotism*, or for verbs such as *explore* or *accept*, or even a word that is used so much with children as *try*.

Multiple word meanings. Children learn that words can have multiple meanings and that meaning can change depending on the context. There can be a *bank* of a stream, a piggy *bank*, or a *bank* where parents transact financial business, or we hope we are able to *bank* on a person. When a teacher says "just skip it" for a problem that is difficult, it means something different from the motor activity of *skipping*.

Words can be used as both nouns and verbs such as *circle* as a round drawing and *circle* as the verb in marking an answer. I recently saw a workbook that instructs children to "ring" the answer instead of circling it. Children with language comprehension problems may become confused thinking of a *ring on mother's finger* or the *ring of a bell* when asked to follow this command.

Function words. Some words can only be understood if they are shown in relation to other words. Prepositions (such as *on, under, behind, among*); conjunctions (such as *and, but, or*); question words (such as *how* or *why*); the auxiliary or helping forms of the verb *to be* (such as *is, are, was, were*), or words such as *has, have, may, might, can, could* are best understood in context.

Prepositions can vary in use and become confusing even for adults. If a person discovered a new idea while reading an article, is it correct to say, "The new idea was discovered *in* reading an article, *by* reading an article, *while* reading an article, *during* reading an article, *through* reading an article?" The notion can be expressed using a number of prepositions, no one of which is the only right one.

We do not easily define *how*, but it has meaning in *how many? how much?* and *how nice!* The word *is* alone does not tell much but is important when connected to a verb as in *is walking* or *is studying*. Transition words between sentences, between paragraphs, and ideas such as *then, next, hence,* and *finally* only make sense in context. Understanding indefinite words such as *later* or *maybe* is also tied to context. These words, called function words or connective words, can also be considered abstract, because they cannot be tied to sensory experiences.

Connected Speech or Sentences

Words must be arranged in conventional order. As children learn about sentences, they discover that they can make statements or ask questions. Questions are special kinds of sentences. *What* demands a name of a thing; *who*, a person, and *how many*, a number; *where*, a location; and *why*, a reason. Later, if an arithmetic question asks *how many miles a person travels*, an answer cannot be in *gallons* or *hours*. Older students must understand more complex questions such as *What is the difference between ... and ...? or Why was ... regarded as a great president while ... was viewed as mediocre?*

Ambiguous Sentences. Understanding ambiguous sentences is usually accomplished easily. Children learn that some sentences can have two meanings. "The striking baseball players were trying" could suggest they were trying to end the strike or that they were annoying their fans by not agreeing on settlement.

Figurative Language. Much of the language we use is figurative and not based in literal truth. Proverbs such as "A rolling stone gathers no moss" and "Let sleeping dogs lie" are figurative. Verbal teasing can be considered figurative language as is literary allusion and metaphor. But daily speech is filled with figurative language as well. "Hang in there," "Shape up!" "Well it's certainly not the end of the world," and "No use crying over spilled milk" are used as part of general conversation. Children acquire this kind of figurative language as they grow.

Understanding colloquial expressions is also important. These words or phrases change rapidly, but it is necessary for children and adolescents to know these expression so they will respond appropriately in their group.

Humor. Children begin to understand humor at an early age. They may first respond to the visual humor of slapstick comedy but soon appreciate verbal humor, clever plays on words, or words used in unexpected ways. Young children may attempt jokes and riddles that make little sense. They have not yet acquired the skill to understand what makes a joke funny or a riddle clever.

Longer units than sentence. Children must begin to understand longer units such as paragraph speech, stories, and factual information. Comprehension of more formal oral language of the classroom, of lectures, and of things literary may precede comprehension for reading. Students learn to understand, relate what they hear to their own experiences, identify main points, make inferences, try out predications, evaluate what a speaker intends, sort fact and opinion, and draw comparisons and contrasts. Skills in understanding speech are put to use for later reading.

Those who have difficulty with oral sentence interpretation may later have difficulty comprehending sentences in text. Any time there are problems with reading comprehension, it is necessary to determine if children understand words, sentences, and longer units in oral language. How we obtain answers about individuals' receptive language varies. We may use tests, generally observe, or analyze responses as we teach. Some of the answers to our questions will emerge only as we work with a child or adolescent over a period of time, while still other answers will be reported by the individuals themselves. We need to be aware of language comprehension as an entity apart from what children and adolescents say. We cannot make assumptions that they understand language unless we specifically ask questions about that understanding.

RECEPTIVE LANGUAGE DISORDERS

Children and adolescents with receptive language problems experience many kinds of difficulty. In the toddler years, they encounter problems in nursery school. As they grow they may have trouble understanding rules and explanations of discipline. Words used for games may be confusing. Vocabulary, concepts, and the grammar of oral directions and questions may be unclear.

As syntax becomes more complex in lectures and texts they are expected to read, they may also have trouble. Multiple meanings of words, colloquialisms, and verbal humor can be jumbled. The specific language of math may trouble them. They may show restricted understanding of words with ranges of meaning, indefinite words, or words related to right and wrong. Teenagers can be regarded as insolent, oppositional, and defiant when they have trouble understanding words used for assignments and those words used by teachers to scold or discipline.

Frequently, children with receptive language dysfunction misunderstand words or have restricted meanings for them. To illustrate: When I asked, "Is anything hard for you in school?" a 7-year-old child responded, "Yeah, a chair is hard in my school." An 11-year-old boy spoke of his summer plans that included camp. He was asked, "Is it a day camp?" He said "No." "Is it a sleep away camp?" and he replied "No." I told him I was confused. He responded, "It would have to be a half-day camp; it's from 9 to 12."

A 10-year-old boy with school problems had been told he had to eat all his lunch before taking his medication. He was a slow eater. One day his teacher told him to hurry so the cafeteria could be cleaned up. He said, "I have to eat all my lunch and then go to the office to take my medicine." She said, "Oh! take your applesauce with you to the office. The workers have to clean up here." The next day he picked up his dessert and began to leave the cafeteria. The teacher on duty that day said, "Sit down and finish your lunch." He kept walking. She said, "We do not take food out of the cafeteria." He shouted, "I do." She became angry, he raced around the school to find his teacher, and located her in the teacher's room. He said, "Tell them! Tell them! I am supposed to take my applesauce out of the cafeteria!" This is an example of interpreting words literally, but it also points to a youngster who did not attend to the nonverbal cues of the second teacher's expression and tone of voice.

Some students report studying and knowing material, but performing poorly on tests. A young teenager said, "I studied. I knew it. But then on the test she didn't ask the question right." A younger child said, "I can't answer it. It's not in the story." We must evaluate how students with learning disabilities understand spoken language.

TEACHING CHILDREN WITH RECEPTIVE LANGUAGE DIFFICULTIES

The following are some suggestions for working with children and adolescents to improve receptive language. Children who comprehend language easily learn from exposure to words. Children with difficulty need words highlighted. Adults must make words explicit rather than assuming the words will be learned naturally. He or she can point to objects or pictures, manipulate objects by putting a toy cup to a doll's mouth, or making two cars crash, or carry out a command through some gross motor activity such as *walk*, *jump*, *run*, or *find*. Later, children can push buttons, draw a picture, or write a word, sentence, or paragraph to show understanding.

- A young child with receptive language problems may not be calmed by words because the words are not understood. It may be better to use one word over and over again such as "all right" or "okay" or just calm the child by holding or patting without words. It is essential in using words of explanation or asking what is wrong to determine that the child does understand the words.

- Present language (say the words) at the same time as the experience. The words need to be provided while the activity is occurring so that they are associated with the action, object, or event. For young children, this means to say "jumping" while the child is jumping or "splashing" while the child is splashing water. For older children, providing meaningful experiences while saying the words is also important. Learning fractions while cooking can be a valuable way to give meaning to concepts that are hard for many. Seeing a glass or plastic measuring cup used to measure liquids and comparing it with cups for measuring dry ingredients is useful to understand how parts are related to wholes and how various shapes refer to the same amount.

- Always expect a response (looking toward the object, pointing at the object, finding a picture, carrying out an action) to be sure the child understands. Speaking is not the only response. Do not assume that comprehension has ocurred unless there has been demonstration of understanding.

- When explaining reasons or teaching a new task, it is essential that not only the content of what is being taught be considered but also the words used for teaching. *Start on the left side of the paper* or *put your name in the upper left hand corner* cannot be done correctly if the child does not understand *left*. *Tell me the first sound* or the *last sound* or *point to the first letter* or the *last letter* do not tell about a child's knowledge of letters and sounds if the child does not understand *first* and *last* in both the temporal (auditory or speech that quickly disappears in time) and the spatial (visual) planes.

- Be sure that children of all ages understand the basic vocabulary that is used for instruction. Words such as *easel*, and *eraser* may need to be taught. A chalkboard eraser and pencil eraser are different even if the same word is used. Words and expressions such as *beside*, *above*, *next to*, *as many as*, *that matches* may need to be explicitly taught. Words such as *lobbyist*, *Gross National Product*, *legislative*, *judicial*, *executive*, *migrate*, *beaker*, *organ*, *splice*, *photosynthesis*, *country*, *continent*, and *longitude*, are examples of words individuals with receptive language problems, at various ages, may not understand and have trouble learning. If they do not understand, they will not remember the words or the concepts they represent.

- Provide meaningful experiences and materials in teaching words and concepts. If individuals do not understand language well, hearing words to describe what they do not know can result in more confusion.

- Use materials that can be manipulated. Individuals learn best from active participation. Names for the materials being used can be taught, and words for the actions can be associated with the activity.

- Use visual support—objects or pictures and also demonstrations—as much as possible.

- Provide multiple examples of an experience and also provide negative instances. Think of how a parent develops the concept of dog. For dozens of dogs that are seen, a parent will say, "doggy." This is repeated many times along with "nice doggy" and then "doggy goes bow-wow (or arf-arf)." Every time there is a dog the young child hears "Doggy. Nice doggy. Pet the doggy." Many instances are provided. One day the baby sees a horse and says "goggie!" The parent says, "No doggy" or "That's not a doggy. It's a horse." So it goes to establish vocabulary and concepts. This provision of multiple examples carries over to middle and high school where, for example, students dissect frogs. They may become proficient in identifying parts in their own frogs. But for the practicum or test, each student walks around the lab and must identify each body part. If the student has only looked at one frog, he or she is unlikely to perform as well as the student who looked at parts in other frogs as well as his or her own. A good teacher or lab instructor has students look at many frogs to learn what something is and what it is not. The same is true when learning through microscope use whether in sixth grade or medical school. Many positive and negative examples must be given until the principle of commonality is learned.

- Relate vocabulary and concepts to children's life experiences. Children with receptive language difficulties tend to learn things in a specific, isolated way. They need help to see how new learning may relate to things they already know. Almost anything that is taught can be related in some way to a child's experiences. A city child can learn about growing things by planting a seed, even a grapefruit or orange seed, in a pot on a window sill or by taking care of a small plant. Learning about a friend's or family member's death can be related to a loss of an important object or pet to help a young child learn how loss feels. Searching for appropriate events in students' lives to be associated with concepts in science or experiences in literature can be stimulating as well as challenging for the teacher and the learner.[8,9]

- Begin work on matching answers to questions including the wh- question forms: *who? what? how? why? where?* Help children learn explicitly if they do not grasp the meaning from casual language. *Who* always requires the name of a person, *what* the name of an object, *where* a location. Students from preschool through graduate school may have problems answering specific questions. The problems are greater for those with receptive language difficulties.
- Some students may need specific teaching to learn when a certain type of response is required such as a single word, a phrase, or a sentence.
- For vocabulary development, teach words from content subjects as well as common words that students are expected to know at a certain age. Words from science and social studies should be taught. They should be reviewed from time to time. Children with receptive language problems may have trouble relating the same word from one situation to another. Pointing out such relationships can enrich meaning and aid memory. (*Menu* in the school cafeteria, plan a *menu* for a party, select from a *menu* at the computer; *set* the table, a *set* of dishes, a *set* in math; *executive* in a company, the *executive* branch of government).
- Additional help for oral comprehension (and later for reading comprehension) should be provided in:
    —following precise oral directions;
    —following printed directions; and
    —responding to questions, emphasizing different kinds of question and the types of answers required (for facts, to make inferences, to use material presented, or to draw on life experiences).
- Help students understand what it means to interpret that which is not specifically stated.
- Teach various classification systems. Objects can be described by
    —perceptual attributes of size, shape, color, texture;
    —function or use; and
    —category.
- These attributes can then be used by children to understand how things are *different* and *alike*. At first, children will need help to see how objects in a group are alike, because all things are *red* or all things are *circular*, or all are *food*, or *desserts*, or *vegetables*. (Children are able to detect differences before finding likenesses.)
- Use similar words and concepts to help children understand analogies. These same attributes can help a child realize relationships among words and ideas. When teaching analogies, provide visual support by drawing lines that connect related words. This helps make concrete the

various ways words for analogies relate. The revisualization of various kinds of relationships is then more likely to be applied.

—up down   in ——

—snow white   grass ——

—snow grass   white ——

—car street   airplane ——

—car airplane   road ——

—cat dog   kitten ——

—cat dog   meow ——

- Provide explicit work with understanding pronoun referents. Help a child understand, for example, how *he* refers to a person, that *he* is always male, and that if two males are being talked about in a sentence, it must be clear to whom *he* refers. If there are several people or multiple actions *they* may not convey meaning to the listener. For instance,
    —Tom and Bill went to the game, and *he* got a cap, but *he* didn't have enough money.
    —Susan's and Sarah's class went on a field trip and *she* brought lunch, and *she* bought it there.
    —The men were afraid of the animal. The animals were gigantic. And then *they* killed *them*.
- Teach figurative language appropriate for age. "Scared to death," "having butterflies," "raining cats and dogs," "that just kills me," "out like a light" are examples.
- Help children understand that words can be used in multiple ways and as different parts of speech. This helps them develop flexibility of language understanding. The word *coach* is used as a noun, it can refer to a person; as a verb, to the act of instructing. But *coach* as a noun can also be a stage *coach* or a *coach* on a train, or as an adjective, for a kind of airfare. A *watch* can tell time, but a person can also *watch* an event.
- Help with understanding the regularities and irregularities of words. The verb tense markers -*s*, -*ing*, -*ed* may be used for many words, but the irregular forms also need to be learned.
- Teach meanings of conjunctions such as *and*, *or*, *but*. These words may be omitted or used incorrectly in writing because individuals do not understand their precise meaning and use.

- Teach meanings of transition words in listening (and later for reading and writing). Lists of such words, called signal words, are in *The New Reading Teacher's Book of Lists*.[10]
- Help students understand how sentences can have words arranged in different ways or use different words and yet mean the same thing. *If you get a good grade, you can go on the trip*, and *You can go on the trip if you get a good grade* mean the same but *If you go on the trip, you will get a good grade* means something different.
- Provide activities for receptive language development to help children and adolescents understand the similarities in meaning of *discuss the contributions made by —— and why were the —— important? What was the 15th amendment?* and *what did the 15th amendment do?* require similar answers.
- Provide practice to decide if there is adequate information given to answer the questions asked or if something is missing. Such problem solving can be with math or with other areas.
- Provide practice in separating fact from opinion. From elementary years through all of one's education, it is essential that fact be differentiated from opinion. Lines become blurred quickly by gossip, tabloids, and television. Those with language comprehension problems may have more trouble than others discerning such differences.
- Specific teaching about the differences between fact and fantasy in language heard and later in reading may be necessary.
- Teach meanings of prefixes, roots, and suffixes. (See Chapters 4 and 5 for further suggestions for older students.)

Receptive language, including vocabulary, syntax, question forms, and content, must be taught. The goal is to teach words, structures, and meanings explicitly so that individuals understand at the level of their peers. It is important to recognize that these recommendations are not meant to imply that the students must always have questions that are easier and more concrete. The questions (and indeed all material) must be gradually increased in complexity, building on the students' successes to allow them to function at higher levels. Those with good intelligence and receptive language dysfunction have the potential to achieve close to the level of their intellect if they have good and sustained help to improve receptive language facility.

AUDITORY PROCESSING

A number of skills are learned by first being processed through hearing. These skills are referred to as *auditory processing*. Included in this area are: *prosody*, *auditory memory*, and *phonological awareness*.

Prosody

Verbal interpretation of language has been discussed. But as individuals comprehend language, there is much conveyed nonverbally—with information that does not consist of words.

Children learn the meaning of different tones in another's speech that convey pleasure, scolding, sarcasm, emphasis, making a statement, or asking a question. They learn to interpret the meaning of pauses in speech and how the length of a pause can carry meaning. Sarcasm and teasing are often communicated more by the tone of the message than by the words used. These nonverbal parts of the verbal message—the pauses, stops, starts, stresses, inflections, and the melody of the language are referred to as *prosody*. They are the *prosodic features* of speech. The melody of speech gives it richness and emotional tone. Speech that shows little variation in prosody is speech that is a monotone or monotonous. This lack of variety in the tone of speech can suggest learning and/or emotional difficulties.

To understand a speaker, prosodic features of speech must be understood. We listen, not only to the words being spoken but also the prosody of speech. The listener must understand the fondness that can underlie such expressions as "You're such a turkey," or "What an idiot!" The tone of voice informs the listener that the message is a lighthearted one. Changing the tone while maintaining the same words creates a much different meaning.

Pauses between words also convey information. "A nice man" is different from "an ice man." A "loud speaker" may annoy us when he or she sits behind us at an event, but a "loudspeaker" is helpful to hear what is going on when there is a large crowd.

Placing emphasis on different words in the same group of words also changes meaning. The white *house* (that is down the street) is different from the *White* House (where the president lives). As an illustration, different meaning is conveyed by emphasis with the following three words. Say them aloud and listen to what you are saying.

> *I* can go. (Even if you cannot go.)
>
> I *can* go. (Although I thought for a while I could not go.)
>
> I can *go*. (I can go by myself, or Hurrah, I really can go, or My mother said I can go.)
>
> I can go? (Do you really mean it, that I can go?)

Interpreting prosodic features of another's speech is essential for development of receptive language skills. Such interpretation must also be carried into reading. It is by processing the prosodic features mentally as we read, that we appreciate the richness of some kinds of text. Text provides few cues to suggest the prosody of speech; only the limited information conveyed by punctuation marks—period, question mark, exclamation point, and comma— and by emphasis that is suggested by italics. Poetry, a different dialect from the reader's own, or dialogue in a play are best understood as processed through the rhythm and inflection of spoken speech.

Teaching Understanding of Prosodic Features

* Teach how the ends of statements (or telling sentences) sound different from questions.
    —I am running.
    —I am running?
    —Am I running?
    —They are on the playground.
    —Are they on the playground?
    —Who is on the playground?
* Present pairs of sentences and ask the children if they sound just the same.
    —Michael is on the playground.
    —Michael is on the playground?
    —Gwen is reading.
    —Gwen is reading?
* Say sentences and ask the children to tell if the sentences are making a statement or asking a question.
    —Do you want to have recess?
    —We will not have recess.
    —We will go to the library now.
    —Should we go to the library now?
    —Is the balloon red?
    —Is the balloon inflated?
    —Is Jennie here today?
    —Everyone is being quiet.
* The children should be given an oral sentence and asked to tell it to someone and then make it into a question.
* Present the same sentences said in a gentle way and an angry way. For example, "I don't like it when someone is sitting in my chair."
    —Ask them to tell if they sound the same.
    —Ask them to tell which voice was the angry one.
* Point out periods, question marks, exclamation points in text and demonstrate using speech to show how meaning is conveyed.
* Show how underlining and italics show emphasis.

Auditory Memory

We usually think of memory as being short term and long term. As we interpret what we hear—a word, a sentence, an explanation—we put it into short-term storage or working memory. Short-term memory is important for participating in conversation, for remembering what is said long enough to act upon it, and in general to appreciate information through listening. We hear and react to what another is saying, and we can immediately respond. We listen and remember briefly when introduced to a person not previously known. We retain a telephone number given us long enough to write it down, dial it, or touch the correct buttons. We remember a short list of a few things we are told to purchase at the market. When engaging in conversation, we know and remember what we have said before. (How important this part of short-term memory is may not be appreciated until we know an older person with dementia, or who has had a stroke, and does not remember what he or she has just said or asked.) For use over a period of time, much that we hear must be held in long-term storage.

Many children who have learning disabilities have problems with auditory memory. Individuals with short-term memory problems have trouble following oral directions, learning from oral input alone, understanding verbal explanations, or remembering a question long enough to answer it. They may also have difficulty taking notes in class, because in order to take notes, a student must listen and remember while at the same time, abstract what is important, and then write it in a form available for later study.

When parents are told that their children have problems with auditory short-term memory, they are often puzzled and report that their sons or daughters can remember places they went two years ago driving on a strange road for the first time. They remember exactly where to make a turn at an old birch tree. These kinds of memory functions are real. It may be helpful to think of different kinds of memory for each kind of experience we have. Some individuals are good with episodic or event memory or with visual-spatial memory but poor with auditory memory.

In helping students with auditory memory problems, we need to first determine how much of the difficulty is with understanding language and how much results from problems with short-term memory. Work with auditory memory needs to consider: length of input, the nature of the input, the level of vocabulary used, and the syntactic or grammatic complexity. Then the nature of expected responses needs to be considered. Situational factors such as whether the task is presented formally, as part of daily routine, or used as casual instructions are also important.

Length of input. The longer the auditory input, the harder it may be to remember. Long sentences are harder to remember than shorter ones. Long lists are harder than short ones. However, length is not the only factor. A short sentence in passive voice, with a negative word, or presented as a question may be more difficult to remember than a longer simple, active, declarative one.

Nature of the input. Individuals may respond differently if the material consists of digits, unrelated words such as a grocery list, or sentences that are meaningful. Some people perform better with nonmeaningful material, while others are aided by the meaning of a sentence format. Those with good syntactic structure in their oral language use it to help with memory for tasks such as repeating sentences or carrying out commands. Those with oral formulation difficulties and problems with syntax may perform better with unrelated material such as numbers or words.

Vocabulary. Unfamiliar words may be more difficult to remember than familiar ones. On the other hand, novel words or emotionally charged ones may fascinate the listener so they will be retained. Familiar material or processes stay in memory longer. For example, a cook can listen to a recipe and remember it, while a non-cook might not remember a major ingredient or a process for preparation.

Expected response. What an individual is required to do with information can determine how well he or she can perform on memory tasks. For instance, repeating exactly what is heard without any attention to the nature of the material is different from hearing information and then using it. Repetition is a parroting response. It can be done with little thought and little meaning. When the material has to be manipulated mentally as in comparing two words, carrying out a command, following oral directions, or taking notes at a lecture, the memory task becomes more complex.

Situation. In a formal situation, such as when individuals are being tested, help is given to be sure the person's attention is focused on the task at hand. The person is cued to be alert. At other times, instructions are part of a daily routine. If a child or adolescent is engaged in a video game or playing in the family room, and at around six o'clock, mother is heard saying something, a child may not need good immediate memory to know that mother is calling the family to dinner. The same thing may occur at the same time each day so little memory is being tapped. A child who is told to "look both ways" before crossing the street or a teenager who is told to "be home by 11 o'clock" has heard the same statements so many times that short-term memory may not be involved. Such commands may be either automatically implemented or ignored.

Casual instructions. Casual instructions are ones that occur at times when the child has not been told specifically to pay attention. The remarks a teacher makes as students are putting books away, or that mother calls out as the child races out of the house or from the car in the morning are casual instructions and may be important, but may be ignored because attention is not focused to listen.

Teaching to Improve Auditory Memory

- Reduce the length of auditory input and then increase it as the child or adolescent can manage.

- Use different kinds of materials (words, digits, sentences). If one type of material is remembered more easily then others, that material should be used to help remember other kinds of material. For example, if the child can remember sentences better than single words, such as items on a grocery list, make the list into a silly sentence.
- Use meaningful materials to improve auditory memory. Unrelated words and digits seldom need to be remembered except for phone numbers and one's social security number.
- Use visual support in teaching so the students do not need to rely on auditory memory alone. A teacher's use of a chalkboard or transparencies to provide visual support helps all students but is essential for many learning disabled students.
- Provide more repetitions for learning to occur. Repetition alone is seldom enough, though. Additional tools or alternative ways of remembering are often necessary.
- Use materials that can be manipulated. Motor memory can assist auditory memory.
- Encourage revisualization of actions and events. Make auditory tapes of paragraphs and stories or tell children to close their eyes while listening. Describe places and actions. Try to stay away from events portrayed on television so they really focus on internal imagery.
- Teach the use of mnemonic devices. Encourage students to develop ways to remember that are unique to each of them. Examples of such devices are:
  —remembering princi*pal* is a pal and princip*le* is a rul*e*, that station*ery* is pap*er*;
  —using the first letters of the names of the Great Lakes—Huron, Ontario, Michigan, Erie, and Superior—to spell HOMES;
  —making up rhymes or silly sentences to remember things in lists;
  —organizing material to be remembered according to categories, for example, a grocery list where items are grouped according to kind or location in the store (cereal versus produce).
- Play games that require following oral directions. Increase complexity and length of input, level or familiarity of vocabulary, and complexity of syntax.
- Provide activities such as listening to sentences and paragraph stories (and later longer stories) to remember facts.
  —At first provide cues about what to listen for as structure for listening.
  —Later, listening should occur without hearing the questions first.

Phonological Awareness

As mentioned earlier, phonology refers to the sound structure of the language, the sounds being those of speech. If children do not attend to phonology, they may have problems with speech production, with reading, and with spelling. See Chapter 4 for specific activities to improve phonological awareness as related to pre-reading and reading.

ORAL EXPRESSIVE LANGUAGE

Oral expressive language is the use of speech to present ideas and feelings. When expressive language develops easily, children make correct words choices, retrieve words as they need them, formulate ideas into sentences, and arrange sentences sequentially for paragraph speech. As soon as individuals begin to combine words, they become increasingly involved in the give and take of conversation. Conversation is one of the most important accomplishments of humans in the evolutionary process.

In studying a child's language, it is necessary to consider both the content and the form. Syntax and articulation are the *form* of language. *Content* is what individuals know in their heads—the cognitive stuff of thinking. What is tested on verbal intelligence tests is the content of what a person knows. An individual can name pictures, define words, use sentences, answer questions, or engage in conversation and thus inform us about what he or she knows. Their responses indicate something about knowledge or content of language as expressed through speech. Good content does not mean that form is good. Some children and adolescents have excellent verbal knowledge with high verbal IQ scores but have trouble with the form of language—retrieving and organizing what they wish to say. Others have good syntax and excellent articulation but little content in what they express.[11]

To make judgments about oral expressive language, we must first have a language sample. This sample must represent the child's typical use of speech. A parent of a preschool child, who is in the test room with the child, can tell the examiner if the language produced throughout the session is characteristic of the language used at home. For an older child, opportunities must be provided for the child both to speak and to interact in give-and-take communication.

Along with results of tests, the person doing the testing also makes judgments about the individual's expressive language with each speech attempt. We observe if an individual has problems with speech production, word finding, and/or formulating ideas. (Some useful tests for spoken language are listed in Appendix A.)

EXPRESSIVE LANGUAGE DISORDERS
Problems with Articulation or Phonological Disorders

An articulation problem occurs when children do not say speech sounds correctly. Errors are classified as ones of substitution, omission, or distortion. Children may substitute *f* for voiceless *th* by saying "fank-you" for *thank-you* or "teef" for *teeth*, or substitute *w* for *r* as "wabbit" for *rabbit* or "cawit" for *carrot*. They may omit a sound as saying "cah" for *car*. Distortion of speech sounds often occur for *s* and *z*. Such a distortion for *s* and *z* is referred to as a *lisp*. Children may put out their tongues and say "thee" for *see* or "thoop" for *soup* or they can make the air come out the side of the tongue and say "shee" for *see* or "zhoo" for *zoo*. Most young children have speech that is intelligible; even with some articulation errors, most of what they say can be understood.

Articulation disorders occur for multiple reasons. Some of these include: *dysarthria* as in children with cerebral palsy or other neuromuscular conditions; *apraxia* for speech, meaning that the child has difficulty in voluntarily executing a motor action for speech, even though he or she can move the tongue and lips for vegetative functioning such as sucking, chewing, or blowing out a candle; motor patterning difficulties; or lack of efficient velopharyngeal closure.

Children who are cognitively limited may have articulation difficulties and hearing impaired individuals will have articulation deviations related to the kind and extent of hearing loss. Many children have delays or deviations in speech production for reasons that are unknown. When children have articulation problems in the preschool years, they may be showing a generalized weakness with managing their phonological system. Thus, articulation problems are now referred to as phonological disorders.[12]

In addition to taking an inventory of defective sounds, it is important that an observation is made about intelligibility of a child's speech—how well it can be understood. Intelligibility may break down in connected speech. A child may show few articulation errors with single words but have difficulty being understood when using sentences or longer units of speech. Speech therapy should not be denied to any child with unintelligible speech, no matter what the age.

Many children have articulation problems that are correctable through speech therapy, and they may never have any later problems with learning. Others, however, through their articulation difficulties, are reflecting generalized problems with their phonological system. They are not making automatic associations between words that they hear and words they need to say. Some of these children are showing the beginnings of a kind of phonological weakness that will affect their later learning to read and spell.

Many children with articulation disorders learn to correct their speech by any method of speech therapy that is offered. A lot of them benefit from auditory stimulation and visual imitation alone, but others do not. Children who are apraxic need specific instruction, often verbal instruction about how to make the motor movements, to help them form the sounds they need to say.

Problems with Word Retrieval

Children and adolescents may score well on intelligence tests and still have expressive language disorders. Problems with word retrieval are common in learning disabled children. Children who have such problems cannot easily recall words that are in their vocabularies. This problem is referred to as a *word-finding problem* or *dysnomia*. Children or adolescents may use circumlocutions, or a roundabout way of expressing the word, such as "little things you put in there to make it work" for *batteries*, "thing you put up in the rain" for *umbrella*, "a thing at hop inna grass" for *grasshopper*, or a "world ball" for *globe*. They may say a word with a similar sound pattern, as "tangerine" for *tambourine* or "period" for *pyramid*, confuse the order of sounds as "bastik" for *basket*, combine word parts as labeling a stagecoach a "kariot" (likely a combination of carriage and chariot), or "candelier" (combining candle and chandelier for candelabra) or give a semantically related response as "key" for *lock*, or a within class substitution as "book" for *magazine*. At times there is semantic confusion as seen in an 8-year-old boy, who, searching for the name of the story, *Cinderella*, said, "Oh! What is it called—the pumpkin turns into a thing—-and the lady was to go to the ball-game." Children with retrieval difficulties often have a difficult time learning to name colors, acquire letter names and letters sounds, and recall math facts or multiplication tables.

To Help with Word-Finding Problems

- Provide practice in naming common objects and parts of objects around the home and school (tools, utensils, foods; knife—handle, blade, point).
- Be sure the words are in an individual's receptive language vocabulary before they are used for naming practice.
- When pictures are used, be sure the child can interpret the visual representation of the object.
- Ask multiple choice questions. This allows a child to show recognition of a target word and also provides practice in saying the word.
- Provide the initial sound of the target word. Again, this allows the person to pull from experience to recognize the word for which he or she is searching and to practice saying the word.
- Provide practice recalling names of movies and stories and characters in stories or movies.
- Give practice naming things to go in specified categories—things to eat, desserts, breakfast foods, meats; jobs that people do, jobs that are done indoors, jobs done outdoors; games; methods of transportation; animals.
- Provide practice in hearing names of things, places, or people and retrieving the category label.

- Help develop alternate ways to speak of an object if the name cannot be recalled.
- If a child or adolescent has a word retrieval problem, he or she needs to study differently for objective tests than for essay ones. For example, in studying definitions, the word should be put on one side of an index card (or folded paper) and the definition on the other. The word should be read and retrieving the definition practiced, but the definition should also be read and the specific word retrieved. The same procedure applies for studying battles and their dates, persons and their contributions, etc. Such studying, both from specific to broad concept and from broad concept to specific is essential for students with word-finding problems. Teaching this manner of learning and test preparation should begin in early grades and will be a skill that is automatic for the student to use later.
- If students cannot retrieve a response, when taking short answer tests, they should go on to the next question and then later come back to the item they could not recall. It is important for them to mark the question in such a way that they will not forget to go back and try it a second time.

Problems with Syntax

Some children have trouble formulating sentences. They may know words to use, but their difficulty is with hanging the words on the structure or the syntax of the language. There can be lack of agreement between subject and verb tense, omission of inflectional morphemes at the end of words, and/or omission of function words.

Other children and adolescents can use sentences but have difficulty formulating longer units to explain an idea, answer a question, or produce paragraph speech. There may be a paucity of content as well as disorganization in forming sentences and in arranging sentences in a sensible order. We can appreciate the difficulty they will have in answering essay questions and writing papers even when they know answers. When children have difficulty with oral expressive language, their reading may not be efficient because their disorganized speech does not allow them to make as good use of context cues as do language-able children. They may not be able to make good predictions about words that might come next in a sentence, and their monitoring systems in getting the sense of what they read can be faulty.

Older children and teenagers with formulation problems may not be able to recall words and organize them to inform others about their thoughts or feelings. Exasperated parents may accuse them of never thinking or having no feelings. It increases a teenager's loneliness to be so misunderstood. Often these individuals have never been identified as having an oral language disorder. When such teenagers get into difficulty, they cannot explain what happened and are often unable to tell that they feel terrible about an incident. They know how they feel, yet cannot put the words together effectively.

Early problems with syntax can appear as later problems in managing complex syntax heard or read, and additionally can have an impact on written formulation. But some learning disabled children and adolescents who have adequate spoken language do not think to monitor for errors in written sentences by using their knowledge of spoken language. They must be taught to do so.

Some examples of problems with syntax include holding on to immature question forms, for example "What for this?" said by a 5-year-old for *What is this for?*, "I going home now?" for *Can I go home now?* by a 4-year-old, or "You both drink them" for *you drink them both* from an 8-year-old. Subtle problems of grammatical usage are often heard in spoken language and then reflected in students' writing.

Here are some additional examples of oral formulation difficulties. One boy at age 7 said, "The other girl kept thoughting I was in a different grade" when he was referring to a female psychologist who had seen him recently. At age 14, he continued to show oral formulation difficulties. He was achieving adequately in school, although below the level of his intelligence, and had not had any speech and language intervention. Asked how you get binary colors, he responded "by mixing firstary colors." He also said, "They should make a law against car theps" (thefts). Speaking of having help in reading an assigned book, he responded, "I read it on my own—only parshinally." In offering a polite close to the session he said, "Anything you need from me else?"

Early problems with formulation may be helped with good intervention, but may never disappear completely. The following are responses over a period of time from one youngster who did have speech and language intervention. He was first seen at three and one-half years.

Age 3 years, 6 months
"Where other train? There down a floor."
"A wheel come off?"
"What for iss?"

Age 5 years, 6 months
"stream thing" for wishing well
"riding thing" for saddle
"fallton" for waterfalls (possibly a combination of *falls* and *fountain*)
"We has to go to art."
"How many more time?" (asking how much more time he had to stay)
"Where am I going? a few more minutes?" (using *where* for *when*)

Age 6 years, 2 months
"How many more time?" for *how much more time*

Age 6 years, 11 months
In telling about the North Pole ""snow—lotsa snow—shop where Santa live—he give every good toy to the childs—gives toys to good children"
In telling about what happened to Pinoccio when he told a lie, "his nose will get real taller" (accompanied by appropriate gesture of nose growing longer out from his face)

Age 9 years, 5 months
Trying to retrieve the title *Robin Hood,* "Don't tell me. I forget! I know it! Christopher Robin. No, not Christopher Robin. It's *Robin Hood!*"
Trying to recall the label *violin* "violet, not violet! lin—violin"

Age 11 years, 3 months
"tangerine" as label for *tambourine*
"syascope—that's not right—stethoscope—I knew it ended with scope and started with s. I just got the middle wrong."
"water surrounding land on three sides" as a definition of *peninsula.*
"two two fifths" for *two and two fifths*
"you take 2000 into 12" for *2000 divided by 12*
"I'm minusing 15."
"I timed six and eight."

TEACHING CHILDREN WITH ORAL EXPRESSIVE LANGUAGE DIFFICULTIES

Children in the normal process of acquiring language do so simply by being immersed in the language around them. Little is explicitly taught with exception of some correction of word misuse. Children with language disorders need to have words and grammatic structures made explicit for them. Some would perhaps never learn to use better language if they did not have special teaching. Children and adolescents must know the target they are working toward and must have practice until they can use the unit (word or syntactic structure) automatically in a structured situation and can then generate it later on their own.

Work with Oral Formulation

• Provide models of correct sentences.
• Provide practice at the imitation level.
• Provide practice in generating sentences without a model.

- Make sentences about single action pictures.
    —The boy is playing.
    —Vary the subject.
      —The girl is playing.
      —The dog is playing.
      —The cat is playing.
    —Vary the verb.
      —The boy is jumping.
      —The boy is running.
      —The boy is eating.
      —The boy is sleeping.
    —Expand the sentences
    —Add modifiers.
      —The little boy....
      —The happy boy....
      —The scared boy....
    —Add objects.
      —The boy is eating soup.
      —The boy is eating cake.
      —The boy is eating ice-cream.
    —Add modifiers.
      —The happy boy is eating cake.
      —The happy boy is eating white cake.
      —The happy little boy is eating white cake and chocolate ice-cream.
    —Use pictures with singular and plural subjects (boy-boys, man-men, child-children, mouse-mice, etc.) with correct verb agreement.
    —Teach children to compose sentences that tell what is happening in a picture, what happened before the picture, and what will happen after the picture—as a way to work with verb tense.
    —Use complex action pictures to stimulate several sentences.
    —Provide several pictures in sequence and have child provide a sentence for each.
    —Provide practice in combining sentences to make one sentence.
- Sentences should be developed to make statements, ask questions, describe, clarify, explain, request, inform, amuse.
- Sentences should be matched to questions asked. The question, *Who wrote Little Women?* requires the name of a person, not "characters in a story."
- Work with morphological endings should be done explicitly for such things as
    — -ed indicates past tense,
    — -s indicates plural or possessive,
    — -er indicates a person who does something or to make comparison

- Practice with fantasy can include such questions as:
  —What would happen if—-?
  —How would —— feel if —— happened?,
  —What do you predict will happen when——?,
  —What happened to cause —— to happen?
- Construct speaking situations to include such things as
  —Ask Tom to tell Bill —-. Who will be doing the talking? What
   would he say.
  —Tell Bill to ask Tom —- Who would be doing the talking? What
   would he say?
- Put several sentences in order to form oral paragraphs.
- Teach function and form along with meaning of parts of speech including
  regular and irregular forms:
  —verbs (*walk, walks, walking, walked* but *run, runs, running, ran*)
  —plurals (*book-books, tooth-teeth, woman-women*)
  —comparatives and superlatives (*great-greater-greatest* but *good-
   better-best*)
- Teach meanings of conjunctions such as *and, or, but*. Most students
  learn meanings of these words easily. Children with language disorders
  may have difficulty.
- Have students construct sentences with clear pronoun referents.
  Children with formulation difficulties often have difficulty in both clarity
  of expression of 'who did what to whom' (in such structures as, in the
  sentence *The girl gave the boy the airplane*, who received the airplane? or
  in the sentence *The cat is chased by the mouse*, who is doing the chasing?)
- Provide practice telling how to make something (paper hat, kite, sand-
  wich, playing a game) or carry out a specific task (how to play a game).
  —At first real objects can be used while the activity is happening.
  —Be sure all objects needed can be named.
  —Be sure all verbs needed are known.
  —Talk about the activity while it is occurring.
  —Teach use of transition words such as *first, then, next,* and *last* or
   finally.
  —After the activity is completed have the child tell what was done.
   Stress the step-by-step instructions that you can carry out on the
   child's directions. This can make the need for clarity of oral
   formulation dramatic.
- For older students, work on oral language to precede written work.
  They need to be consciously aware of, or have a sense of, how sentences
  are put together. They may learn this best through imitation and practice rather than learning about subjects and verbs specifically. Others
  may learn better with explicit instruction about subjects, verbs, and

parts of speech. The only value in learning parts of speech, which is very hard for many learning disabled students, is to allow communication about how sentences are put together and how to correct errors. Individual teachers will need to decide if spending time in this area will be worth what the students can learn from the exercises.

- Help children learn to describe objects according to:
    —how they feel, sound, taste, look, and smell;
    —function and use; and
    —superordinate category.
- The objects can be categorized in the same way.
- After proficiency is developed in describing concrete objects and experiences then the same procedures could be used to *compare, contrast, discuss, list, evaluate, explain* actions and ideas rather than objects.
- Encourage children to use figurative language once they understand it. Language impaired children and adolescents frequently enjoy work with figurative language and begin collecting examples on their own.
- Play a game where there is a barrier (piece of cardboard or easel) blocking the view of the table directly between the child and teacher. An object or picture is placed in front of one person. The other must describe it by giving clues. The first person must guess what is being described.
- Use the same set-up as in the previous example but have each person ask questions in an attempt to guess what the object or pictured object is, or what an imagined object or person is.
- Review concepts of time, days of the week and months of the year, holidays and months in which they appear, and if not mastered teach them.
- Develop exercises to increase skill in acquiring information through questioning. Provide activities for multiple situations in which questions are asked. Encourage practice in formulating the questions. For example, how would you call a friend's mother and ask if he can come over to spend the night? How could you ask a teacher for additional help? How could you explain that you have trouble remembering an assignment and it would help if the teacher could write assignments on the board. Start with a *Twenty Questions* type exercise and proceed through role playing.
- Some of the time, it helps if the material used for spoken language is shown in print. Seeing words in print can stabilize speech production for some children. Printed sentences can support correct formulation. Speaking and reading combined may reinforce each other.

PRAGMATICS

Pragmatics is the use of language in a social situation. Young children who have difficulty with pragmatics may have trouble understanding and using the language of instruction, of discipline, and social interaction. They may not have the words to say such things as "I don't know. Help me. Say it again. I'm tired. I'm hungry. I'm scared. I'm sad. I'm disappointed." In addition to failing to attend to cues of displeasure from an adult they may not interpret the multiple cues used by peers and adults to say "I like you." Older children may not know how to ask questions to gain information they need, to request clarification, to expand a point, to change a topic, or to direct anger appropriately using words. Excellent vocabulary and good syntax mean little if the words and sentences are not used appropriately for the situation.

Some children with language learning disorders do not use "kid-talk." Their linguistic usage may be formal and controlled so they do not use current colloquial expressions. They do not say "buzz off," "cut it out," "stop right now," or other appropriate phrase if they are being bothered. They can become figures of fun for other children because their formality in using language is inappropriate. Children and adolescents can be regarded as outcasts. They often have no awareness of why others do not like them or why their manner of using communicative interactions annoys others.

Developing Pragmatic Skills

- Help children develop vocabulary and concepts to be associated with experiences as they occur.
- Teach words and syntax to convey expressions of joy, pleasure, excitement, sadness, anger, disappointment, fear, tiredness, boredom.
- Help children improve their vocabulary related to feelings thereby allowing easier communication about times when things are going well or poorly.
- Teach the language of good manners such as *please, thank-you*, and *excuse me*. A wide variety of such words can be taught with shades of meaning to be used at appropriate times.
- Teach "kid talk" or appropriate ways to respond to teasing or hurt feelings. Expressions in use with other children of the same age should be taught.
- Exercises should be provided to help children and adolescents understand how:
    —to modify language interaction with peers, authority figures, strangers, family members, etc.;
    —to ask questions and learn when such questions are appropriate and how to word them;
    —to request clarification and what to say
    —to expand a point;
    —to express feelings related to learning;
    —to direct their anger at the task rather than at themselves or others and what language to use; and

—to learn flexibility of language use—that things can be said in different ways, that there are multiple ways one can express displeasure, joy, etc.

- If children have trouble understanding humor, teach them what it means and that verbal humor can help them be part of a group. They may need assistance to understand how words can be used in different ways, how shades of meaning can make what is heard funny. Some students, with receptive language disorders, are so literal that they need help to grasp the idea of verbal humor. Some comic strips and cartoons that use words can be helpful. For older students, cartoons from the *New Yorker* can be used. For some students, visual humor in cartoons can be used as a step toward appreciating humor that uses words.

- Provide exercises showing the difference between literal interpretation of a rule, a command, and instruction and what is actually meant. "Write a paragraph with 50 words" usually does not mean exactly 50 words, but it is implied that there is an acceptable range. A lot of language has a range of meaning implied; little can be divided into "either/or" categories.

- Review or teach meanings of words such as *maybe* an event will occur, we will leave at *about* 4:00, or it weighs *about* a half-pound.

- Teach children and adolescents what teasing means, how expressions commonly used by peers are not insulting or as hurtful as they sound from the literal words used.

SPECIAL CONSIDERATIONS ABOUT LANGUAGE DIFFERENCES
Speakers of Languages Other Than English

Anyone who sees children with language and/or learning disabilities will be asked to see children from backgrounds other than English speaking. Parents of these children may speak only the language of another culture at home while peers in school speak English. It is wonderful when individuals grow up to be bilingual. They have a richness in their lives denied those who speak only one language. But there is a controversy about teaching such children. In some places English is taught as a second language. Some educators advocate teaching children in their first or home language rather than teaching them to understand, read, and write English. In order to achieve school and job success, children need to learn to speak, read, and write the major language of school and the workplace. To provide them with programs that do not teach them such basic survival skills in language understanding and production is discriminatory.

Children with problems in form and content in one language may show similar problems in their second language. They may need to learn one language in its spoken and beginning printed form before being able to add the second language. I am often troubled by the willingness of clinicians to accept the judgments of a bilingual translator or parent as to whether or not a child is being "correct" in the other language when the clinician does not speak that language. We often see young English-speaking children whose parents report their young children understand everything they hear, when upon evaluation they understand little.

Children who are growing up bilingual but who show problems in school should be given adequate evaluations. If they are in English-speaking classrooms, they need evaluation of their understanding and use of English. But they also need evaluation in their first language. Many children show a spoken language disorder in both languages. Then the choice must be made as to the language in which they are to be educated. It should be the language of the society in which they will grow and hope to be employed.

Speakers of Black-English Vernacular

There are other children in the United States, particularly in our cities and some rural areas, from African-American backgrounds who are speakers of a dialect that differs from standard English used in formal situations and in printed texts.[13,14] Their fully developed linguistic system may have some slight differences in articulation such as "bruvuh" for *brother*, "teef" for *teeth*, "dem" for *them*, "ax" for *ask*, and final consonant clusters reduction so *test* and *desk* are said "tess" and "dess" making the plurals "tessez" and "dessez." But there is often greater variance in rules of grammar. There are different ways of marking plurals so that "two book" is correct instead of the redundancy of standard English where "two books" has both number given as *two* and also the *s* as a marker for more than one. Rules for verb tense are different as well. One example is the sense of continuous action over time such as conveyed by "he be working"—a kind of marker that is absent in standard English.

Since the 1960s, information has been available describing characteristics of dialects of African-American speakers, particularly as spoken in our cities. More recently movies are being made in which such dialects are used appropriately by actors to evoke the reality of some neighborhoods. Actors who perform and writers who develop novels and scripts can, when they are interviewed on radio or television, switch codes from standard English to dialect, appropriate to the characters portrayed, or to the point they wish to make. Characters in movies express ideas admired by children and the way they talk can serve as powerful models. But this does not mean that children should be discouraged from using standard English speech. Standard English, rightly or wrongly, is considered the speech of textbooks, of commerce, and of the educated person. One may be granted or denied job interviews and jobs because of the way one talks.

Those who speak only a dialect of English that uses a different grammar may not have the same system of spoken language when they enter school as that used in books. The language of text for them does not represent "talk written down." They are at a disadvantage when asked to write, since they may be graded on how they write, using a standard English model, when indeed their spoken speech does not have the same rules.

In all linguistic groups there is home language, language that is used with intimates, family and friends, that is different from formal speech. Being able to make the shift is what is important. Those who are successful automatically change to a more formal manner of talking when with unfamiliar persons or when engaged in public speaking, for example. Those of us who teach, have an obligation to help children appreciate the dialect they use but also to help them learn formal and Standard English. To deprive them of learning Standard English is a kind of racism. They need to have standard spoken language skills to acquire jobs and progress in the professions or in business to the level of their abilities and desires. They should not be held back because of judgments about dialect differences. They should have the option of learning Standard English, to have it available even if they decide for social and political reasons never to use it. It would then be their choice.

Information about dialect differences has existed for some time. Yet at the time of this writing, I continue to hear well-meaning, caring professionals speak of "bad English" spoken by inner city children. Dialect differences are not spoken about these days as easily as in times past. Refraining from such discussions is again a way to hurt children. Some of these children do have language disorders and learning disabilities in addition to their dialect differences. To deprive them of the best of our knowledge in linguistics, cognition, and language disorders is unjust.

SUMMARY

Oral language forms the base for later verbal learning. Our language comprehension and production provide an intimate reflection of our culture and who we are as individuals and as part of a group. Hence, evaluation of oral language should always be considered when students have trouble in school. Parents need to pay attention to how their children use language to talk about thoughts and feelings, to express pleasure, fear, and regrets. Parents and teachers should observe how children use language for thinking, learning, and social interaction. Teachers use language in reading, math, music, or physical education in the classroom, the playing field, and the tutoring session. When we use language to teach we must be sure those who listen to us understand what we say and know how to respond.

CHAPTER 4

DISCOVERING THE CODE
Reading

Learning to read is a basic reason we go to school. Technology can translate text to computerized speech. News, current events, entertainment, and sound bites that form public opinion are available on television. Many books are accessible on audio-tape, but reading text remains a major way to acquire knowledge. To respect how the past influences the present, to appreciate variations in words of public figures, to learn from previous and current research, to acquire kinds of knowledge in depth, to treasure great literature or delight in escapist fare, as well as for daily information and safety, we read. Comfortable reading is essential for success in school and out of school. Perhaps one of the best reasons for learning to read was proposed by a first grader who said, "You need to read so when you grow up, and your kids ask you questions, you can read stuff so you can tell them answers."

We are constantly bombarded with print. Readers practice reading in a nearly subconscious way on the street, in the marketplace, and on the job even when not purposefully deciding to read. If there is print, it is read. This automatic pull to read can be observed at food market check-out counters as few of us can refrain from reading tabloid headlines on display.

Universal literacy is a goal for those cultures that have their language represented by print, and the assumption is made that everyone can learn to read. Such an expectation is relatively recent, because in earlier times it was not believed that everyone needed to read. At times, it was thought important that individuals read, because to save their souls they needed to read the word of God. At other times, only those in power could or should read.

Slaves were kept subservient by being forbidden to read, although during other periods they were given the job of teaching children to read. In the not so distant past, women did not need to be educated, so learning to read was not regarded as necessary for them. Such an attitude may still persist to some extent, since until recently, fewer girls were referred for reading or other learning failures than boys. Currently the unemployed or under-employed are often under-educated, especially in reading. The state of being a reader is still a powerful one. Reading seems so simple for those who learn it easily, but is a painful struggle for those who find it difficult to crack the code.

DEVELOPMENT OF READING

History

English text is based on an alphabetic system. Before alphabets were developed, there were pictographic (or picture) representations of objects or conditions. Some of these kinds of communications are seen in early cave paintings, in some old Native American drawings, and in some parts of the characters in Chinese writing. Logographic systems developed as marks to stand for whole words or phrases.

Reading methods used in the 16th century were similar to those used by the earlier Greeks and Romans. The beginning reader learned names of letters, letter sounds, then syllables, and finally words. At various times, philosophers and teachers wrote that reading could be taught in just a few days. Similar attitudes exist today as clever advertisements and endorsements suggest that the code of print can be mastered effectively and quickly if a family invests in a few audio or video tapes.

The ABC method of teaching reading has included various kinds of activities. For instance, in ancient Greece, slaves might have been used to move their bodies to represent each letter in a word to be learned and later in 18th century America, letters were made of gingerbread for children to eat as a way to approach mastery. Early reading instruction consisted of much drill, and reading material often represented advanced ideas and adult thoughts. Horn books (wooden paddles with letters and words attached and covered with thin layers of horn), the New England Primers, and the 19th century McGuffey readers all included topics related to religion and morality. For the most part there was little attempt to make the content of reading materials appealing to children.[1]

Child Development and Reading

There are two major components of reading—decoding and comprehension. Decoding is looking at printed words and associating that print with speech. Comprehension is getting meaning from print or from the words that are decoded. Pronouncing printed words, but with no meaning is not really reading. Once children learn the code, they will, for the rest of their lives, add to their knowledge through print as they read with understanding.

A rich oral language base is important for reading. Children should be skilled in using the language they are expected to learn to read. The language used in their books should be familiar to them in speech, because they must translate the code of marks on paper to words that can be spoken. Then they must understand what these printed words mean.

The environment in which children grow influences their attitudes toward reading and, in addition, develops a cognitive readiness. In some homes, children are provided with rich language models that constantly stimulate new vocabulary and concepts. When they see adults they admire engaged in the act of reading it is one more adult activity they wish to imitate. Children learn not only the structure and purpose of language at their mother's lap or knee, but also begin to value reading as they see adults read to gain information, follow instructions, understand ideas, and to relax. Through having books read to them, children develop a sense that the printed marks on paper stand for the speech they hear. They learn to appreciate story development and understand a notion of completeness, that a story begins and ends, as demonstrated through pages of a story-book.

All activities in which preschool children participate prepare them for beginning to read. This preparation is part of the process that relates to reading before letter names and sounds are introduced. Learning through sensory motor discoveries, detecting slight visual differences in objects, drawings, and marks on paper, interacting with objects and people to solve problems, and learning to understand and use spoken language with its rhythm and melody all contribute to a readiness for managing print.

Just as children play with toys and learn how building blocks and puzzle pieces fit together visually, they play with the sounds of speech. They are accomplished in knowing how speech sounds represent experiences; they demonstrate this knowledge in their understanding of words and in their talking. As they manipulate speech sounds they start to discover similarities and differences in words they hear and may begin experimenting with rhyme. This becomes one more kind of play that is repeated, because it is fostered by adults, and it is fun. It is an important step in pre-reading.

While exploring and manipulating speech sounds, children also become attentive to visual representations. They start to realize, for example, that logos stand for places of business or products, and that shapes and squiggles made with a crayon, pencil, or computer have meaning. The advertisements for food markets, fast food chains, and car dealerships are learned from television or encountered while riding about in cars or buses. Many young children demand to be told what words on cereal boxes and street signs say.

They may begin to pick out words on packages of toys, on menus in restaurants, and in books. As they sit next to parents who repetitively read favorite books, they may begin to notice the way that print represents speech—that groups of letters in print stand for words they hear.

As children develop a sense of visual discrimination and categorization, noting differences and similarities, they learn that although an object in any position is the same object with the same name, marks on paper that vary only slightly in shape have different names—*n* and *h*, *k* and *h*, *t* and *f*; or if their positions are changed in space they also have different names—*p*, *q*, *d*, and *b*. Just as children begin to respond to temporal qualities of the stream of speech—speech moves over time and into auditory memory—they begin to learn the importance of the spatial arrangements of printed letters. As they can segment speech into meaningful units and words, they see visual units surrounded by space in books, thus developing a sense of individual words and their boundaries in text. They acquire a sense of order, of how text moves from left to right in English, how letters must be ordered to make a word, and how words must be ordered to make a sentence. This integration of print with speech is the beginning of reading.

An adult observer can count the words read and retained as a young child learns the first few printed words. Just as in recording the first few spoken words and word combinations, parents and teachers can keep track of words read, but quickly children begin to read words they have not been specifically taught. With exposure to text, they begin on their own to make generalizations about print and can read words for which there has been no direct teaching. Although it seems almost magical, Gibson and Levin wrote that "The only magic in learning to read is the magic that the child supplies himself when a rich and responsive environment gives him a chance."[2]

Anyone who has watched a child learn to read can be shocked by the ease with which reading success is achieved. The converse is also true. Those who have observed only adept beginning readers are dismayed by the extreme difficulty experienced by one who does not learn the code easily.

Once children start to read, reading habits begin to develop. When they see print, they will try to read it. They become interested in print materials and will read what is available. During this time, having access to books is essential. Children who find reading fun and are directed to seek out books that inform or give pleasure will read and become better readers. Reading gets better with reading. Thus, good readers become better readers, while poor readers continue to lag behind. Once able to read to learn, individuals can be in charge of their own reading and select what they wish to read.

Some feel that being deprived of reading would be one of the worst things that could happen to them, and indeed taking away a person's books has been used as punishment and a kind of torture in some cultures. Many skilled readers show a preference for settling in with a book as a leisure-time activity rather than a movie, television, or a sporting event. But there is nothing inherently good about being able to read. Many adults function quite well without ever reading books, magazines, or the daily newspapers. Not wanting to read is different from not being able to read, however. One goal in working with children and adolescents having learning disabilities in reading is for them to read at a level that allows them to choose what they read or whether or not they want to read at all.

Jeanne Chall,[3] a prominent teacher and writer in the field of reading, describes stages of reading that include: Stage 1—Initial Reading, or Decoding at grades 1 and 2; Stage 2—Confirmation, Fluency, and Ungluing from Print at grade 2 and 3; Stage 3—Reading for Learning the New: A First Step at middle school ages; Stage 4—Multiple Viewpoints' during high school; and finally Stage 5—Construction and Reconstruction, A World View, which occurs at college age or at 18 and older.

From birth to about six, or when children start to school, stimulation is provided to prepare them for readiness to read. (See Chapter 1, Getting Ready for School). For the decoding stage, children are taught about how printed letters represent sounds of speech, and at this time Chall writes, they have better listening than reading skills. At the second stage, they begin to develop an automaticity—looking at print and translating it to meaning. Children understand more, and monitor for the sense of passages, although they continue to understand more through listening than from what they read. Two examples can illustrate this step.

A graduate student recently spoke of his struggles with beginning to read. He recalled that he had tutors and help from home, but did not really know what he was supposed to accomplish. Then one day in second grade, all of a sudden, with a favorite book, it made sense. He understood what reading was all about, what teachers and tutors had been trying to get him do. Once he understood, he reports having no further reading problems.

Donald Hall in *The New York Times Book Review* wrote of being home from school with whooping cough at age seven, and tired of listening to 1930s radio soap operas, he began reading a story book he had brought home from school. "...in my boredom I read it over and over. Thus I became fluent in reading for the first time, and discovered the bliss of abandonment to print, to word and story."[4] Both of these anecdotes represent what Jean Chall refers to as becoming unglued from print. When individuals have severe reading disabilities, they often struggle so with figuring out the words that they never achieve this kind of reading, reading for the pure joy of it. Those with weak decoding may become frustrated in their attempts as they try to guess at or fill in the many words they do not know.

By Chall's stage 3, children add to knowledge through reading, although at the beginning of the stage they still comprehend more of what they hear than what they read. Toward the end of the stage, listening and reading comprehension are similar, but for some, reading will be more advanced than listening. At Stage 4, they read widely, nonfiction as well as stories. Comprehension while reading becomes better than while listening, especially for complex material. The final stage lasts the rest of a person's life where reading is efficient with a good rate. The reader selects a wide variety of material to read and can master complex material in familiar and unfamiliar texts. Some people never reach this last stage because they do not read critically or to learn complex new material. The preparation for reading begins at birth, and reading's utility and enjoyment continue for as long as one can hold a book and see the print.

Teaching Reading

There is an enormous body of literature about reading. For the amount that has been studied and written it would seem that there should be agreement about how reading develops, how to teach reading, and what to do if children fail to learn to read easily. Such is not the case.

Reading teachers and researchers usually agree that most children learn to read whatever reading method is used. There is nothing superior or inferior about any reading approach and the final goal of reading remains to gain meaning from print. School reading programs change over time. There have been extremes in recent years, and indeed throughout history, in the initial way of teaching children to read. There has been and continues to be disagreement about the beginning units to be taught—stories, words, or single sounds. When Chall wrote her classic book about teaching reading, *The Great Debate*,[5] she offered an observation that is important. That is, that when a completely new reading program is instituted in schools, classroom teachers tend to integrate techniques and procedures from previous programs they used. So any new program in the hands of skilled teachers is likely to include older elements in addition to specific approaches outlined in new teacher manuals. This blending of previously successful teaching techniques with new ones probably accounts for the fact that most children do learn to read with ease. How they are taught seldom becomes an issue.

Approaches to reading have been categorized as *bottom up* or *top down*. A bottom-up approach has been referred to as being *synthetic*, while top-down approaches are regarded as *analytic*. A bottom-up approach focuses on individual letters and sounds while the top-down approaches begin with larger chunks of meaning such as the word or sentence.

As this is being written, the way reading is being taught in schools across the country is with *whole language*, a top-down approach that is literature based and uses stories as beginning units to be read. (Children are also encouraged, as part of this approach, to use invented spellings and to try to express ideas in their written attempts rather than worry about correct spelling and mechanics of writing. This results in first grade children writing long and wonderfully creative stories.) Most children will learn to read using whole language as they will with most other approaches.

Another top-down approach uses basal readers. The child learns whole words and makes generalizations from already learned words to unstudied ones. The words are then quickly embedded in stories. Most adults can read, and, depending on a person's age, basal readers helped many to become skilled readers. No matter how much they have been vilified and made into figures of fun, Dick and Jane, Sally, Spot, Puff, and Tim taught a lot of us to read, and to read quite well.

One bottom-up approach is referred to as synthetic phonics. The sounds for the letters are taught and a child is helped to blend the sounds into words. This learning to build words from single letters and sounds is called phonics. Miriam Balmuth makes a point of providing two definitions of *phonics*, one being the sounds that letters make while the other refers to a technique of reading instruction.[6]

Some phonics is taught in most reading methods and has been throughout history, but how it is taught varies in the amount of structure used, the unit to be taught, and the way of judging mastery. In some phonics approaches, a few sounds are taught specifically. A brief time is spent on a basic sound unit, a short vowel, *a*, for instance, with perhaps a worksheet or two. But quickly children are expected to make generalizations to unknown words on their own. Many children read in this way. They are taught some principles of decoding, generally for short words and then, on their own as they read, they decode longer words. In other phonics approaches, time is spent on having children master each sound and new sounds are introduced slowly. Each generalization to new sounds and words is taught. Children are taught to read words of two or more syllables; they are not expected to read the words without direct instruction. Nothing about reading words is left to chance.

READING DISABILITIES

Decoding Problems

The study of reading disabilities through the 20th century has been influenced by the changes in psychology from the psychoanalysis of Freud to the behaviorism of Skinner to the current emphasis on brain-behavior interactive relationships. A child with a learning disability in acquiring the code that print represents speech has *dyslexia*. He or she has good ability, is free from significant hearing or visual impairment, has been exposed to adequate teaching to which others have been responsive, and has no emotional problems of a kind to cause reading failure.

Dyslexia is one kind of learning disability, a disability in decoding words (translating print to speech), with related deficits in spelling. Dyslexic individuals show a discrepancy between intelligence and their ability to decode words and to spell.[7] The assumption is made that dyslexia results from some difference in the way the central nervous system, or the brain, is put together.

Early reading disability or dyslexia results from problems with phonological awareness and processing. This means that the young dyslexic child has difficulty looking at letters and in an abstract way relating these letters to the sounds of speech. He or she cannot easily relate letters to the structure of sounds. [8,9,10,11]

The classic dyslexic child is easy to recognize—often a boy, bright, talented in many areas including math and nonverbal learning, and a good user of words. Development is on target or advanced with the exception of learning to read and spell. Such a child needs special teaching, often with a phonics approach that is organized and explicit in teaching how print represents speech. There is much repetition until the code is learned. After that it is smooth sailing, although spelling may continue to be a problem for life. There are some children like this, but they are a minority of those who fail in reading. Many classified as dyslexic have other learning disabilities as well.

Whatever we label the condition, there is a group of cognitively able children who fail to learn to read with typical approaches used in the classroom. If the educational subdivision uses *learning disability* or *reading disability* instead of *dyslexia*, the same assessment processes and teaching procedures for reading apply. Every dyslexic individual is different, and the unique combination of strengths and deficits must be taken into account when teaching him or her to read and spell. A child and a teacher set up an interaction with text that leads to reading success or failure.

A problem with decoding or translating print to speech may be dyslexia, but all those who fail to decode words are not dyslexic. Some adults never had the opportunity to learn to read. Others were slow in acquiring the code and rapidly fell behind. All reading assignments were difficult; they refrained from reading.

It is common to find auditory or visual deficits discussed as causes for the decoding problem. Reading involves translating the code by interpreting and remembering visual shapes—the letters—and understanding how these visual shapes relate to speech. The input is visual, but the reader translates the visual print to language, which has an auditory base. Trying to force reading patterns as reflected on tests or from observations as being either auditory or visual is a simplification that does not help in understanding the poor reader. At some point there may be ways of defining subtypes of dyslexia, but for the most part, the categories now described are not clinically or educationally valuable and are of more interest to researchers than they are useful to teachers.

Reading Comprehension Problems

The goal of reading is to acquire meaning from print. Beyond accepting that, reading comprehension has been studied less than decoding. The importance of reading for understanding depends on what one wishes to read. A person who reads only newspapers and magazines may not comprehend professional journals or texts in science or higher level mathematics or even want to read or understand them. The person who pursues education beyond high school needs to have better facility in comprehension of text than one who does not choose advanced study; although level of education does not determine the level of a person's reading comprehension. There are also differences in kinds of reading comprehension among those who have graduate degrees. An educator would not necessarily understand texts about economics or medicine. An engineer may have little comprehension of either classical literature or best-selling novels. Of course, we could say it is not that these individuals cannot comprehend, but rather they have no interest. I am not so sure. We are usually interested in those areas in which we perform well. Nevertheless, this can illustrate the point that it is hard to define a maximum goal for reading comprehension. To decode words, for example, a goal might be to read any word that is printed in English. A similar goal is not as easily established for reading comprehension.

Readers can have problems comprehending text for various reasons. They may have trouble understanding, because they are poor decoders. If they cannot read the words, they cannot assign meaning to them. Sometimes individuals who had earlier problems with decoding, but can now decode words well are very slow in the decoding process. They have trouble holding words in memory as they read them, so the individual words decoded do not really become language for them. This can be observed in young children who struggle with printed instructions on worksheets and assignments. They need to read repeatedly until the words make sense. But this struggle and slow rate is also seen in older students and adults who can decode but only in a painfully slow fashion.

Another reason for failing to comprehend text is the presence of oral language comprehension problems. Young children generally know meanings of words so that when they confront words in text they make a match between the words read and the words in their heads. If they do not have the words in their oral language, the words will have no meaning when they read them. This is true for early reading and typical readers. Once we read well, we increase general vocabulary knowledge through reading. Speakers whose first language is other than English and who have learned most of their English through texts, may not recognize a word they hear because it is not pronounced as they think it would be; it is unfamiliar to them except in text. They may not pronounce the word correctly when they have only seen it in print. Some children show similar patterns. A 7-year-old precocious reader was asked if he knew another word for *cocoon*. He responded "kris-all-us" a word he knew from reading but had not heard spoken, or if he had heard it spoken, did not relate the word he heard to the printed word, *chrysalis*.

In order to understand text, readers must also be familiar with complex grammatical constructions. If a reader has trouble understanding oral grammar, he or she will have the same problems with the structures in text. Typical daily conversation does not provide practice with formal and more complex syntax. As with most things, readers must have practice with complex sentences in order to understand them. Such practice comes primarily through reading. I am convinced that some of the students who perform poorly on standardized tests such as the MCATs and LSATs may do so, not because they do not know content, but rather because of trouble understanding the syntactic structures of the questions asked.

Another reason for possible reading comprehension problems is an oral expressive language problem. Some children do not have a good *sense of sentences*. Oral language may not be developed enough to make predictions about text or to understand how ideas can be expressed chronologically or conceptually by sentences that are formed in a certain way and then cohesively tied together in paragraphs and longer units.

Limited experiences on the part of readers is another possible cause of poor comprehension; they are not able to bring an adequate knowledge base to the task. Some experiences, and some level of awareness about these experiences, are necessary to begin reading about the thoughts and feelings of others. Children with learning disabilities or those from impoverished backgrounds may not have a sense of the merely possible or of worlds that can be imagined. Some children with no learning disabilities may have limited experience with imagining and thinking about behaving "as if." Before television presented growing children with images of families, events, and situations, children who read, had their imaginations tickled in ways that television may have taken away. Those growing up before television have mental images of settings in houses, cities, or rural areas; how characters look, and how they go about solving problems in the stories they read. Often as adults, they still visualize these settings from imagined places. Television may have robbed children of an imagery that adds to reading. Now, development of images may need to be specifically taught.[12]

Skilled teachers help children understand how experiences they read about can relate to their own lives. Almost any subject can have relevance to a reader or can encourage potential interest. New information in science, a concept from history, the inspiration of a biography, or the enjoyment of a well-written short story or novel may stimulate new thinking and perhaps even open career possibilities.

Finally, some readers can decode, have adequate oral language and ample experiences and still have trouble with comprehension of text. There is something about the structure of text that is hard for them to master. The form of text is different from much of speech. When we interact with a speaker, even in listening to a formal lecture, we receive many cues from the style of speaking, places of emphasis, changes in facial expression, and uses of gesture. Similar cues are not provided in text except for punctuation, use of italics, bold-faced type, and headings that are sometimes included. Sentences in text are often longer and more complex than speech. Text differs in the style of organization, the formality, and the density of meaning. Text does not have the redundancy that is present in speech so there are fewer opportunities to clarify meaning. What is read may be unfamiliar; therefore, meaning must be derived from both the vocabulary and the structure of sentences. An overall sense of structure of text is necessary to read with comprehension.

When we read to comprehend, a level of attention focused on, and an interaction with text, is required. This means that more is involved than just looking at the page or reading the words. All of us have had the experience of reaching the bottom of a page and realizing we have no idea what was on that page. Sometimes this happens repeatedly. Generally, we are distracted or uninterested in what we are trying to read. When I ask middle-school-age and older children if this ever happens to them, they often respond with "All the time." When some of them are in their rooms studying, this may be what their studying is. They really do have books open and think they are reading, but are not. Although attention must be focused on text, a certain relaxed sense must be present as well. Just as holding a pencil requires tension on the pencil to hold it, but too tight a grasp causes problems, tension or anxiety when trying to read can impede understanding.

Some good students seem to develop personal ways of understanding what they read, while others need explicit instruction. Students with learning disabilities may need a greater focus on comprehension early in their reading instruction than do others. Comprehension is dynamic. The reader interacts with text in an aggressive and tenacious way.

Staying only with the known can result in being stuck both personally and vocationally. Reading can enrich thinking and inform about the merely possible. Children and adolescents need instruction in how to approach text for comprehension, to struggle with what at first they may regard as too hard or boring. Then they need practice in reading. Teaching for comprehension must be more than having a student read a passage and recognize facts, the main idea, and a good title for the selection. It is also more than reading and writing answers to questions. Unfortunately, this is what many children think reading comprehension is. Other children I see, I am convinced, think reading means to say the words. They have not made the leap to the next step, the recognition that words that are pronounced, or read, have meaning as do sentences, and that sentences in text have relationships to other sentences. They must be helped to see that what we must do in reading is to read with a purpose—this will allow us to gain new information, to think about a subject or person in a different way, or to appreciate the pleasure of printed language. Maria wrote, "To fail to teach children how to use text to gain information is to render them illiterate in an advanced technological society like ours."[13]

ASSESSMENT FOR READING PROBLEMS

In testing an individual who has trouble with reading, we must find ways to understand how the reader approaches the printed code to pronounce words and how, or if, he or she comprehends or understands what words, sentences, paragraphs, stories, and other kinds of texts mean. Each person who tests children has different procedures to use and certain preferred tests. There is no one right way to test children for reading problems, but an attempt needs to be made to gather as much information as possible that will lead to appropriate teaching, so the individual can be helped to read as well as he or she can. Any time a person is tested, the tester formulates certain questions to be answered and then selects tests or devises tasks to answer the questions. One such set of questions follows. They are presented in some detail, because it may help parents understand the complexity of what is involved with reading. It also may help those who see only children who read easily consider some of the issues that contribute to reading success or failure. The order in which the questions are presented does not imply that the questions are asked in this order for testing, and there does not have to be a different task or test for each question, but in the process of the evaluation many of the questions will be answered. Those that are not resolved during the testing will be answered by mainstream or special teachers as they work with the children in the process of teaching them to read. Three major questions need to be answered first:

1.   Who thinks there is a reading problem?
2.   Is there a reading problem?
3   If there is a reading problem, what can be done about it?

Who thinks there is a problem?

The first question we need to ask is: Who is concerned that there may be a reading problem? Before we can regard a behavior or activity as being a problem, someone must express a concern. Is it the reader, a teacher, or the parents? When any one of them is anxious, the concern must be addressed. Sometimes it is the student who expresses worry. This worry can range from the disappointment of a first grader who comes home from school on the first day of first grade distressed at not having learned to read that day, to a child or adolescent who never wants to go to school again because of reading failure.

Students let parents or teachers know they are worried about a problem with reading in various ways. Some children—from age six through high school age—express their concerns verbally while others show their concerns through such behaviors as crying, withdrawal from friends, or saying negative things about themselves. Often these behaviors occur at a time of school change when demands for independent reading of more complex texts are greater.

Adequate reading is reading that an individual needs to function. A child in school needs to read to learn and to read what classmates read. Adults need to read to meet requirements of their jobs and to manage material for recreation if they so choose. I often receive calls from adults who have failed in college, are employed in jobs that are unsatisfying, or who go from job to job—all because of unidentified reading disability.

Sometimes it is a teacher who has concerns about students' learning. Specific attention to reading problems occurs most in the early grades, although it is not uncommon to see a middle school or secondary student with previously unidentified poor reading. A teacher generally observes that the student functions at a certain level in class discussion, in learning and retaining information, but is not reading at that same level. Bright children can fill in an enormous amount with limited reading skills. Their reading problems become apparent only as the requirements become greater in manipulating read material, and greater amounts must be read within limited time.

Often it is the parents who first express concern. They are puzzled about why their child, who has always been enthusiastic about learning new things and learned them effortlessly, struggles so with print. With young children, such an observation is usually made when they practice reading aloud or are doing homework. But later, parents sometimes observe by chance and with shock, that their son or daughter cannot read as expected. They may notice the poor reading when they ask to have directions read for completing a task or casually ask that a piece from a magazine or newspaper be read. Often young and not-so-young children are, because of their basic brightness, accused by parents and teachers of not putting forth adequate effort in trying to read. The attitude is that if the children tried harder they could do all right. This is discouraging to those trying as hard as they know how.

Whenever a student, a teacher, or a parent suspects a reading problem some testing should be done.

Is there a reading problem? How does the reader perform when asked to read?

I.   What are scores on standardized achievement tests of reading?
     A. Group tests
     B. Individually administered tests
II.   Are scores from testing discrepant
     A. with expectation or ability?
     B. with age?
     C. with grade?
III. Is the rate of reading adequate for the individual's needs?
IV. How is performance on oral reading tasks?
     A. Single words
        1. Is reading better for content as opposed to function words?
        2. Is reading better for real words as opposed to pseudo-words?
        3. What is the nature of reading errors?
           a. Are words read as ones with similar visual configuration (words that look the same)?
           b. Is there transposition of letters or syllables?
           c. Are there real-word substitutions?
        4. Are there attempts made to read words that are not automatically known?
     B. Context
        1. Are there errors of omission for
           a. Words?
              1) Content words?
              2) Function words?
           b. Word endings?
           c. Lines of print?
        2. Are there substitution errors for
           a. Content words?
           b. Function words?
           c. Word endings?
        3. Is there monitoring for self correction?
           a. By syntactic cues?
           b. By semantic cues?
        4. Is a word read correctly in context but not in isolation?
     C. How developed are isolated phonics skills?
        1. Can sounds be provided (said orally) for printed letters?
           a. Consonants?

        b. Vowels?

        c. Vowel combinations?

        d. Consonant blends?

    2. Can sounds be recognized (by pointing to letter or letters) for

        a. Consonants?

        b. Short vowels?

        c. Vowel combinations?

        d. Consonant blends?

    3. Can sounds be isolated from within words and associated with printed letter (by pointing to letter) for

        a. Initial consonant?

        b. Final consonant?

        c. A medial long vowel in a nonsense word?

        d. A short vowel in a consonant-vowel-consonant (CVC) nonsense word?

    4. Is isolated phonics knowledge applied to:

        a. Real words?

        b. Nonreal words?

D. How developed is phonological awareness for:

    1. Paired word short vowel discrimination? (Do these two words sound just the same? Yes or No. *fat–fat, fat–fit, pin–pen.* etc.)

    2. Sequencing sound within words? (Say: *basket, animal, spaghetti,* etc.)

    3. Rhyming?

        a. Recognition (Do these two words rhyme? *cat—bat, cat—can*)

        b. Recall (Tell me some words that rhyme with *cat.*)

    4. Blending? (Put these parts together to make a word: *base—ball, ta—ble, f—a—t*)

    5. Segmentation? (Divide these words into parts: *snowman, baby, fat*)

    6. Deletion? (Say supper without "per," bus without" s," fan without "f," snail without "s")

E. Is structural analysis used

    1. For common endings (-ed to mark past tense, -s to mark plural and possessive of nouns and present tense of verbs, -ing to mark present progressive of a verb)?

    2. For other common suffixes?

    3. For common prefixes?

F. Is there awareness of meaning of these morphological units?

V. How is reading comprehension?

A. For comprehension of vocabulary?

    1. Antonyms?

2. Synonyms?
3. Analogies?
B. For comprehension of text?
  1. In a cloze procedure for:
    a. Supplying a word?
    b. Selecting a word from an array of words?
    c. Selecting a correct answer (phrase or sentence) from an array?
  2. For formulating a phrase or sentence response orally?
  3. For formulating a phrase or sentence response in writing?
  4. For formulating longer units orally or summarizing in writing?
  5. For understanding chapter of text or a book
    a. By taking notes?
    b. Using the information to
      1) Relate to what is already known?
      2) Re-tell content?
      3) Summarize content?
      4) Question for clarification?
      5) Compare and contrast ideas read?
      6) Function well when tested over the material?
  6. For using printed material read for own purposes in gaining information and spending leisure time?

Oral Reading

Content versus function words. In oral reading of single words, we consider if more errors are made in reading content words or function words. Content words are nouns, verbs, and sometimes adjectives and adverbs. For many of these words, it is possible to associate strong sensory and perceptual impressions to the word. The word *dog* can be associated with all dogs a child has known, how dogs look, smell, sound, feel, and act. The same is true for *alligator* or *basketball*. Strong personal positive or negative associations can affect memory for many content words. In contrast, function words do not have strong sensory experiences to be associated with them. The lack of strong sensory and perceptual associations can account for the complaint of some parents that their second grader can read *alligator* but not the word *were* even though "we've studied it hundreds of times." The function words are best learned in meaningful context. They are words that tie sentences together and make longer pieces of text cohesive. Teaching them in isolation is seldom successful for children who have trouble learning to read.

Pseudo-words, nonreal words, nonsense words. Giving the reader nonreal words to pronounce is a way of evaluating the application of decoding rules, or word attack skills, or phonics knowledge as applied to novel words. Nonreal words are used because it would be impossible to devise a real-word list with a high likelihood of unfamiliarity to a large number of readers. Nonreal words must be those that have a universally agreed upon pronunciation. Syllabic stress or accent is not as necessary as in real words, so some readers may read nonreal long words better than some advanced real words. Familiarity with specific words, a visual memory for them, or vocabulary knowledge about them cannot be called into play when reading nonreal or pseudo-words. Therefore, they are useful for testing application of decoding knowledge.

Oral reading errors. A reader might confuse a word with one that has a similar visual configuration. These are errors such as reading *costume* for *custom*, *banquet* or *boutique* for *bouquet*, *deceive* for *decisive*, *biography* for *bibliography*, *experience* for *experiment*. Other common errors may be transposing letters or syllables in words such as *was* and *saw*, *dog* and *god*, *abroad* and *aboard*, or of *spot*, *stop*, *pots*, and *tops*, or *paternal* and *parental*.

Some children monitor their reading of words to the extent that the errors they make in reading are substitutions of real words. As words become more advanced, some children may be comfortable in giving a nonreal word thinking that it is a "hard word." But children with serious language disorders, particularly receptive language disorders, are comfortable reading without monitoring at all; often what they read is nonsense and they are not bothered by that.

Additionally, an important observation when evaluating how readers approach unknown words is whether or not they make attempts if they are not sure of the word. Some refuse completely, which makes error analysis difficult.

When readers are engaged in reading passages in *context* it is useful to observe if they are aided by the structure of sentences. They may be helped by semantic cues or the meaning of known words or by syntactic cues in the way words are arranged. They may make sense of short passages, reading a minimal number of words. In contrast, other readers become quite anxious if they are not sure of a word and refuse to continue unless they can know, or are told, the word. They must read every word with equal weight and refuse to guess at all.

When there are *omissions* in oral reading, we ask if the omission is with content words, function words, word endings, or lines of print. If lines of print are omitted, the reader needs to be encouraged to use a marker such as an index card, piece of paper, or the eraser end of a pencil. When words or endings are omitted we can ask if the sentence as read makes sense. Word endings omitted in reading and writing sometimes reflect a lack of awareness of their meaning in language. How much meaning is preserved in what is read can indicate how the individual approaches reading in general and if getting meaning from text is important to him or her.

When there are *substitutions*, we ask if they are with content words, with function words, or with word endings. It is also useful to consider if the errors make syntactic sense. Do sentences as read make sense grammatically? Do word substitutions make sense semantically so meaning is preserved? It is also important to observe if, while reading, the individual monitors what he or she is reading and makes any self corrections. Sometimes children and adolescents do not seem to pay attention to meaning at all.

   Oral as opposed to silent reading.   When evaluating reading in students from 6 years old through college and adult years, it is useful to know if there is a difference between performance for oral and silent reading. Young children are expected to read aloud, so parents and teachers have some notion about how they approach words. But if they have significant oral language problems or have problems with retrieval of information, some attempt should be made to determine if they read better silently. Words can be put on cards to be matched to pictures of some nouns, commands can be presented for the child to read and carry out, and printed sentences can be matched to action pictures. If a child performs better reading silently, this must be taken into consideration and opportunities need to be provided for silent reading. In class, they should not be expected to read aloud until they can manage oral reading with some sense of comfort.

   When older students make errors of substitution, or pause incorrectly between words so that meaning is changed while reading aloud, it is possible that the same kinds of errors are made in silent reading. Omitting negatives such as *not* or the prefix *un-* obviously changes meaning dramatically. If student's when reading aloud, make self corrections for meaning, some monitoring for the sense of what is being read is taking place. Perhaps they may then also check themselves when they are reading silently. Of course, where this process can break down is when the material to be read becomes technical or complex. We need to help students evaluate for the sense of what they read as soon as they begin reading sentences. This helps them regard reading as an active process.

   Reading single words versus context.   It is useful to note if a student reads both single words and context easily. One way to determine if individuals can read words in isolation is to provide them with a list of words that they are required to read aloud. This is also the process that is necessary on vocabulary tests; the reader must read the target word and each of the words in a list from which they choose an antonym or synonym. Having a poor vocabulary score may have less to do with vocabulary knowledge than with poor decoding. Reading isolated words that have several syllables creates difficulties for many reading disabled students when they take standardized tests such as the SATs, MCATs, or LSATs.

   Sometimes readers can read words in context that they fail to read in isolation. If a word that is misread in isolation can be read in the context of a phrase or sentence, such awareness should be incorporated into the remedial program. Skilled readers often confront words that are unfamiliar in text, but determine what the word means from the context. Depending on motivation, level of organization, or access to a dictionary such a reader may or may not look up the word to determine its precise meaning. However, a certain level of reading is necessary for readers to decide whether or not they know the words. Determining word meaning from context may fail when reading such technical material as science. Words in biology and names of medications and illnesses must be read correctly in isolation. A substitute word or one similar in meaning is not good enough. Knowledge of the words is essential in the sciences, but also in reading literature. An occasional word can be determined by context, but poor readers cannot depend on this as being efficient. Readers must understand vocabulary and grammar of both simple and complex sentences. They must be able to conceptualize ideas read in some relationship to their own experiences. Readers build meaning from the text they read.

Some children with difficulties in decoding make maximum use of context cues to aid reading comprehension. They can score fairly well for a time in school and on tests. However, as demands become greater in the material to be read and as it becomes more technical, as in science, and/or less familiar as for long and complex sentences in literature, it is not as easy to gain meaning from context cues. The reader is constantly engaged in a process of filling in what the text might say from the words that can be read. This results in a guessing game that is inefficient. To read, we must be able to read the words.

Phonics

We could next ask what the reader knows about phonics or about how printed letters and letter combinations represent the sounds of speech. Show an individual printed consonants, vowels, vowel combinations, and consonant blends and ask him or her to say the sounds of that letter or letter group. If there are problems with these tasks, show the reader groups of printed single consonants, short vowels, consonant combinations or blends, and vowel combinations and ask him or her to listen to the pattern presented orally and select the visual representation of what is heard. The child may indicate knowledge at the recognition level, even if he or she cannot recall the correct sound to say it.

Ask a child to listen to a word and then point to a letter within an array of printed letters that represents a short vowel in the middle of the word, or a consonant that is at the beginning of the word, or at the end. This is one way to know if the child is able to hear a word, segment it into parts, and relate the isolated unit to its visual printed letter equivalent. Children who can accomplish such a recognition task with successful segmentation are often those who score a bit better for spelling words than for reading them. The objective for these tasks is to understand how much a child knows before asking him or her to apply known skills to read real words and nonreal words. With better recognition than recall, a reader shows knowledge about the code in the same way a person "knows" a word but cannot retrieve it because of a word-finding problem.

Phonological Awareness

Phonological awareness tasks are often referred to as those involving auditory processing or auditory perception. Some descriptions of kinds of tasks referred to as *phonological awareness* or *auditory processing* follow. For a paired-word *short vowel discrimination* task, a child could hear paired words and tell whether they are the same or not. Pairs such as *fat–fat, fat–fit, pin–pen* are presented so that the tester's mouth cannot be seen. An individual makes judgments based on what is heard, not by looking at the tester's face or the position of the mouth when pronouncing the words. With *sequencing sounds within words*, the observer notes any confusions in the sequence of sounds when the child speaks. In addition, a repetition task could be given where a child is asked to say such words as *basket, animal, spaghetti, hospital, aluminum*, and *statistics*. For *rhyming*, a child is asked to provide words that rhyme with a given word. For *blending*, a child is given word parts and asked to make them into whole words. Examples include such words as *base—ball, ta—ble*, and *f—a—t*. A child could be given words to segment into parts. Words such as *snowman, baby*, and *sun* are presented. A final task is one of deletion. The child is asked to say the word with a part omitted. For example he or she could be asked, "say the word *supper* without *per*," say *bus* without *s*," "say *fan* without *f*," say *snail* with *s*." It is worthwhile doing these phonological awareness tasks with middle school students, adolescents, and adults with poor decoding. For some, it is quickly observed that they have no idea how print fairly regularly stands for the sounds of speech.[14,15,16]

Structural Analysis

Knowing how words are put together is important to early reading development and later reading, as well. (See discussion of morphology in Chapter 3.) Children could be asked to demonstrate an ability to read and understand early frequent endings including -*ed* to mark past tense, -*s* to mark plurals and possessives, -*ing* to mark present progressive form of a verb, and other common suffixes and prefixes that are age appropriate. I find that children who omit endings when they read and when they write sentences often do not really understand that such endings convey important information about meaning.

In the process of testing, we must provide enough items to learn if the individual has internalized a rule or principle. This is easier to accomplish with decoding than comprehension. For instance, if we are interested in knowing if a child can read CVC short *a* words, then we present many words with short *a*. Then the short *a* words are presented among an array of other short vowel words. The short *a* words are presented in context or phrases and sentences. If the reader manages these tasks easily, we can be fairly sure he or she knows and can apply the rule for reading one-syllable words with short *a*.

Reading Comprehension

Vocabulary.   In assessing reading comprehension, there are different kinds of tests available. For *silent reading* tests we must be sure the reader is actively engaged in the task. Some tests that measure reading vocabulary require marking a word that represents a picture, while others require selecting words from a group of words to assess understanding of antonyms, synonyms, and analogies. Each of these can be called silent reading vocabulary tests, but the cognitive demands are different. Children generally understand opposites before they understand words that mean the same. Analogies need explicit teaching for some, while others have an intuitive sense and can reason through words in analogous relationships. Accurate decoding is important for these tasks. A reader must correctly read the target word as well as all the words presented as choices, or at least as many of them as necessary until a choice is made.

In addition to general words, readers must also read vocabulary specific to classes. Each science, social studies, shop, or English class in elementary or secondary school or in post-secondary situations has its own core vocabulary that must be read and understood. Sometimes older students try to remember the visual form of a word and try to learn a printed definition for that printed word; they may have no idea that a word they try to remember by its shape is a same word a teacher has said in class. Relating the words in print to the words they hear in class can sometimes make a big difference in their understanding.

Text.   Some reading comprehension tests involve a *cloze procedure*—the reader must insert an appropriate word to fit in a blank space in a passage. Other comprehension tests require a reader to read a passage and then select words, phrases, or sentences from an array of answers. High scores on reading comprehension tests do not mean that a reader is equipped to handle all kinds of reading comprehension. These tests only measure the kind of tasks that they present—generally short passages, often with a cloze procedure. A student with a high score on a reading comprehension test does not inevitably have functional comprehension at that level. High scores are often misused by parents and professionals, including physicians, who believe the scores indicate that the readers handle all reading at an advanced level. The tests only inform us about the kind of reading measured by the tests. Standardized reading tests with short passages do not simulate reading a chapter or a book and preparing it for study. Any implications we draw from test results must be evaluated in the classroom or the situation in which reading is required.

Reading with comprehension is a major requirement to complete a person's education. To show that they have understood what they have read, students from early grades through college may be expected to formulate phrase or sentence responses orally or in writing, verbalize orally, or summarize in written form to demonstrate their comprehension of print.

Texts have structure and some sense of that structure can help with understanding. If we wrote a number of sentences about a topic in a list, this set of sentences will not necessarily form a paragraph. Helping students understand this can help them begin to appreciate how sentences are strung together, either chronologically or by ideas. Stories have a structure distinct from science or history texts, so they are read differently from textbooks. Particular kinds of questions need to be asked about the text to be read and different kinds of preparation may be necessary.

Reading Rate

An evaluation should include some observation about whether rate of reading is adequate for an individual's needs. Sometimes students who have learned the code well are slow in the process of decoding, particularly for unfamiliar words. Speed reading courses are not effective for those who have been or are dyslexic. Dyslexic readers may persist in being slow at decoding words. Readers can't read any faster than they can read the words, but they will pick up speed over time as they practice reading. For slow readers, extended time, without penalty, for in-class reading and tests is essential.

Compensation by using books recorded on tape is one way for literature to be enjoyed and textbook material to be mastered when a lot of reading must be completed in limited time, although all slow readers should practice reading. They will never develop better reading, and get practice with the reading skills they have, if they do not read. Dyslexic individuals cannot skim as effectively as able readers, because words must be decoded to determine what weight should be given them; they tend to place equal value for all words printed. To skim, we know that some words or parts of text are more important than others.

TEACHING INDIVIDUALS WITH READING DISABILITIES

The final question to be asked after testing and determining that there is a problem for decoding and/or comprehension is, what can be done about it?

And then, of course, who will implement the plan? After we have gathered information from an assessment, a teaching plan is developed to best help the individual learn to read. Children reading below grade level are in trouble as are those adults who do not have reading skills to manage the reading they need.

Reading specialists, special education resource teachers, or Title I teachers in public schools provide special instruction to supplement reading taught in the regular classroom. In some places reading disabilities are treated as part of general education, and children with reading problems are not regarded as having a learning disability. In other places reading disabilities are managed in special education. If schools have Title I services, reading disabled children may receive those services. But they are usually designed to give children more exposure to reading as it is taught in the regular classroom and do not provide specialized teaching techniques to aid the dyslexic reader.

Often the nature and extent of a reading disability does not determine placement for children. Children with reading problems will need various kinds and intensities of help to learn to read. Some parochial schools have reading or learning disabilities specialists on staff, but most do not. Non-public schools do not have the same funding that public schools do and often do not have specific programs for reading disabled students, except for those schools that are especially for students with reading disabilities or dyslexia. Some independent schools are able to make modifications and provide some support services for reading disabled students, while others are not. If a child's school does not have services to supplement what is provided through group instruction, or if children do not make progress with school-provided programs, then parents may decide to use private tutors. There are no accreditation requirements for tutors as there are for other such specialists as physicians, psychologists, and speech-language pathologists, so it is not easy to select one. Generally the professional(s) who evaluate children for reading problems can suggest resources for tutoring. At times, the child's school will have a list of tutors. Armed with a report that describes the nature of the child's reading disability and suggests teaching approaches, parents can select a tutor.

Phonological Awareness

Because it is generally accepted that facility with reading and spelling require phonological awareness, or an awareness of how speech is represented by print, the following activities are suggested. They are only suggestions and are not meant to be inclusive. The goal is to encourage play and pleasure with language and the sounds of speech before children confront print. It is controversial as to whether the following activities should be auditory activities or if they should be combined with printed letters. I believe some work with how words sound and how they can be taken apart and put back together should be provided orally before presenting the activities along with print. Different children may take different routes to success in these tasks. Not all will handle them in the same way. If children perform some of the tasks successfully, these tasks can serve as review. It can also be pointed out to them that they have already learned important skills related to reading. These activities should be tried with older children and adults with reading problems. Many of them will have difficulty. When working with older individuals, it is important to choose pictured materials that are appropriate to adults and are not just for very young children.

Rhyming. Children should repeatedly hear words that rhyme—in word pairs and in rhymes that are said or read. At home, parents can read rhyming books again and again, having the child sit beside the parent. With repetition, children develop a sense of rhyme and may notice the similarities in the way words look as well as how they sound.

- Make up silly rhymes while riding the car.
- Say a word to the child. Present two other words orally and have the child tell which one rhymes with the target word.
- Say a word and have the child say a word that rhymes.
- Say a word and have the child say as many words as possible that rhyme with the target word.

Blending. The progression for blending should start with compound words (base—-ball), progress to syllables (ta—-ble), and then to sounds (f—-a—-t). Care needs to be taken at the single sound level not to add a schwa ("uh") after the consonant sound but rather to clip it short. Initial consonants that can be sustained such as *f*, *s*, and *m* should be used first.

- Say a word divided into parts. Have the child point to a picture of what the whole word represents.
- Say a word divided into parts and have the child say the whole word.

Segmentation. Present sentences orally, and have the child indicate how many words he or she hears. The child is segmenting a stream of speech into units of meaning or words. Sentences could be ones such as: *I run. He walks fast. A hippopotamus is gigantic.*

- Say a compound word and indicate awareness of the parts.
  —Use words such as *Batman*, *toothbrush* and *cowboy*.
  —Say words of two or three (or more) syllables and have the child indicate the parts. Use words such as *table*, *yesterday*, and *multiplication*.
  —Have the child indicate awareness of the parts by moving markers of blocks, sticks, or pennies or tapping with hand, finger, or mallet.

Deletion. Ask the child to say a word without one of its parts. The order could go from compound words to two syllable words to CVC words, and finally to words with blends. For example,

—Say cowboy without cow.
—Say snowman without snow.
—Say toothbrush without brush.
—Say baseball without ball.
—Say mat without t.
—Say fun without n.
—Say boat without b.
—Say phone without n.
—Say smile without m.
—Say fast without s.

- Say a word. Show him or her many pictures that start with the same sound. Say the name of the pictures. Have the child say the name of the picture.
- Say a word. Ask the child to repeat the word.
- Say a word. Ask the child to repeat the word. Ask him or her to select which of two pictures starts with the same sound.
- Increase the array of pictures from which the child should choose.
- Finally, ask the child to say a word that starts with the same sound.
- The same procedure can be done with final sounds.

All of these phonology activities occur before the child is expected to read or deal with phonics (or at the same time but in a different part of the lesson). For such play with sounds, it is important that children have the sense of temporal order and what *first* and *last* mean by the time they are listening for first and last sounds in words.

Teaching Decoding

Some children will require direct instruction in decoding and the application of phonics in order to be successful readers. The amount of direct teaching necessary will vary. Some children will quickly make generalizations on their own. From reading a relatively small set of words, they will begin to see patterns and identify words they have not seen before or that have not been specifically taught. Children who are slow in acquiring initial reading skills, but catch on quickly, may be in this group.

Dyslexic students do not learn in this way. They cannot easily take a few words they can read and make generalizations to unstudied words. Indeed, children who are slow in initial reading at age six but catch on quickly are unlikely to be dyslexic. How the letters and sounds are presented, the order of their presentation, the number of consonants taught before presenting vowels, and how soon sentences are introduced will vary with different phonics approaches.

Many dyslexic children cannot learn using whole words or stories. This is particularly true of older children who have not learned to read. If they could have learned using whole words, they would have learned already because words are everywhere to be read. Often dyslexic children and adults need to have an approach that focuses on the speech sounds of the language (phonology) and how these sounds are represented by letters. This is referred to as phonics. There are different phonics approaches.

- When children require a specialized approach to decoding, they need to be taught sounds of consonants, vowels, consonant combinations (*sh, th, ch*), vowel combinations (*ee, ea, ai, ay, ou, ow, oi, oy*, etc.), consonant blends (*tr, str, pr, pl*, etc.), and later syllables and prefixes and suffixes to be built into words.
- After there is mastery of the regularities of language in print, then the rules for irregular words are taught. Instruction continues until the code of print reaches a level of mastery. Some of these phonics approaches designed specifically to teach dyslexic individuals include: the Orton–Gillingham approach, the Slingerland approach, Alphabetic Phonics, and Project Read.[17] These are bottom-up approaches starting at the level of letter sounds. They are highly structured, systematic, multisensory, and cumulative. The multisensory nature of these approaches means that children learn to read by seeing, hearing, saying, and writing the sounds of the letters. They quickly learn to blend sounds to form words. At higher levels, once basic decoding skills for single words are mastered, syllable patterns, and other rules of English orthography are taught. Generalizations from known words are specifically taught; nothing is left to chance. Spelling is an integral part of these teaching approaches although the emphasis placed on spelling seems to vary among them.[18,19]
- It is essential for dyslexic students that spelling and writing are integrated with reading. Parents and teachers sometimes say that spelling is not important because it is possible to look up a word in the dictionary or use a spell checker on a computer. However, it is important to recognize that a person must have a fair command of spelling and/or reading to begin to look up words in a dictionary or make choices from the lists provided by spell check programs. But spelling also offers a window on how an individual approaches text—the rules the reader knows about printed language, and how he or she relates speech to print.
- Before children begin a phonics approach they need to have developed a level of phonological awareness—an understanding about the sounds of speech.
- As individual words are taught they should also be presented in phrases and sentences, on cards or lists, to be practiced for reading. This repetitive practice with cards or lists develops automaticity. It also proves to the reader how sight vocabulary is increasing. Although it seems as

though this is boring rote drill, it is something children enjoy because they can see and feel their sense of mastery.

- Words should not be given for home practice until they begin to be retained in sight vocabulary. Home practice should be just that, practice of what has been taught. A child should see the stack of known words grow, not see the stack as ones to be learned.
- The same words taught for reading should be used for spelling. Practice in writing learned words not only teaches spelling but reinforces reading.
- Words that are not phonetically regular, such as wh-words, conjunctions, and prepositions, need to be taught in the context of phrases and sentences.
- Attention also will need to be given to early structural analysis and to the endings of words such as -ed, -ing, -es, -s, -ly, -ful, etc.
- Later, attention needs to be focused on more advanced structural analysis including word derivations. This helps both with reading and with meaning.
- As the highly phonetic words are learned, it is important that they be quickly embedded in printed sentences. Initial sentences need to be meaningful and use the grammatical structure of the way we talk; this allows spoken language to be used as an aid to reading.
- Providing work with comprehension of what is read must begin when a student is reading at the sentence level.
- It is important that classroom teachers as well as parents understand the approach the children are experiencing as they learn to read. Both parents and teachers can reinforce words that are taught. If the special reading teacher is in a school it is likely that the teacher knows the approach that is being used. When tutoring is provided privately by the family, it is still helpful for teachers to know how the children are being taught. There should be no mystery about special help provided for children. Reading approaches for dyslexic students may be complex in their theoretical base, but they can be understood by any interested parent.
- Parents need to know how to help the child practice at home and what should be practiced.
- Teaching decoding cannot stop with one-syllable words. Specific instruction must be given to dyslexic students to learn long words.
- There are generally accepted types of syllables that most students learn implicitly but other students need to have taught explicitly.[20,21,22] These include the following:
  —Closed (VC) syllable with one vowel and ending with a consonant. The vowel is usually short as in one syllable words *bat*, *cup*, *fan* or in words with more than one syllable as *tab—let*, *nap—kin* and *es—tab—lish*.

—Silent-e (VCe). A silent -*e* syllable has one vowel followed by a consonant and then by an *e*. The *e* is silent and makes the previous vowel
long as in *bone, fade, cute,* or *tale.*

—Open (CV). An open syllable ends with one vowel. The vowel is
usually long as in *si*lent and *re*member.

—r-Controlled (Vr). An *r* controlled syllable has a vowel followed by an
r, which changes the vowel as in *term, dirt, fur, cord, farm.*

—Consonant-le (Cle). A consonant-le syllable is a final syllable in which
the *e* is silent so the syllable sounds as a consonant-l as ta*ble*, bu*gle.*

—Double Vowel (VV). A double vowel syllable has two vowel letters
that make one vowel sound as *paid, treat, boat.* These vowel combinations are sometimes called *digraphs.*

- Teach students to read word parts that can be blended into words.
Words with regular syllables, with word parts that are represented regularly or consistently should be taught with the word parts shown in print
and then put together to make words. Words such as *trum—pet, mag—
net, pub—lish—er* can be used. It helps some children to have the word
parts printed on cards. They can then move the parts together to form a
word and separate the cards into word parts. These word parts should
be manipulated before they are presented in a list.[23]

- Teach students the meanings of prefixes, roots, and suffixes. They need
to learn about these word parts early, as soon as they know rules about
syllables. Common ones are derived from Latin and Greek. Mastery of
some of these forms means that there is less to remember in learning vocabulary. Knowing that the word part *auto-* refers to *self*, the student
does not have to learn separate and new definitions for *automobile, automatic, autobiography, autograph* and *autonomy*, or that if *de-* means
down, away from, or *negation*, student may be able to figure out meanings for *depart, deport, depress, deflect, deflate, denounce.* Students with
learning problems often do not notice these similarities on their own.
Specific teaching to make word derivations explicit is necessary.

- Teach students to understand how words in different contexts have related meanings. A *margin* is found around the edge of a page and when
something is *marginal* it is on the edge of being acceptable or included.

- If students understand underlying relationships among words such as
sign, significance, significant, signify they are more likely to both read
and spell better. In addition, they develop better knowledge of word
meanings.

In order to read, we must be able to read individual words, at least most
of them. Guessing at what printed words might be is not efficient. "...no matter how a child is taught to read, he comes sooner or later to the strait gate
and the narrow way: he has to learn letters and the sounds for which they

stand. There is no evidence whatever that he will ultimately do this better from at first not doing it at all." [24]

Teaching Comprehension.

Decoding words is essential for being able to read. But once the words can be decoded, the reader must understand the words that are read. Pronouncing the words has no value if the words mean nothing. Readers must have an adequate vocabulary including multiple word meanings and figurative language. They must also understand long sentences and the complex ones that are used in text. They must understand how sentences are held together in certain ways to form paragraphs and that paragraphs are tied together to convey ideas in a sensible way. Teaching for reading comprehension may begin with oral language understanding but with recognition that text uses more complex and formal structure. There is some overlap in teaching comprehension for oral language and reading, but there are differences as well. Printed text demands different kinds of knowledge in addition to what is provided through oral language.[25] Maria wrote, "If children are not exposed to long words, long sentences, difficult constructions and structures, and new genres, they will never learn to understand them."[26]

As adults read to young children:

- Ask the child to tell what the story might be about from the title or from pictures on the cover.
- Ask the child to point to pictures as they are named.
- Ask the child to show what in the picture demonstrates specific verbs.
- Ask the child to tell what might happen next in the story or on the next page.
- Early on, parents might just talk about pictures on the page but some children need help to pay attention to the stories. If they are not willing to sit still to listen to a story, the activity should stop, but be tried again in one week.
- Through being read to, children begin to understand how stories are constructed, how a story moves over time, and what a problem might be and how it is resolved. They learn the different ways that information is conveyed.

As children begin to read for understanding:

- Reading comprehension work can be done first with sentences and then move to longer units.
- Practice should be provided in the cloze procedure. It is helpful if words are on cards first with a space left to be filled in. The cards could then be manipulated. Later the work can be presented on worksheets. For example, if the student can read *The rabbit ran*, he or she should fill in the blanks:

—The ————- rabbit ran.
—The rabbit ran ————.
— ———— rabbit ran.
—The ———— ran.
—The rabbit ————.

- Have the child move words on cards around to unscramble sentences.
- Have the child arrange words to tell or to ask. (Punctuation marks can be on separate cards.)
  —The ball is red.
  —Is the ball red?
- Have the child read words to describe the subject of sentences.
  —The big dog
  —The tiny dog
  —The black dog
  —The mean dog
  —The nice dog
  —The scary dog
- Have the child read sentences where the verb varies.
  —The dog can bark.
  —The dog can run.
  —The dog can bite.
  —The dog can play.
- Add modifiers to tell about the verb.
- Form longer sentences as *The big scary spotted dog that barked was nice to me when I patted its back.*
- Provide practice for sentences that have words rearranged as
  —The dog chased the boy.
  —The boy chased the dog.
- Provide practice with a single printed instruction to follow.
- Increase the number of steps in directions telling how to make or do something. Picture cues can be given.
- Take away picture cues and give several instructions.
- Use recipes for following directions.
- Help students understand that drawings and diagrams help with some activities such as building models or connecting computer components but at other times words may be more useful. They need to learn both.
- Point out the sense of flow over time of a paragraph in expository text or of a story to aid comprehension beyond the sentence level.
- Teach function words in context, with meaning emphasized.
- Teach transition words. A resource is *The New Reading Teacher's Book of Lists*.[27]
  And later as readers continue reading:

- Poor readers are often understimulated. Poor decoding does not mean they cannot handle ideas. They need to be challenged at the level of their intellect. Questions can be asked to help them manage complex concepts even while they are reading simple material. With constant intellectual challenges, they will be ready to handle advanced texts once they can read the words.
- An early goal is to determine if the student really understands what it means to read with comprehension. Children who have some difficulty with early decoding believe that if they read (say) the words, then the job is done—that saying the words is reading. They do not have the notion of reading for understanding or that the text they read has meaning.
- The reader must constantly ask "does it make sense?" This kind of monitoring may need to be specifically taught.
- Readers need to have practice with visually similar words for both reading and learning meaning. For example, *inspired, inspiring, inspirational.*
- If they do not know the meaning of each form of the word, they should be taught the meaning. Have the student read or read to him or her, "The teacher encourages students" and ask, "Which is correct? The teacher is *motivational* or He is *motivated.*" Read "The student cares about doing well. Which is correct? He is *motivational.* He is *motivated.*" Read "He has a prominent position in the school community." Is he *influenced* or *influential,* or both, but how does the meaning change?
- Work with sentences before moving on to longer units. Focus attention on
  —unscrambling sentences or making sentences from words presented out of order. At first provide words on cards to be made into sentences. Later print words on paper and require the student to use mental manipulation to unscramble them.
  —changing a word to change meaning (*Tom is eager to see. Tom is easy to see.*)
  —using different modifiers to change meaning (*The generous man ... The selfish man ... She completed the task carefully. She completed the task carelessly.*)
  —changing word order but maintaining meaning (*Mother walked the dog. The dog was walked by Mother.*)
  —changing word order to change meaning (*The boy chased the girl. The girl chased the boy. Mom showed the girl the boy. Mom showed the boy the girl.*) The goal for reading at this sentence level is for the reader to understand the importance not only of single word meaning but of word order as well.
- Some readers must be helped to realize that they must read every word particularly for reading comprehension tests and when reading some kinds of technical material.

- Readers may need explicit help to learn that fiction and nonfiction should be read differently . Stories have a kind of structure and features that can be identified. Nonfiction must be read for facts and the relationships among them.
- Work with using pronoun referents (*it, he, she, they*). Children with reading comprehension problems may have difficulty in both clarity of expression and comprehension as far as 'who did what to whom' (in such structures as *The girl gave the boy the book* or *The cat is chased by the dog.*)
- Teach the use of figurative language in reading.
- Teach multiple meanings of words to contribute to general vocabulary knowledge.
- Provide practice in having the child follow explicit printed directions.
- Provide practice in making inferences and how we infer from only partial or limited information.
- Provide practice in reading to note fact versus opinion. Newspapers and news magazines are good sources of material. Have the student study differences among styles on the editorial page, letters to the editor, and front page stories.
- Teach meanings of prefixes, roots, and suffixes.
- Help the student predict what might occur after the event, paragraph, or story.
- After reading, the student can tell how an event or action that was different could result in a different kind of outcome.
- Provide practice in re-telling first sentences, then paragraphs, then longer units of stories or expository text.
- Help the student develop questions to be asked about a section of text or a chapter before reading begins. Provide the general topic that the passage covers and have the student formulate questions that might be answered when the selection is read.
- Help the student relate new or unfamiliar information to his or her own experiences. This is particularly helpful when reading literature, stories set in another time and place, or involving a culture or lifestyle different from the reader's own.
- Help students realize how much information is supplied by looking at the story or chapter before reading it—titles, headings, topic sentences in paragraphs, etc. Encourage them to scan these markers every time they begin to read, teach them that this is not just an exercise.
- Provide practice with reading to recall specific facts. At times fact questions need to be asked before the reader starts to read the text until he or she learns what it means to read about facts. Later he or she can read text and be asked a factual question after having finished reading.

- If needed, give specific instruction in answering questions that are based on what the reader knows versus answering by what is specifically stated in the passage read.
- Visual plans or outlines, story maps, time lines may support text that is read.
- Students may need specific help to understand the differences in what is conveyed in factual material such as science or history and in stories. They need to read differently for each type of task.
- The difficulty of questions asked should increase. Even with limited reading, children should have an opportunity to practice thinking about ideas at the level of their ability rather than at the level of their reading.
- Readers with learning disabilities may need help in building from concrete to more abstract questions to guide their reading, or if they cannot yet manage reading at the level of their listening comprehension. Just as many dyslexic children will not learn to read unless they have a highly structured phonics approach, so some children need more direct instruction in how to approach comprehension of what is read. Poor readers may be understimulated in their thinking since questions asked about text may not be advanced enough. They may need work with structured questions that increase in complexity.
- Adults need to continue to read to children, particularly dyslexic children, so they can continue to learn at the level of their ability until the time they can read on their own.
- Teachers and parents cannot assume that once children can decode, they will easily manage to comprehend text. Many of them will need to be taught how to read with understanding.

SUMMARY

All children must be taught to read. Most will learn easily. Some will find it extremely difficult. We must help poor and reluctant readers become better at reading so that they have the option of reading or not. It has been suggested that children do not learn to read in reading class; it is only with practice reading about topics of interest and importance that they really learn to read. Poor readers need to be taught to master the code and then have enough supervised practice until reading that code is automatic. Then they need exposure to a wide variety of print materials so they can become readers, if they wish, of any book in print.

CHAPTER 5

SHARING THE WORDS
Written Expressive
Language

"I wish trees were never invented, and then there wouldn't be pencils" stated an 8-year-old boy at the time of his testing. Many children feel this way when they are asked to write. Written expression is the last of the language arts skills acquired. For writing to develop, children must have some sophistication about language and the organization of ideas. They must appreciate how the stream of speech is represented by print and how images of the printed words are retrieved for spelling. They need a sense of how thoughts are given life through sentences and longer units. They must know how to write for specific purposes, whether the product is a note from a telephone message, a letter, an answer on a test, a homework assignment, an essay, or a story. They must have a sense of what the reader or reading audience knows about the subject. Finally, they are required to have some mechanism of transmission—pencil, pen, or keyboard. All previous language learning, including comprehension of speech, oral expression, and reading, comes into play when we write.

Spoken language existed for many thousands of years before humans began to communicate in a written form. Ancient cave drawings that provide indications about the lives of early civilizations are marks of communicative intent. Campbell, who spoke about the power of these drawings, said that although inferences about early life are made from the drawings, "...until you have writing you don't know what people were thinking."[1]

As far as we know, the first written expression was pictographic, using pictures to represent objects and experiences. There is disagreement about

117

whether writing systems emerged from the pictures or if the drawings have no relationship to later writing systems. After pictures, logographic representations, in which a mark not connected with the represented object or experience, were used. We still use logographic representations such as dollar and cents signs and the shapes that become associated with soft drinks, cars, food markets, and fast food chains.

There are indications that written forms were used in some parts of the world but then faded away to re-emerge later. As beginning writing was retained by societies, it was then available to be modified within a culture and in different areas of the world. Civilization moved forward in its ability to communicate information through syllabaries in which marks stood consistently for spoken word parts. Finally just a few thousand years ago, alphabets were developed; a mark came to stand for a part of a spoken word, often referred to as a speech sound.

As societies began to regard it as important that children learn to write, slaves taught children of the nobility to read and write. Later still, writing preserved cultures and was carried out largely by the clergy. For a long time, there was no consistency of either spelling or letter formation. Spellings of words did not become standard until they were set in type. When the printing press was developed, written materials could be both standard and accessible to more people. The making of a lasting mark that could communicate with others, the discovery of materials to be written upon, and the invention of the printing press were major developments in human communication. But the increase in rate of information sharing may never have changed so rapidly as in the past two decades. Computers affect every aspect of our lives, so much so that one of the worst things to hear when one is in a hurry is that "the computer is down." Facsimile (FAX) machines are commonplace and messages can be shared instantly. Such rapid transmission of ideas has affected how we gain knowledge and how quickly we learn of world affairs. A natural disaster such as fire, flood, or earthquake in one part of the country or blazing guns and killing in another part of the world can be observed as soon as a video camera and someone to run it are on site. However, there are negative aspects to information being shared so quickly. Little effort may be given to contemplation or reflection before sending a message, and of course confidentiality is difficult.

No matter what advances in technology have been made, the basic need for writing has not changed. It is a mark of a literate person to be able to read and also to express ideas through writing. Writing clarifies thinking as well, allowing the writer to share thoughts and feelings with others.

Whether considering normal development or disabilities, there are many ways to discuss written expressive language. Some investigators write about writing as including components of planning or pre-writing, writing, then revising, and later making a final copy that can be shared with others (the latter often referred to as publishing). Others make distinctions between mechanics of writing including capitalization, punctuation, and spelling on one hand and fluency on the other hand, with fluency being essentially the amount written, whatever unit of measurement is used. Another way to conceptualize the writing process is to regard it as having components that include handwriting, spelling, and written formulation of sentences and longer units of discourse. This latter approach will be used in this chapter.

HANDWRITING

Luria wrote, "For adults writing is an automatic skill, a series of built-in movements which I call 'kinetic melodies.'"[2] Each of us develops a style of writing that is unique and ours alone. Children are presented with the same basic letter models to copy, yet each develops a personal handwriting style. Our handwriting is ours for life. Indeed, if we try to make our writing look exactly like another's, it is called forgery and we could wind up in jail.

Handwriting is regarded as one of the mechanics of writing and as such is often afforded little consideration as part of a writing process. However, as children pass through school, they must expend energy in learning to write and to express their ideas in writing. A problem with handwriting, which has no impact on an adult who has easy access to secretaries and/or word processors, can be a serious one for developing children. Students must write for in-class activities, for homework, and for tests. A problem with the motor act of handwriting can cause a child or adolescent to resist writing anything at all because it is hard and tiring, or they may write the minimal amount possible. Often children who find it hard to master handwriting in early school years, resist all writing. They may then hold onto the resistance toward writing even when the act of handwriting itself is perfectly adequate. Computers are helpful, and they are continually decreasing in both cost and size, but they still are not as available to every child in school as are pencils. So, for now, children must write using their hands and some implement.

Beginnings of Graphomotor Skills or Visual Motor Integration

The term *graphomotor skill,* or skill of visual-motor integration, refers to making marks with an implement on a surface such as paper, with the marks having a sense of purpose. Children move or tap a crayon, pencil, pen, or marker on paper and observe that they leave a trace. Once such traces are made deliberately, a child has some visual memory that the pencil will leave a mark and some motor memory that the implement must be held and then moved in a particular way. Provided with the tools, children repeat making marks on paper. They do this again and again until they begin scribbling.

Gardner[3] relates this early playing with marker and a surface as analogous to 2- to 3-year-old children playing with language just for the joy of saying words which often occurs as they are resting in bed before sleep. In the same way young children enjoy play with pencil or crayons and paper. They practice the visual and the motor skills that will later lead to drawing and writing.

Children's marks on paper have been studied as art, as ways of assessing personality and emotional growth, and as reflections of developmental stages. Kellogg and O'Dell described and illustrated young children's drawings from under 2 years of age through 7 years as art.[4] The delight of children's manipulation of media to make pictures or just to express joy with an implement and paper leaps from the pages in many young children's drawings. Lowenfeld[5] related children's marks on paper to intellectual, emotional, social, perceptual, aesthetic, and creative growth as soon as the children regarded the marks as representational, or as standing for something.

Once children have records of what they have completed, these records are available to be evaluated in a way that speech, their other output system, is not. As soon as sounds, words, or phrases are said, they are completed and off in time. At some stage of pre-writing, the visual image and the motor act become integrated and repeated.

Emergence of Geometric Forms

Out of free scribbling, lines and shapes emerge. Children first make vertical lines at about 21 to 24 months, horizontal lines at about 24 to 30 months, circles at about 36 months, a cross by 48 to 54 months. A square occurs at 4 to 5 years, an oblique cross (an X) at close to 5 years, a triangle at about 5 years and a diamond at 7 to 8 years.[6,7] First they may imitate the shapes and later copy them. To *imitate* them means that an adult presents the line or shape while the child watches, and then the child attempts to make the same line or shape. *Copying* occurs when the child sees the line or shape and tries to make one like the model, but without observing another in the motor act.

Before children can make marks on paper, they must hold a pencil with enough tension so it does not flop over. Children, when first presented with a pencil or crayon, may hold it in any number of ways. A child may first hold it in a grasp in which a fist is tightly wrapped around the pencil shaft. This has been referred to as a dagger grasp. It is an extension of the reflexive act of the newborn in curling their fingers around the parents' fingers and then any cylindrical object. Children may also hold the pencil shaft as though they are going to shovel something from the paper, and this is known as a shovel grasp. In order to hold a pencil in a traditional grasp, the child must use the first two fingers and the thumb in a pincer movement, the kind of movement that is used for lifting ice with ice tongs. Once this pincer motion is established, a pencil can be put in place and the child begins to use a conventional grasp.

Children use the forms they make to represent people, often with circular shapes as faces first, and then lines coming out from the face as legs and arms. Pleasure is derived from such activities, and if fostered, young children experience great delight from what they produce with paper and pencil. With encouragement, they can create and at the same time increase their ability to hold an implement for later writing. It is important to promote this creativity for its own sake, to give pleasure, and to encourage any innate talent, while at the same time encouraging a pre-writing activity.

Those who work with young children disagree on whether children should be permitted to play with pencil or crayons until they begin using a correct grasp or they should be taught to hold a pencil correctly from the time they pick it up. Many children will, through their exploration and manipulation, discover a comfortable conventional grasp, while some children with special needs would never discover a correct pencil grasp on their own and do require specific teaching.

Assessment of Pre-(hand)Writing Skills

One way to measure visual motor or graphomotor skills in children is to have them copy forms. A common test used is the *Developmental Test of Visual Motor Integration*.[7] This test was designed to measure children's visual motor integration developmentally. An earlier test was the *Bender Visual Motor Gestalt Test*, which also involved copying designs.[8] The early interpretations of the *Bender Visual Motor Gestalt Test*, according to Lauretta Bender, who developed the test, were clinical and used diagnostically in adults with neurological and psychiatric problems as well as in developing children. The strength of this measure was shown best when it was in the hands of clinicians who used her guidelines for analysis. I had an opportunity to interview Dr. Bender for a videotape series sponsored by The Orton Dyslexia Society, and I asked her if she approved of some of the attempts to standardize scoring of the designs of her test. She said that the forms themselves and the developmental ability to copy them is so powerful that there is nothing that can be done to destroy the value of such a copying task and what it can tell about kinds of perceptual organizations and productions.

Development of Handwriting

Apart from using the pencil for artistic expression and perhaps to indicate their feelings, children begin to notice that marks on paper relate to marks in books, that the marks have some value for communication. They start to have some sense of marking to make letters.

They will naturally, through their exploration of implement and paper, make many pre-letter forms that will develop as parts of later letters. As they sort out some of the squiggles, parents will label them and the child has the experience of beginning to write. Legrun and Hildreth observed developmental stages in pre-writing in young children.[9] The stages progressed from unorganized scribbles, to zigzag lines across a page, to some separation between the zigzag marks, to occasional insertion of a real letter, to more real letters within the array of marks, and finally all letters. Some children make their scribbles on paper look like items on a list and others have the format of a note or letter. Children seem to pass through these stages with little difficulty and as part of play, unless there are problems with the visual-motor act.

As children make marks on paper in any plane—on a flat surface or on one that is vertical such as a chalkboard on a wall—they may start to label them as letters. These forms may be right-side-up, up-side-down, or written backward. It takes a while for children to realize that a mark must be made in a consistent direction to be labeled as a specific letter. But this behavior of mixing up the spatial direction of shapes is logical for a young child. Up until this time, they have been aware of *object constancy*. This is the notion that an object in any position remains the same object with the same name. A chair turned in any way remains a chair. Crawling under it, looking down on it, or jumping on it, the object remains and is still called a *chair*. So there is no reason for a child to understand immediately that when a line and a circle are placed together, the resulting marks can have different names—*p* or *b* or *d*, or *q*. As children begin to learn letter names, they learn this new rule of directionality fairly quickly, but some will continue to confuse letters and show reversals until they are about 7 years of age. It is when these confusions remain after the age of 7 that there may be reason for concern.

Handwriting Problems

Some children do not make easy transitions in the use of a pencil from drawing to forming letters. In early school years and into middle school they may have trouble with writing when compared with their agemates. Letter formation may be inconsistent. There may be a mix of upper and lower case letters and cursive and manuscript. They may have trouble with consistent shape, size, and slant. Some hold the pencil so tightly that their hands tire quickly after only a few words are written. Some write with tiny letters that are hard to interpret or in a sloppy way as a mask for poor spelling.

Handwriting may be regarded as a fine motor skill or a task of visual motor integration. Yet there are those with excellent fine motor skills for building with small blocks and manipulating small objects who have poor handwriting. There are also children who show superb use of a pencil for drawing whose handwriting is exceedingly poor. It is the formation of shapes or letters as symbols that may be hard for them.

Dysgraphia is a term sometimes used to describe problems with writing. It is used here in its narrowest sense as being an apraxia for pencil use.

(*Apraxia* means a problem with voluntarily executing motor tasks.) An individual knows how the letter or word should look, but he or she cannot voluntarily execute the motor act. Other professionals use dysgraphia to refer to spelling and written formulation difficulties as well. It is essential that both parents and teachers know what the person using the term *dysgraphia* means by their use of the word. How broadly or how narrowly dysgraphia is defined makes a difference in how it is managed.

Something as unimportant in life as handwriting should not be of great concern. Yet there are many children and adolescents who are in big trouble in school because they do not have handwriting that can be executed at a reasonable rate and in a way legible enough to be interpreted by one's self and others.

Evaluating Handwriting

In evaluating pencil use and later handwriting we might ask the following questions.

What hand does the child use for writing? Is this hand used consistently? Establishment of handedness emerges at varying times in children. Some are strongly right or left handed and show the preference in their high chairs. Others show mixed use of left or right hand through preschool years. Others do some tasks consistently with their right hand and other tasks with their left. Some individuals remain ambidextrous throughout their lives, which can be a benefit to athletes and surgeons. More learning problems in left-handed individuals are reported by some investigators but not by others. It is probably best to let nature take its course and wait for a child to decide which hand he or she will use to write. If a child reaches school age without making the choice, analysis of which hand he or she uses for most tasks can be made and the child encouraged to use the dominant hand for writing.

Is the pencil held in an appropriate grasp? The pencil grasp or grip needs to be one that is comfortable so that the child can write without tiring. When children begin regarding their marks on paper as letters they should be helped to develop correct grasp. Any motor act practiced many, many times becomes a habit. Thus, we need to have children use the correct pencil grasp from beginning stages of writing. If they do not, they can develop idiosyncratic ways of holding a pencil that make their hands fatigue quickly and interfere with the amount they are able to write. Children may hold a pencil in what looks like a traditional grasp but with the pencil between the third and fourth fingers rather than the index and second fingers. Some curl their thumbs tightly around the pencil held between the fourth and little fingers. Others fold their fingers around the pencil too close to the point while others try to hold it in the middle of the shaft and the pencil wobbles all over the place with little control. There are many odd ways that children can hold pencils. The reason for encouraging a consistent grasp is for the writing act to be, not only efficient and automatic, but also comfortable. Comfort reduces the chance of fatigue and resistance or refusal to use a pencil.

Is appropriate tension used in holding the pencil? Tension of pencil grip has to be present to some degree or the pencil will fall out of the hand. The pencil must be held so it stays between the fingers and is anchored by the other fingers. Pressure needs to be heavy enough that the marks made can be seen but not so heavy as to make holes in paper or to make the hand tire quickly.

Is the paper positioned correctly on the writing surface for right or left handed writing? Paper needs to be positioned differently for a right and left handed writer. Diana King[10] suggests folding over a corner of the paper—the lower left hand corner for a right handed writer and the lower right for a left handed writer. The fold should then be placed along the bottom of the desk or table in front of the writer for correct positioning of paper for writing.

Is the non-writing hand used to anchor the paper? It is important that the non-writing hand is used to hold the paper. If it is not used, the paper will wiggle all over the place. Some children never seem to notice the moving paper as they write and must be helped to develop the habit.

Is posture correct? Posture also needs to be comfortable until writing patterns are established. This means that feet should be on the floor, and the writing surface should be large enough to hold the paper.

What is the writer's preferred writing, cursive or manuscript? There continues to be some controversy about whether cursive or manuscript writing should be taught initially. I have seen children with severe reading disabilities show confusion when seeing printed letters for reading while learning to write in cursive. For most children it probably does not matter if they learn manuscript or cursive first.

What writing is required by school and can the individual execute it? What is important for the child to learn is the script that is required in his or her school. If manuscript is used by the other children, the child should learn manuscript. Consistency of script is important. Because it serves to reinforce reading and spelling, it is important that the same motor movements are used all the time to create strong motor memories. Many learning disabled children at middle and secondary levels have notebooks that show a confused mess of cursive and manuscript with little that can be interpreted and used for study. With ordinary students mixed cursive and manuscript may never be a problem. But learning disabled youngsters who have trouble with reading as well as writing are helped when their writing is consistent. They should be encouraged to select a style of script and then stick with it for all writing.

Are letters formed consistently? Letters must be formed in a consistent way every time they are written. It is only when they are consistent over many renderings that the patterns become automatic and can be used as writing rather than drawing. When cursive writing is used, it becomes important to establish not only skill in forming individual letters but also the connections between letters.

Are letters formed correctly? The correct formations of letters for whatever script is used have been developed as the ones that are most efficient. Starting letters at a specific place in relationship to the space and line is useful. Starting the letter in the same place each time contributes to reinforcing the motor habit pattern.

If cursive writing is used, are connections between the letters correct? Some of the connections between letters are more difficult than others. For example, connecting *b* and *l*, *v* and *e*, or *x* and *i* can be hard for some writers.

Is size consistent? Size of letters is modified to fit within a certain space on lined paper. Some children will need help to use the lines to assist them with making consistently sized letters.

Is slant consistent? Consistency of size and slant is important along with letter formation. Until there is uniformity and automaticity, handwriting does not exist as a tool. It is almost as though every act of writing letters is new.

Are letters positioned correctly to use lines and spaces when lined paper is used? Some children write as though they do not perceive the lines. It is as though the lines do not exist. Later, when paper is used with a red line down the left side of the page, many children will not use that line to help them with the left-side margin. They need to see the lines as aids, not as marks to be ignored.

If there is a problem with handwriting, does the individual have trouble in copying or with remembering how to form the letter? Children who are dysgraphic will have trouble forming the letters even with copy present. They know what they want to put on the paper but cannot make their hand and pencil produce the image of what is in their heads. Instruction for such a child will need to involve tracing letters, and they may be helped by giving verbal instructions to the hand as the letters are written. A child whose problem is with memory will easily form letters with copy present but needs help to remember the shape of the letters. The pencil may be moved with good coordination, but the motor patterns required cannot be remembered.

Are spelling errors really ones of handwriting? Errors such as *nap* for *map*, *veb* for *web*, *clear* for *dear*, and *kat* for *hat* are likely to be handwriting errors rather than mistakes for spelling. Uniformity in letter formation will help reduce such spelling errors that are errors with handwriting. For some writers with learning disabilities, it seems at times as though some letters are formed in a way that is almost random. If habit patterns are established for letters they are more likely to be available to the writer for spelling.

If there is trouble in any one of these areas, some intervention needs to be provided. Such support must be given as early as possible before the writer develops a motor habit that makes changing it difficult.

In recent years, handwriting has received little emphasis in our schools. This is probably good in many ways, because there is so much of importance to learn. Most children learn to write in a way sufficient for their needs. However, if children have trouble with learning to write, they require direct instruction and practice. Unless they get it, they may reach teenage years with inconsistent motor patterns for writing. They may be inconsistent enough in their writing that they cannot take notes that they can later read and may have such poor writing that teachers cannot read their homework and tests, so their grades are reduced. Some level of efficiency with handwriting that can be read by oneself and others is essential. The writing act must also be executed at a rate that is efficient for the task requirements. Some examples of handwriting problems are shown below.

TEACHING CHILDREN WHO HAVE TROUBLE WITH HANDWRITING

- With preschool children and beginning writers in kindergarten and first grade, various implements should be made available. Included should be felt-tip markers, crayons, pens, fat pencils, small pencils, chalk, and finger paints. A finger can be used to make marks on a dirty chalkboard or a paintbrush can be dipped in water and used on a chalkboard. Children begin to develop the sense that by moving an implement held in their hands a visual form will be produced.
- Provide paper such as newsprint, construction paper, tissue paper, rolls of inexpensive shelf paper, the classified section of the newspaper, or used computer paper.
- Provide various sizes of pencils, crayons, and markers. Different children may respond better to one size than another. Julia Molloy, a well-respected educator of cognitively limited children, said that little fingers need little pencils[11] and Diana King refers disparagingly to primary pencils as being "the size of fence posts."[12]
- Provide practice in scribbling. Children should be encouraged to scribble. If they did not scribble as toddlers they should be encouraged to use such freedom of movement in kindergarten or first grade. The goal is to have some freedom in motor movements but with the movements leaving a consistent mark that can be repeated. Children must have sense of motor control with the pencil before they can imitate or copy.

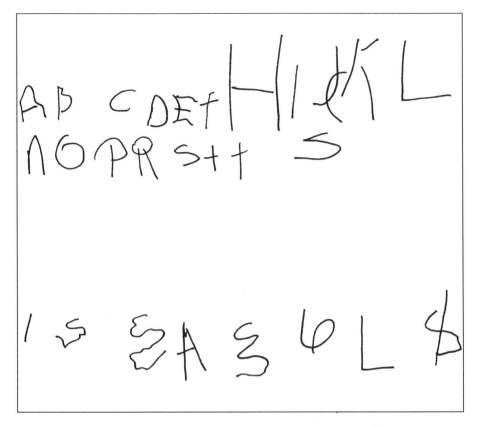

The alphabet and numerals 1 through 8 written by a 6-year-old boy with dyslexia and a strong family history of dyslexia

- Children can imitate adults by producing a particular kind of line or shape. A child watches an adult and then imitates the movement that has just been made. Included can be vertical lines, horizontal lines, circles, and diagonal lines.
- After children can imitate they could be encouraged to copy the same lines and forms—the shape is presented, and while looking at it the child copies it.
- Additional forms to be copied are the X, cross, square, and triangle.
- Later, at about age 7, children should be encouraged to copy a diamond.
- Copying forms has no value in itself, but rather shows a developmental level of integration by interpreting a visual form and relating it to the motor act. The forms are also parts of strokes that will be used in forming letters.

go

cat

in

boy

and

make

cook

Words written as dictated by a 7-year-old boy whose reading and spelling are fine, but who has both visual memory and visual-motor problems for writing.

already

animal

because

children

Words extracted from spontaneous writing of a 14-year-old boy whose handwriting is illegible

- As children become adept with imitating and copying designs, they should practice pre-letter forms—the lines used to form letters—until there is motor control for using a pencil or marker to make these forms. Some pre-letter forms are shown on the following pages.
- Have a child practice tracing over dotted letters.
- When children know number names and their order, dot-to-dot pictures can be used.
- Have a child make shapes, pre-letter forms, and letters in trays or cookie sheets containing sand or salt.
- Some children will find tracing sandpaper shapes and letters helpful.
- Finger paints can be used for practice as well. A place that is safe for making a mess is important. Some children will need to be helped to accept the feeling of the paint on their fingers and hands.
- Some teachers put shaving cream on a surface and have children practice the forms and letters in the cream.
- You may need to provide some children with a verbal cue such as "up, over, down, over" (to make a square) or "up, down, around, up, finish" (for cursive *d*)
- Learning rhymes to go along with the movements helps some children.
- After children have control of some of the motor patterns, they need to learn to begin at the left side of the page. Some teachers draw a green line down the left side of the paper to represent *go* or *start* and a red line down the right side of the page for *stop* or *end*.
- As children begin to show interest in using a pencil it is important that:
  —Posture is correct.
  —The pencil is held in an appropriate grasp.
  —The paper is positioned correctly on the writing surface for right or left handed writer.
  —The non-writing hand is used to anchor the paper.
- Triangular pencil grips are available for those children who have difficulty learning correct pencil grasp. There are also grips that look like squashed bits of clay that fit over pencils and can be positioned for both right and left handed writers. Metal wire devices help some children learn correct pencil grasp. Be sure that children understand the reason for using the devices, that is, to help them until they have mastered a pencil grip that will be comfortable and efficient. Establishing any habit or changing to a new one takes much practice for it to become automatic.
- The traditional grasp of a pencil is efficient, comfortable, and has served most of the population well. There may be times when an alternative grasp should be considered. Thurber, who developed the D'Nealian method of writing, advocates a different pencil grip.[13] He states "The

Some pre-letter forms for manuscript writing

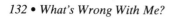

Some pre-letter forms for cursive letters

pen or pencil is held between the index and middle fingers with the barrel resting on the web between the fingers. It is then grasped with the thumb, index and middle fingers about an inch from the point. The thumb gently holds the pencil in place against the other two fingers. The hand rests on the heel of the hand and slides on the tips and nails of the fourth and fifth fingers. The pencil is held with about a 25-degree slant from the vertical position." At times it may be more efficient to change a grasp to this unconventional one rather than changing finger position to one that is close to the way the child is holding the pencil. Learning a completely different way may be easier to learn. In the D'Nealian writing method letters are made with minimal strokes, appropriate slant, and once mastered makes it easy to connect the letters for cursive writing, although it can be used for printing without ever changing to cursive writing.

- Introduce letters once there is good control for pre-letter forms. It is important that correct motor patterning for each letter be learned from the very beginning of handwriting instruction. This is necessary to establish a motor habit or automaticity that leads to efficiency in writing.
- Group letters according to similar strokes.
- Make up rhymes about how to form letters.
- When students have trouble with the motor act of handwriting, it is essential that teachers understand the impact of the writing problem on all areas of learning. Some modifications of requirements may need to be made *while* special help with the writing is provided and *until* the act of writing is mastered. Such modifications include:
  —additional time to complete tasks and in-class work without penalty;
  —liberal acceptance of projects rather than written work;
  —oral reports rather than written ones; and
  —work as part of a group rather than individually so that creative ideas can be contributed while another student with good handwriting can execute the writing.
- It is important that such modifications are offered only until students can write on their own. Students will not get better in writing until they write and patterns become automatic and comfortable.
- It is boring and sometimes painful to re-copy a lengthy assignment, especially when the motor act of writing is hard. Recopying should be kept to a minimum.
- It is difficult for children with less than adequate handwriting to do well with writing tasks when they must think of ideas, correct spelling, and neat handwriting all at the same time.
- Some writing should be required in school, but a limited amount. There needs to be a balance between expectations for a reasonable amount of writing and allowances for the writing difficulty.

- Children with handwriting problems do need practice writing. They will only learn to write through practice.
- Control the requirement for writing so that the act of writing does not become confrontational. One of the most difficult situations that can occur is when a child refuses to write. One cannot force the reluctant writer to put pencil to paper.
- There may be times when teachers and parents should accept the quality of the writing, and the fact that it does not look age appropriate, that there is not space between words, that letters are not formed consistently, with the goal initially being to request an amount of writing that is complete. Some children are so perfectionistic that they refuse to write, because they think that what they write is not good enough. It is possible that if teachers and parents do not comment on the quality of handwriting, the child will be more comfortable and willing to try to write and to be accepting of what is produced.
- Over time, students with handwriting problems need to come to understand that there will always be writing requirements for school and that they will need to do some writing.
- As students mature, they can understand that writing occurs in one's head and that a pencil, typewriter, or computer is only a tool. It doesn't matter which is used but "writing" must be done. There are situations when a student must use a pencil; at other times, a computer/word processor might be preferred.
- Until an effective writing output system is developed, some alternative responses may be acceptable such as:
  —Doing written assignments by committee with a student with good handwriting being the scribe, while the one with poor handwriting supplies ideas.
  —In a few instances, permitting the student to dictate to parents can be helpful. This is important when there is a lot of important knowledge or creative ideas to share such as for creative writing or some reports.
  —Allowing alternative ways of responding such as oral reports or construction projects some of the time.
- Using only oral testing and oral presentations and projects should not be a goal. Students need to write to learn to write. Personal laptop computers are too expensive to be readily available for all students with handwriting problems and most will not need them.
- Visual motor integration problems may cause serious obstacles in math. It is important to separate math knowledge from the visual-spatial-motor act of putting numbers on paper. Some possibilities are as follows:
  —Turn paper sideways with lines on paper in a vertical rather than

horizontal direction so numbers can be lined up correctly within columns between the lines.

—Alternatively, graph paper could be used.

—Place paper under problems in a book so work can be shown without having to copy problems.

—If a lot of problems are involved, make a photocopy so problems do not need to be copied from a book.

—Permit parents to purchase math text so the student can write in the book.

Help with handwriting can be provided by classroom teachers, special education resource teachers, occupational therapists, and/or parents. No child should fail in school because of a problem with handwriting. No child should be kept out of programs for the gifted and talented because of poor handwriting. Handwriting is only a tool. Its proficient use should not loom as large in the lives of children as it often does. This is the one area that can allow compensatory, or substitute systems such as word processors, without compromising cognitive functioning.

Using a computer/word processor

Every student needs to learn keyboarding and how to use a computer/word processor. The use of the computer/word processor should

—allow compensation for poor handwriting;

—permit ideas to be expressed in neat copy; and

—increase knowledge about the editing process and develop facility to expand and change what is written to make it better.

• Keyboarding should be learned so that there can be maximum skill in using the computer. Efficient use of a keyboard needs to be learned and the skill will be of benefit to students for the rest of their lives. No child should grow up using the hunt and peck system of finding letters on the keyboard as do so many adults today.

• Motor coordination problems that exist for handwriting may cause difficulty as well with typing or keyboarding, so a skillful teacher is essential to teach keyboarding to students who have trouble with fine motor skills. Often, a student is in middle school or above when formal typing/keyboarding is taught, and it is usually done in groups. Students taking such classes may not look different, and the teacher may not know that a particular student has a learning disability that can affect the fine motor system. Teachers at the secondary level often have little or no exposure to the field of learning disabilities; they know their subject areas but may know little about different learning styles and learning abilities. The teacher must be informed when there is a student who has basic problems with fine motor skills. Such students may not learn the sequential motor movements and patterns as fast as others. They are likely to experience extreme frustration. Frustration can lead to explosive reactions on the part of students. A teacher who does not understand, or has no wish to understand, students with learning disabilities may over-react to what such distressed students may say or do. Expulsion from school has occurred when a student, experiencing extreme frustration, made an inappropriate remark to his typing teacher. If students with learning disabilities are enrolled in keyboarding classes, the parents, or a special teacher or counselor must inform the teacher of the nature of the problems. This is a serious issue and must be managed as such before the student gets into trouble with an inflexible teacher.

- Permit major writing assignments to be done on the word processor at home.
- It is helpful, if systems permit, for the student to have his own floppy disk for writing assignments that can be worked on in computer lab at school but also at home. This is effective only if the student has the same system at home and school; many families purchase computers to be compatible with what students are using in school.
- Some students with poor handwriting need to use a computer for all writing activities. Parents supply a laptop computer and it becomes an extension of the student's hand for taking notes, completing assignments, and writing exams. Efficient use of the computer must be learned before it is this useful, however.

SPELLING

From time to time, spelling has been regarded as either very significant or of little importance, being relegated to the unimportant mechanics of writing. Often parents tell me they do not care about their children's poor spelling. Their reasoning is that spelling is without value, and students growing up today will have access to computers and word processors with spell checkers. These kinds of remarks are likely to reflect limited knowledge of both poor spellers and computer spell-checking programs. For example, a word processing program I once used often showed an array of more than twenty visually similar words for my typing errors. If a word is misspelled or mistyped, a person must be able to read fairly well to select the correct word from such a visual display.

Spelling may or may not provide accurate appraisal of a person's educational level, but it may reveal some of what a speller knows about reading because poor readers are also poor spellers. How a student spells provides a window on what the speller knows about print representing speech. We can begin to hypothesize about approaches to teach reading, as well as spelling, by observing how an individual person spells.

Good spellers write words almost automatically; the words seem to flow from the ink in the pen. Occasionally for long words, they may divide the word into syllables to aid spelling. For words retained in visual memory, they may write the words and decide if they look right. Moreover, most good spellers recall at least some rules to assist them in correct spelling. As with all learning, we do not really know how individuals master spelling. Most people can spell words they need with few errors. They do this without being able to tell the rules for why they spell as they do. Often if asked to reflect upon a rule of spelling, they say they have no idea, yet at some level the rule has been learned and can be applied.

Development of Spelling

Some writers regard reading and spelling as reverse processes of each other. Others disagree. Peter Bryant and Lynette Bradley, who have studied reading and spelling of young children in England, suggest that in the beginning stages of learning to read and spell, children may show different cognitive processes for reading than for spelling.[14] Beginners may spell some words better than they read them. They suggest that early on children may use phonological processing for spelling, relating how the word is pronounced to their writing of it. They try to write letters that represent the way they say words; they relate the sounds of their speech to the letters. In contrast, they use visual chunks, or groups of letters retained by sight, for reading. Most children seem to combine both phonological knowledge (relating speech sounds to print), rule learning, and visual imagery when they spell.

Charles Read, who has studied invented spellings in young children, has written that spelling is not the inverse of reading. He writes that young children, before they can read words and even when they can read some sight words, construct spellings for themselves. They are not bothered when others cannot read what they write or when they are unable themselves to read what they write. He states that the "key difference between reading and writing is that in reading, someone else has chosen both the message and the level of representation, while in writing as young children do it, no one else is necessarily involved."[15]

From the work of Read and others, common features of these early invented spellings have been described. Beginning writing, including invented spellings, is illustrated by Bissex in a charming book, *Gnys at Wrk*, tracing initial writing in her preschool-age son.[16]

In early attempts to write, children may produce marks on paper that resemble grocery lists or letters. As they learn about letters and know a few they may group some together and label the attempt as a word. Soon they are able to write some of the letters that are in a target word they are attempting to write. They may use a letter name to represent a word or part of a word such as *U R lat* for *you are late* or *sanD* for *sandy*. They may over-generalize rules as they did earlier in spoken language when they may have said *I ran*, but, as they learned the rule for past tense, may for a while have said *I runned*. Finally, with varying programs and varying amounts of effort, most children learn the conventional rules of spelling.

In many schools, young children are permitted to use invented spellings without being penalized for incorrect renderings. A child who writes that something is "prtE" for *pretty* does make her point even with the misspelling.

Children, in first or beginning second grade, who are encouraged to use invented spelling often write long stories that reflect imagination and creative thinking. They are wonderful to read. A 7-year-old boy showed good vocabulary and freedom to express ideas comfortably using his own spellings. He wrote:

> Sond trvls throo the eare.
> It bunbs agsnt the molucools
> in the eare. you can toc throo
> water an rel her it. Toc
> throo a tab adn mac som but-
> e lisn in the uthr ud

Translated this is:

> Sound travels through the air.
> It bumps against the molecules
> in the air. You can talk through
> water and really hear it. Talk
> through a tube and make somebody
> listen in the other end.

In contrast, this is a sample from a 10-year-old boy who had marked problems with phonological awareness. He had trouble blending word parts and sounds to form words, trouble segmenting words he heard into parts, and confused the sequence of sounds in words when he talked saying "hosapal" for *hospital* and "cimmin" for *cinnamon*, for example. He wrote,

> The litte boy is play wite is toy he
> like to play wite polpe toy. He like to
> make then mofe like we do. The little boy play
> wite then afatday afat school in hes room.
> He like then very much.

Translated this is,

> The little boy is play with his toy(s). He
> like(s) to play with people toy(s). He like to make
> them move like we do. The little boy play(s)
> with them every day after school in his room.
> He like(s) them very much.

It is important to inform parents when invented spellings are accepted, and indeed encouraged by school. Often they tell me their children are not being taught and are angry with the teacher and the school because of uncorrected wrong spelling. They do not see these spellings as being cognitively advanced. When children are in a language arts program that encourages invented spellings, the assumption is made that at some point they will learn conventional spellings. Most do, but dyslexic children often cannot make the shift without explicit instruction.

There is not as much known about the development of spelling as there is about developing early speech or about the initial stages of learning to read. But in some way young children without learning problems acquire the ability to spell. At first, many relate the sounds of speech to what they know about printed letters. As they begin to read, they hold some of the words they learn in visual memory and will reproduce them. Gradually, they learn spelling rules. Some of these rules are specifically taught, while others seem acquired at a level that the speller may not be aware of in any conscious way. As they learned in early speech how to use inflections on words to show verb tense and to make plurals, they notice or learn that there are consistent ways that tense and plurals are shown in what is read. Then they begin to incorporate this knowledge of language into spelling.

Words to be Spelled

Words to be spelled cannot be easily arranged in a sequence of development. Highly familiar words, those often referred to as easy words, are often those that cause the greatest difficulty. Words such as *who*, *how*, *when*, *where*, *were* are common and yet may be harder for children to spell consistently than the long name of a dinosaur. Spelling depends on the conventions of the language spoken. The way words of a language are represented in print is referred to as the *orthography* of the language. The printed letters that represent the sounds of speech are called *graphemes*, just as the word *phonemes* is sometimes used to refer to speech sounds. The speller must also have some sense of the morphophonemic principles of the language. Both inflectional and derivational morphology must be considered in spelling. Derivational morphemes are not applied as consistently as inflectional morphemes.[17,18]

Marcia Henry[19] presents a plan that helps students read and spell words but stresses meaning at the same time. Her materials can be used after students have some knowledge of sound and letter correspondences. This is an economical approach in that a number of important cognitive points can be learned at one time. She organizes words to be taught in layers with letter-sound correspondences being on one layer, syllable patterns another, and morpheme patterns of prefixes, roots, suffixes, and compound words arranged as they are derived from Anglo-Saxon, Latin, or Greek influences on another layer. The words used in her texts are useful and up-to-date. She also suggests, in her word lists, those words that are sensibly omitted for younger students. These materials are inexpensive and invaluable for those teaching spelling alone and spelling as it relates to reading.

All spelling words cannot be learned in the same way. This fact becomes important for parents to understand when they are helping children learn spelling words and is important for teachers as well. Both teachers and parents can help children group words according to some common principles as ways to practice them and hold them in memory.

Some words are learned by relating the way a word sounds to how it is represented with printed letters; the sounds of the word are represented consistently by a printed equivalent. *Sat*, *web*, *magnet*, and *establish* have a letter or group of letters to stand for the sounds or syllables. This knowledge of a regular association between sound and print helps spell many words.

Some words are learned by rules of English spelling such as "*i* before *e*, except after *c*, or as sounded as 'ay' as in *neighbor* or *weigh*." Other spelling rules tell about adding suffixes or endings to words. For example, "if a word ends with -e, the -e is dropped before adding an ending starting with a vowel."

There are some words that must be retained in visual memory such as *said*, *does*, or *enough*. Spellers need to commit such words to memory; drill and cues to memory need to be provided.

Disorders of Spelling

It is assumed that a person can spell when a certain level of education is reached. Because most people spell almost automatically, they make harsh judgments about those with poor spelling. Often dyslexic individuals, even when they have learned to read quite well, persist in having terrible spontaneous spelling. But with good decoding skills they are more likely to select a correct word from an array of words on spell checkers and/or have enough of a sense of the word to use a dictionary.

Some individuals who have never had problems reading can have spelling problems. Uta Frith in England has written about children and well-educated adults who never had trouble reading but are terrible spellers.[20] Adults I meet with no history of reading difficulty but with persistent poor spelling often seem to have learned to read by using whole words. They were often self-taught readers who began to read before starting school. They may have responded to partial visual cues when reading, but having a sense of only parts of words did not help them spell. Retrieving only parts of a word results in incorrect spelling. Initially, they may have remembered how to spell words by retaining visual images of them, but this approach cannot hold up as the burden placed on visual memory increases with more words to be remembered.

Some young dyslexic children do not have the joy of playing with writing and representing ideas by inventing their own ways to spell. They do not produce long written sentences or stories because they cannot invent spellings. They have difficulty in segmenting the stream of speech—the words they wish to spell—and relating it to letters. This does not mean that these young children do not have ideas to express and wonderful stories in their heads. Often they are highly creative, and parents and teachers need to guard against the children becoming unwilling to express themselves, because they fear poor spelling.

Some poor spellers will hold on to primitive patterns of spelling, because they do not consciously understand the rules of how print represents speech. There are some poor spellers who may never be able to discriminate between isolated short vowel sounds, and it can be a useless endeavor to expect it. Some cannot hold words in visual memory. Many have not learned the rules that would help with spelling, while some children with learning disabilities can verbalize the rules easily but never apply them as needed.

Without some sense of letter and sound relationships, some spellers try to retain a picture of a word. Some older learning disabled students who have had limited or no remediation make enormous efforts in trying to retain images of words, and the memory load for them becomes overwhelming.

In addition to knowledge about how speech is represented by print and a good working visual memory, writers must also have knowledge of the morphophonemic rules of language by having some sense of how morphology and syntax govern spelling. Throughout the United States spelling is taught in various ways. Many language arts programs are not systematically teaching spelling. Even special teaching approaches for children classified as dyslexic vary in the emphasis placed on spelling.

An additional stressor for children (and equally for their parents during the week of studying) is preparing for the special words, bonus words, or extra-credit words that must be known for Friday's test. Such words can be names of states, words from current events, or tricky words that the teacher knows are hard to spell.

In most schools for both regular and special education, children are expected to spell words on weekly tests, usually given on Fridays. How children learn to spell words for the Friday test varies. Little direct instruction may be provided. In many situations, a pre-test is given and the student then studies only words for which errors are made, usually by writing them several times. There is no emphasis in determining if a student has mastered a rule or if correct spelling occurred more by chance than plan. Then on Friday, the spelling tests are given. If these tests constitute the report card spelling grade, some of the worst spellers can have A grades for spelling. With effort they can retain the words until the test, but the words flee quickly from memory.

Many of the spelling word lists that children share with me are arranged alphabetically. They are expected to know how to spell the words by a certain time, but no instruction is provided in how they might best practice to learn to spell them. Able readers and spellers seem to develop ways to study words that allow them to be successful. Those with problems must be taught how to study the words so that they can be remembered. Grouping them according to common principles is one way to start managing long spelling lists.

Sometimes students are asked to write only single words for a test, while at other times sentences are dictated, or the child is required to use one or several words in good written sentences. We need to help students and their parents understand that they may be adept at holding the words in memory for the test but not for later spontaneous writing. To really master a word for spelling, a student must be able to spell it, not only for the test, but for any later situation in which the word must be written.

Although there is much research about beginning reading, investigation of spelling has begun more recently. There are standardized spelling tests of some kind on most achievement tests, but they do not follow current knowledge regarding what is known about spelling and rule acquisition. Spelling tests are often scored by counting the numbers of errors, but without analysis beyond statements about errors based on whether or not the speller uses phonics to spell words. It may be observed that the speller does or does not write words phonetically. Existing tests do not offer enough samples of spelling principles to determine if a speller is applying rules. Until tests are developed based on current knowledge, teachers and clinicians are left to make do with current spelling programs and tests. Careful observation of correct spelling and spelling errors can inform a teacher or clinician regarding what a student knows about spelling rules.

Spelling cannot be separated from reading and writing. Students tend to use words they can spell, and often their written work does not reflect their levels of vocabulary or their ideas because they fear being marked off for spelling. The encouragement of invented spellings has permitted young children to write more at the level of their ideas rather than at the level of their spelling, at least until their peers begin to use conventional spellings. But young dyslexic children do not have the luxury of being rewarded for long creative stories. Because they have poor phonological awareness of the relationship between print and speech, they are unable to render many good invented spellings. If they are willing to try, they become discouraged easily, because what they attempt bears little relationship to the words they are trying to put forth.

Some older students report using spell checkers on computers effectively. One man said he misspells a word many times and has the same set of words from which to choose the correct spelling; therefore, he gets a lot of practice with the correct spelling by selecting it repeatedly. Others have said that their spelling is so bad that they get no benefit from the spell checkers, just as they cannot look up words in the dictionary.

Some errors do seem to be more a result of failing visual memory. Children who write *gril* for *girl*, *wnet* for *went* are retaining some visual image of the words they try to spell. Sometimes older teenagers or adults with fairly good phonological knowledge but with marked problems in visual memory for retaining the shape of words, try to spell words the way they sound. For instance, they may write *fizishun* for *physician*. Although the word *physician* is seldom spelled correctly by those I see, most of the time it does start with *phy-* or *phi-* showing at least some visual memory traces about the word from their reading. Some teenagers and adults continue to show weaknesses in their phonological sense of words, which results in errors such as "soot" for *smooth*, "shougetion" for *suggestion*, "creant" for *correct*, "cosmter" for *customer*, "attion" for *attention*, "chactiar" for *character*. By middle school age, dyslexic students who have been in some synthetic phonics approaches to reading, often spell quite well phonetically but fail with words that must be retained in visual memory or learned by rules.

Major errors made by older learning disabled students often occur for unstressed syllables of words that can be spelled with any of the vowels. Errors persist with words pronounced the same way but spelled differently, as with *their* and *there* or *two*, *to*, and *too*. Other older spellers show continued problems understanding how print represents speech. They reflect a confusion of word boundaries. This results in the not infrequent "wonsaponatime" (*once upon a time*) to begin a written story or "how depites" for *how deep it is* or "somishfun" for *so much fun* written by a 12-year-old boy with poor decoding and spelling in the presence of a high IQ.

ASSESSMENT OF SPELLING

Questions to ask about a student's spelling when considering a spelling problem follow.

How is Spelling Measured or Graded for Weekly Tests and for Report Card Grades?

How spelling is graded on Friday spelling tests and on report cards varies. Some children are required to write only single words that are dictated. They are words that they have studied all week. Others must write dictated sentences as well as single words. Still other children have their spontaneous spelling included as part of their weekly and report card grades.

How is Spelling Tested for Standardized Diagnostic Tests?

Some standardized spelling tests are ones of recognition—an individual is required to scan a group of words and indicate which one of them is spelled correctly. Other standardized spelling tests require that words are written as each one is dictated; such a test measures recall of the spelling. In evaluations designed to guide teaching, we must present enough words of a certain type to know if the speller has mastered a particular rule—that of doubling a final consonant before adding an ending, for example. Finally, sometimes spelling is assessed by analyzing errors in spontaneous writing from samples that the speller has written over a period of time.

Can the Individual Read the Words He or She Is Required to Spell?

This always seems such a foolish question. Yet many children reading two to three years below grade level may be in a proper reading group in the classroom or as part of a pull-out special reading program, but be expected to spell the same words as the able readers in their class. Often they cannot read the words they are expected to spell.

Is There a Difference Between Oral and Written Spelling?

Sometimes children are helped by spelling orally. At times, this is the way they have been taught, but at other times it is a way they have discovered on their own to help themselves. If oral spelling helps they should be encouraged to use it; they can spell subvocally if they are in a classroom.

Are Errors Ones of Visual Memory?

When individuals have trouble holding visual sequences of letters in mind they may need general practice to improve visual memory. Some errors are easy to recognize as those of problems remembering the visual picture of words. For example, spelling "gril" for *girl*, "luagh" for *laugh* show an attempt to retrieve the visual shape of the word.

Are Phonological Skills of Discrimination, Sequencing, Rhyming, Blending, Segmentation, and Deletion Efficient?

Tasks of sequencing, segmentation, and deletion specifically relate to spelling. A child who mixes the sequence of sounds to say "ax" for *ask* is unlikely to spell it correctly. Another who says and segments the words *basket* as "bas—set" and *equipment* as "e—quit—ment" will spell the word the same way. Teenagers who have never had specific remediation in how print and speech relate, can continue to display marked difficulty in tasks of phonological awareness in contrast to those who have had a lot of phonics instruction.

What Is the Nature or Pattern of Errors?

It is useful to know what kinds of errors the speller makes and if those errors are consistent. Some students will make the same spelling error over and over again, while others may write a word five different ways in a report or story if the word is used 15 times. If the same error is made, there may be faulty learning or the individual may be applying a rule, but the wrong rule. If there is no consistency, it generally means that a rule has not been learned. The word is spelled more by chance than plan.

Some errors are those in which the speller uses fair representations of speech or how the words are pronounced. Such errors as *ballenses* for *balances*, *fizishun* for *physician*, and *olowens* for *allowance* show a speller trying to spell words the way they sound. Some spellers get stuck at this stage.

Errors may be those of recognizing inflectional morphology in the structure of words? Errors such as "walkt" for *walked* or "dresstup" for *dressed up* or "wonet" for *wanted* suggest a possible problem in appreciating the reason for using inflectional endings.

Errors may result from failure to know common rules about the regularities of English spelling—rules such as "i before e except after c, or if sounded as ay in neighbor and weigh." We must help children with learning disabilities strive for consistency.

Some spelling errors are attributable to handwriting rather than spelling? Errors such as "munber" or *number*, "clear" for *dear*, or "darade" for *garage* suggest a problem with remembering how to form letters rather than a specific problem with spelling.

Consistency of errors under different conditions should be considered. It may be easiest to spell the words if they are dictated one at a time. It may be more difficult when sentences using the word are dictated, because the speller must hold in memory the sentence to be written as well as the patterns of spelling for all the words. It is even more difficult when spellers must generate a written sentence using a spelling word; they must formulate a sentence, remember the sentence while they write it, recall how to spell the word, and render it in a form that can be interpreted by the reader

TEACHING SPELLING

- Remediation with spelling needs to include work with words that:
    —are spelled the way they sound (that have a close phoneme-grapheme correspondence);
    —follow rules of English spelling (such as "i before e except after c...,");
    —need to be retained by sight (does, said, enough);
    —require knowledge of inflectional morphology (such as -ed for past tense, -er for a comparative form or a person who performs a task, -est as the superlative form of an adjective); and
    —demand awareness of derivational forms (Such errors are seen most in spontaneous written work).
- Words to be spelled should be in the spoken language of the speller.

- Words to be spelled should be in the reading vocabulary of the speller.
- Words should be grouped according to common principles.
- Syllable types can be taught (see Chapter 4).
- Provide practice to develop improved phonological skills (spelling words the way they sound). Polysyllabic words could be used. Present the words divided into syllables visually. Say the word divided into syllables to the student. Have the student say the word in syllables. Then present the whole word visually. Say the whole word. Have the student say the whole word. Say the word in syllables and have the student write it. Cover the word as written in syllables. Then say the whole word and have the student write it. This approach improves decoding for longer words as well as improving spelling.
- Spelling demons, words that are frequently misspelled, need to be practiced using a fading approach in which the word is spelled aloud as it is written with copy present. The word should then be covered and written while being spelled aloud.
- Provide practice spelling and writing homonyms (*there-their*) and frequently confused words such as *where, were, we're* since they are frequently used incorrectly in spontaneous writing.
- Practice structural analysis of words with attention paid to regular and irregular verbs and changes in endings.
- Teach meanings of prefixes, roots, and suffixes. Common ones are derived from Latin and Greek. Specific teaching to make learning explicit is necessary. Such knowledge increases word meaning, improves reading, and aids spelling.
- If students are not sure of a spelling of a word they should write the word as they think it is spelled and underline it. They can then go back and try to recall the correct spelling or look up the word. In this way, the flow of thinking is not interfered with by the burden of trying to think of the correct spelling during the process of formulation. Teachers may permit such marking of words on tests, as well. Wilson Anderson refers to this as the underlining option. [21]

Very poor spellers may never become good spellers. However a goal for them is that they learn enough about how words are constructed that they can effectively use a computer spell check or have enough of a sense about their spelling that they monitor their writing for possible errors and then either look up a word in the dictionary or have a good speller proofread their work.

WRITTEN FORMULATION

"...writing is but a line that moves haltingly across the page, exposing as it goes all that the writer doesn't know, then passing into the hands of a stranger who reads it with a lawyer's eyes, searching for flaws." [22]

Young learning disabled students may have difficulty with either hand-writing or spelling or both, so they begin to think it is hard to write. They may resist writing, particularly for homework. Even after they can move the pencil easily and spell acceptably, they may tend to refuse to write. This then becomes a behavioral problem as well as one with writing. Attentional issues and oppositional disorders are often seen in students with writing problems. Writing has been hard, and may continue to be, and that begins the patterns of resistance and refusal.

When we read about writing, terms such as product and process are often used. The *product* is what is written—a list of words, a sentence, a paragraph, an essay, or a report that can be re-read by the writer or read by a reader. The *process* is what goes into writing, the act of putting ideas on paper or computer screen. Writing is part of a linguistic process. As such, all that students have learned about spoken language and reading will be called upon. In addition, they will need to learn principles unique to writing. There is a formality to expressing ideas in writing as opposed to the informality often possible with speech. It is common for parents to report that their son or daughter can "tell you anything. He (or she) just can't get it on paper." Yet if we assess formal linguistic expression, such as telling a story, sharing an important idea, or telling a sequence of events, there may be similar problems in oral expression.

Although written expression shares commonalities with speech, it is different. Jack Rosenthal in the *New York Times Magazine* wrote that "to base thought only on speech is to try nailing whispers to the wall. Writing whether clear or clouded, freezes thought and offers it up for inspection."[23] It is this record offered for inspection that troubles many learning disabled students.

In addition to the formality of written, as opposed to oral expression, there is also a need for the writer to develop a *sense of audience*. The writer must understand writing for an absent reader rather than relying on partial sentences and nonverbal cues possible with a speaker and listener. However, it is of value and help to some learning disabled students, as for all writers, that with writing, there is the opportunity to both plan and revise.

Writing has recently received more attention for children in the general curriculum and also for children with special needs. As the last of the linguistic skills acquired, writing is the hardest to learn. Writing is used in school but often does not receive the practice that reading does. We are surrounded by print all the time and unless we are oblivious, we see printed material and can practice reading (at least if we are good readers). We do not get the same kind of practice with writing. Writing letters to share ideas has been replaced by using a telephone. But with the widespread use of computers, with many business and professional people formulating their own reports and business letters, and with the reliance of FAX messages to replace the telephone, perhaps written formulation of ideas will again be used.

Formulation of ideas for written expression may be different for a child or adolescent who has trouble with the motor act of handwriting or who is a terrible speller. We need to begin at a young age with learning disabled students to help separate the expression of ideas from poor handwriting and atrocious spelling. They must learn to value their ideas as they learn the tools to share the ideas.

The book, *Reach for the Moon* presents a dramatic example of a young teenager whose mother and English teacher discovered the girl's wonderful creative expressive abilities that had been hidden beneath poor spelling, handwriting, and punctuation and a learning disability in arithmetic. The poetry and prose are written by Samantha Abeel, age 13, to accompany watercolors by the artist Charles Murphy.[24] It is a book that should be shared with learning disabled students and their parents and teachers, because it shows the wonderful creative mind and writing in the presence of poor spelling and mechanics in writing.

Many learning disabled students have wonderful stories in their heads that never find expression because of poor spelling and handwriting. I have been impressed with some of the poetry students with learning disabilities have written when they have both encouragement and some instruction. It may be that they are more positive toward poetry than prose because many forms of poetry are expected to be, or are valued, when they are short. For those with writing problems, short is always best.

Once young children learn some spoken words and a bit about sentence structure, what they say begins with an idea they wish to express. In the same way, once children can write and spell, they may express ideas. All too often, good ideas are stifled by the dread of handwriting and spelling. With or without good handwriting and adequate spelling, learning disabled children need help with learning to express their ideas comfortably.

In the formulation of ideas for writing, we can consider the sentence and then extended discourse. Before children can write, they must have a sense of what a sentence is. This is a hard concept to teach. The most common definition that many of us learned is that "a sentence expresses a complete thought." Very few complete thoughts can be expressed in a sentence. If we speak of a sentence as a unit with a noun and a verb, students are often unclear about what a verb is and what a noun is. Being able to find the verb in a sentence and to understand its function and then how words relate to the verb may be one way to talk about sentences. Importantly, it is now widely agreed that learning grammar and parts of speech does not have any relationship to whether or not a person can write well. Laboring to learn parts of speech does not make us writers.

A problem facing a tutor or teacher beginning a writing program for students with learning disabilities is to help them understand that a first draft is only that, that anything that is written can be made better or different. We know from those who make their livelihoods writing that their pieces go through many drafts until they decide that it is finished. If writers waited until they were satisfied with what they had written, we would have little in print. One well-regarded writer said, in an interview, that he made changes in the margins of his own published books. This sense of making it better or making it different is an important one in teaching writing. Having writers purposefully write poorly can sometimes free them to see the difference of what it means to change what has been written to make it better.

Evaluating Written Formulation

Any time we read what another has written, we make some judgment about the writing, and teachers must make judgments about students' writing all the time. There are some tests of written expressive language. The first test of written expressive language was the *Picture Story Language Test (PSLT)* developed by Helmer Myklebust.[25] A later test, *The Test of Written Language-2 (TOWL2)*, by Donald Hammill and Stephen Larsen[26] is the one most widely used today. Both of these tests require that the individual write a story for a picture stimulus. These tests simulate creative writing rather than the kind of writing most often expected in school—expository writing or writing a report. In actuality, children often do not really write a story but provide a description of the picture.

A valuable test for assessing written formulation is the *Writing Samples* from the *Woodcock-Johnson Psychoeducational Battery-Revised(Tests of Achievement)*.[27] The beginning writer is asked to complete sentences with a word or phrase and older ones to write sentences. The writer is asked to write sentences that tell about pictures, complete partial sentences, use specified words to form a sentence, or to compose a sentence that would fit between two given sentences. Most children taking this test write 15 sentences. Since they write them one at a time they generally do not object. If they were told before they began writing that they would have to write that many sentences, few would even begin the task. *Writing Fluency*, also from the *Woodcock-Johnson*, is a timed test in which the writer sees pictures and three words and must write sentences using the specified words for each item. This latter task sometimes shows a nice discrepancy for an older writer taking time to compose sentences (on the *Writing Samples*) versus writing as quickly as possible. It can provide evidence for some students needing extended time for writing in class.

Many of the writing tests devised by states and individual school districts require subjective judgments. The writing is often judged holistically, and at times it is hard to understand why some writers pass and others fail these writing tests. When the goal is to share information, it is important that these tests and their rating scales are described so that parents and others understand what is being communicated about the students' writing.

Writing is being studied in many places by professionals with various interests and competencies. The most basic question is always one of whether an individual can write well enough to meet requirements of what he or she needs day-to-day. New measures of written expression are likely to emerge. But to teach or to help with homework, there are some questions we could ask that help with judging writing. One set of questions follows.

Are There Problems with Oral Language?

If there were earlier problems with spoken language, the written formulation weakness may result from a basic linguistic deficiency. A continuing problem with oral language can affect written formulation of ideas. If deficits in receptive language persist, there may be global weaknesses in all verbal learning including vocabulary development, reading comprehension, and written expression. I have observed children I have known in preschool years with significant problems in oral syntax who, in adolescence, show problems with written syntax. Many of them do not show obvious language problems that would easily be heard in casual conversation. Unless there is extreme shyness or some emotional difficulties, we generally speak better than we write. Children I see who have had intensive work with oral formulation often show good improvement in writing sentences and sometimes longer pieces, even if they have not had direct work on written formulation. Such improvement, of course, depends on how well the child is able to apply what is learned about oral formulation to their writing.

Here is an example of a story written by an 11-year-old boy who had early problems with oral syntax. Although oral grammar is adequate now, the earlier problem is affecting his written formulation.

> "The Boy And The Toys"
> One day this boy home Matt wanted to play
> with his toys. But had take a nap so he went
> bed "but" not for long he got of bed and said I
> will get my toys and play with them. But his
> dad heard that and got suff got ready and Matt
> the door and there was a bear and the bear
> went g-g-g-g-g-g-g ɜ ɜ ɜ ɔo Matt anther door
> there was a ghost and he went boobooboo
> ran to the window as was a which and
> she went heeheeHehee go bed Matt
> and Matt did and he heard heeheehee it was
> his dady he said. I did it and Matt started
> laugh too

Are There Problems with the Motor Act of Writing?

If the writer has problems using a pencil, if the pencil grip is so tight and tense it causes fatigue, or he or she does not know the keyboard well enough to find the keys, it is hard to uncover the writer that may be inside that child.

Is There a Reading Problem?

Problems with reading may affect vocabulary, spelling, and, indirectly, written formulation. If students' reading vocabularies are limited, obviously they will not have a variety of words to use in their writing. If they fail to pay attention to endings on words when they read, they may fail to mark endings in what they write. Omissions of -ed for past tense or -s to mark plurals are common. If students do not have wide experiences with texts containing many different kinds of writing, it can be difficult for them to see any value in writing or to understand various kinds of writing.

Are There Problems with Spelling?

Some students with spelling problems write using only words they are sure they can spell. If they worry about spelling, they will use short words. Students who worry about correct spelling and use simple words often have much better oral expressive skills than written ones.

Are There Problems with Capitalization and Punctuation?

This is a major area of difficulty for many children and adolescents with learning disabilities. They seem to lack an appreciation of the need to use these conventions. I sometimes question if they are aware of these cues in texts they read because they seem content to write with no punctuation at all except a seemingly random insertion of a period. It is as though they see no purpose in using capitalization and punctuation. We need to know if they recognize when to use capitalization and punctuation correctly. We ask: Can they recognize correct use of capitalization and punctuation? Can they then use correct capitalization and punctuation in their writing?

Are There Differences Between Oral and Written Expressive Language for the Same Types of Task?

When this question is asked, it must be with an awareness that speaking and writing are different. Speaking can be casual, as in conversation with intimates, or formal as public speaking. In conversation, use of single words and phrases is acceptable and, indeed, if speakers are too formal they are judged as having inappropriate use of speech in a social context. Support is provided to listeners by the speaker's melody of speech with its pauses and inflections and by gestures and facial expressions. Even in a formal speaking situation, important parts of messages are conveyed through inflections and gestures. In both casual and formal speech, redundancy can be appropriate. If we do not understand what is being said immediately, we can give the speaker a cue, and it is likely that he or she will say it in a different way. In contrast, writing is more formal and follows conventions not required for speaking. I think we need to assess informal spoken language situations, responses to structured questions, but also look at more formal speech. Formal speech can occur when informing another about an action or event, telling a story, telling a joke, or explaining how to do something with no visual support present. Often when learning disabled students are presented with formal oral language situations, they show formulation problems, indicating that the problem is not just "with getting it on paper." Newcomer and Barenbaum in a 1991 review of composing abilities of children caution, "The oft-repeated hypothesis that subjects with learning disabilities know more than they show when they write because of the restrictions imposed by their deficiencies in the mechanical aspects of writing is neither supported nor refuted in the studies that compared dictated or retold stories with written stories."[28] This is an area that awaits further clarification.

What Written Expressive Language Tasks Cause Difficulty?

We need to know where the writer believes he or she has difficulty as well as where an identified problem may be, as seen by the teacher and/or the parent. A writer may need help for one or all of the following situations: writing answers on tests, taking class notes, summarizing what has been heard or read, completing homework, writing a report, or creating a story.

Can the Individual Write a Sentence?

It is useful to know if students have a sense of what a sentence is. Even when a writing problem seems to be with long written pieces, there is value to analysis at the sentence level. We could also ask if they use a variation in types of sentences. Some young children write only sentences of the type "The (noun) is (verbing)" as *The dog is barking*, *The girl is running*, or *The boy is laughing*. Such sentences suggest they do not know how to vary written sentences.

Are Errors Made in Word Usage?

Such errors can include problems marking plurals, possessives, and comparative forms of adjectives, for example. But errors in usage can also include confusion about word meaning. For example, those who wrote "There is a lot of humid (for *humidity*) in the air" or "You shouldn't put more on your

plate than you can assume (for *consume*)" or "I can't even make a rash decision" are showing problems with word usage. In contrast, writing that there
was an "axinent on the stressway" may be a stronger way of telling about an
accident on the expressway but suggests problems with phonological processing and spelling rather than a lack of understanding of word meanings.

What is the Holistic Impression?

We are asking if overall the piece holds together? We can also ask if the
writing makes sense. Sometimes students write at length, but what is written
makes little sense. At times, this results from their having forgotten what
they set out to write. At other times, ideas are confusing or sentences are
mixed up.

Does the Writer Impose a Sense of Organization?

To write, there must be some sense of organization. Some people with learning disabilities seem to start to write and then arbitrarily decide to stop. They
impose no sense of order or organization. Often it is because they have not
had enough practice or because they really do not understand that what is
written must have some order. There are many different ways of organizing
similar information, but there must be some plan.

Are Referents Clear?

Often, even at a single-sentence level the reader has no idea to whom or
what the *he*, *she*, or *it* refers. However, with longer pieces, it is as though
some students forget about what or whom they are writing.

Are Vocabulary Words Used Appropriately for Age and Grade?

Teachers within classrooms, whether first grade or graduate school, have a
sense of what vocabulary the average student uses. Sometimes oral vocabulary is limited and that is reflected in the writing. At other times, short words
are used because of fear of spelling failure. Worry about spelling is more
likely seen in older students and those who have never been exposed to the
idea of invented spellings.

Are Transitions Used Among Sentences in a Paragraph and Among Paragraphs in a Longer Piece?

We consider whether or not the piece shows a flow of ideas. Are transition
words used to show passage of time (*first, next, then*, and *finally*), or to show
that opposing ideas are being presented (*in contrast, contrariwise*), or that
the piece is ending (*in summary*).

Does the Piece Reflect a Student's Understanding of the Task Expectation for either a Story or an Expository Assignment?

Sometimes a student writes in a way that shows no understanding of what the assignment has been. Other students write in a quirky way or choose to write from a different angle than has been assigned. At times they say the assigned topic was boring so they wrote about something else or in another way. But I often question if they really fully understood the assignment.

Can the Writer Find Errors through Proofreading What Has Been Written?

Which one of us has not carefully read and re-read a letter or paper and felt it to be perfect only to find a glaring error the next day. Such a situation is magnified many times over for a student who has a problem with written expression.

TEACHING WRITTEN FORMULATION

- Even young children should use writing for practical purposes—taking telephone messages, writing shopping lists, writing notes or letters, writing notes to oneself to remember things to do or things to buy, and crossing items off the list as they are bought or completed
- Writing lists can be helpful. Diana King[29] provides suggestions for possible lists including: things in your room, fast-food restaurants, things that run on batteries, and excuses for not doing assignment.

Writing Sentences

- Help students develop better writing by having them write many, many sentences. They can learn the variety of messages that can be expressed by a sentence and the power of a basic building block of writing. That they are only expected to write a sentence is manageable for them, and they can approach the writing task with some sense of the possibility of completing the task well. Give examples, and encourage children to first tell as many sentences as they can aloud. An adult can write the sentences as they dictate. They are often impressed by how much they have dictated. After orally producing sentences, they can later write them
- How many sentences can be written about a single action picture?
    —The boy is sitting.
    —The little boy is sitting.
    —The little boy in the striped shirt is sitting.
    —The little boy wearing a striped shirt is sitting on the step.
    —The little boy wearing a striped shirt who is sitting on the step is eating.

—The little boy wearing a striped shirt who is sitting on the step is eating a sandwich.

—The little boy wearing a striped shirt who is sitting on the step is eating a ham and cheese sandwich.

—The little boy named Sam wearing a striped shirt who is sitting on the step is eating a ham and cheese sandwich for his lunch.

- Sentences can be expanded using modifiers of single words and phrases. Using *The clown*, children could write

—The old clown

—The fat clown

—The cheerful clown

—The fat cheerful clown with a dog

—The fat cheerful clown with a big dog

—The fat cheerful clown with a big dog and an umbrella

—The fat cheerful clown with a big dog and an open umbrella

—The fat cheerful clown with the big dog and an open polka-dotted umbrella

- The verb can be varied.

—The clown walks.

—The clown strolls.

—The clown saunters.

—The clown stumbles.

—The clown trips.

- The verb can be modified

—The clown walks.

—The clown walks *slowly*.

—The clown walks *carefully*.

—The clown walks *carelessly*.

—The clown walks *lightly*.

—The clown walks *heavily*.

—The clown walks _____ at the circus.

—The clown walks _____ around the ring.

—The clown walks _____ in the street.

—The clown walks _____ across the park.

—The clown walks _____ on the playground.

—The clown walks _____ in the hallway.

—The clown walks _____ to school.

—The fat cheerful clown with the big dog and an open polka-dotted umbrella strolls slowly across the park to school.

- Have children write different kinds of sentences to make statements, to ask questions, and to show excitement. Appropriate labeling of sentence types—declarative, interrogative, exclamatory—should be taught at appropriate times with their meanings made clear. An "excitement mark" for an exclamation mark is fine to make the point clear but children should learn the correct name. Children often enjoy learning this as a new word and a long one, at that.

* Move parts of sentences to show how they are flexible. *The boy made a plane*, and *The plane was made by the boy* mean the same thing, just as do *The boy carrying the heavy load fell off his bike by the creek*, and *The boy who fell of his bike by the creek was carrying a heavy load.*
* Partial sentences can be given for completion such as:
  —I saw_____
  —I heard_____
  —I felt_____
  —I tasted_____
  —He failed because_____
  —He had to sit on the stage while_____
  —The girl who_____was sorry.
* Provide practice in unscrambling sentences. Put words (or phrases) on cards that can be manipulated before expecting the child to unscramble them in his head. For example,
  —tall Bob is
  —the The not ride cat airplane like did
  —test driving disappointed she Susan was not that could her take
* Provide practice with combining several sentences into one compound or complex sentence. For example,
  —She got a present.
  —She was happy.
  —She was happy that she got a present.
  —The boy is scared.
  —He rode his bike.
  —He fell off his bike.
  —He got hurt.
  —His parents told him not to ride his bike today.
  —The boy was scared when he fell of his bike and got hurt, because his parents told him not to ride today.
* Provide practice that emphasizes subject-verb agreement. For example, the following can be the subject of a sentence. Which ones tells about one subject? Which ones tells about more than one?
  —a girl
  —girls
  —the boy and girl
  —they
  —students

—student
—suitcase
—suitcases

Now read the following out loud (or repeat when you hear them) two times each.

—A girl runs.
—Girls run.
—The boy and the girl run.
—They run.
—An athletic student enjoys physical education.
—Athletic students enjoy physical education.
—A student with many activities likes school.
—Students with many activities like school.
—The suitcase full of many clothes was lost.
—The suitcases full of many clothes were lost.

Now choose the correct verb form:

—A girl (run runs)
—Girls (run runs)
—The boy and girl (run runs)
—They (run runs)
—He (run runs)
—She (run runs)
—The students (like likes) history.
—The student (like likes) history.
—They (like likes) history.
—He and she (like likes) history.
—He (like likes) history.
—She (like likes) history.

Write sentences using the following for subjects.

—The girl
—Girls
—Boys
—The boy
—The students
—A student

Write sentences combining the above listed subjects with the following verbs:

—see, jump, walk, chase, find, collect, notice, receive, cook, sew, scare, disappoint.

The goal of such an exercise is to make a rule explicit and then to practice it until it approaches automatic use, at least in a formal structured situation.

- Beginning at the sentence level, help students write sentences (and later paragraphs) to describe, inform, explain, complain, request, demand, amuse, annoy, frighten, soothe, convince, etc.

Writing Paragraphs

Once a variety of sentences can be written, work can begin with writing paragraphs.
- Give specific instructions about what a paragraph is and how it is developed.
- Using partial paragraphs can sometimes help students begin writing. For instance, they could be asked to write about a movie, book, or TV program. For example,
   —Last night I _____. It
   was_____. The main characters
   were_____. The story took place
   in _____. It was mostly
   about_____. I thought it
   was_____because_____. Others
   might_____.
- Provide practice with formulating a concluding sentence for a group of sentences.
- Provide practice with formulating a topic sentence for a group of several sentences.
- Provide practice inserting a missing middle sentence in a three-sentence paragraph.
- Have a student write sentences (and paragraphs) first by looking at pictures and then for structured ideas presented by the teacher.
- Some of this work in providing topic sentences and concluding sentences can be done orally. The goal is to establish the skill through appropriate reasoning and formulation.
- Have a student write a topic sentence, two or three supporting sentences, and a concluding statement.
- Some students may be helped more if they can start free writing of their ideas rather than using the structured approach just discussed.
- Once good paragraphs can be written, show students how a paragraph can be expanded into an essay by writing a topic paragraph, two or three supporting paragraphs, and a concluding one. They need to know that there is no specified number of paragraphs needed for a report or essay.
- Teach students what colloquial language is. It should not be used in formal text and papers; it may be used in a written piece to show every-day language or dialogue.

- Help students think of the audience who will read what is written—a peer, an adult, a young child; someone familiar, a stranger. What does the audience/reader know about the subject?
- Provide instruction about the difference between creative writing (a story or essay) and expository writing (a report). Practice each.
  —Teach the required format for writing reports in various subjects.
  —For creative writing, students need to experience the freedom of writing to the limits of their imaginations. Obviously, some will be more creative than others but all children should experience this kind of free expression.
- Students should keep a list to be checked off for every writing assignment to include such items as
  —Are complete sentences used?
  —Are capital letters present and used correctly?
  —Is punctuation present and used correctly?
  —Is the beginning of the paragraph indented?
  —After indenting the beginning of the paragraph do the rest of the lines begin at the margin?
  —Has the passage been read aloud for errors?
  —Are subjects and verbs in agreement?
  —Are pronoun referents clear?
  —Is there a topic sentence?
  —Are supporting sentences used?
  —Is there a concluding sentence?
  —If what is written is longer than a paragraph, are correct transitions made and transition words used between paragraphs and ideas?
  —Does what is written make sense?
  This list should be added to as needed for different situations and as advanced writing is expected.
- Before expecting a student to find errors in his or her own writing, have the student proofread for errors (of word usage, misspelling, run-on sentences) in typed copy prepared by the teacher.
  —Require a separate reading-through of the work for each type of error, at least for a while.
  —Have a student detect errors in single sentences before requiring proofreading of longer units.
  —The student should be encouraged to read aloud pointing to each word as it is read to pick up word omissions.
- Students must learn to detect errors in their own work. Each piece written must be proofread. It is not a sometime thing.
- Be explicit when teaching principles of writing. Receiving comments about what is wrong such as "run-on sentences," "choppy sentences,"

etc. is not helpful to students who are having difficulty with writing. Good students can take such comments and incorporate them into their next writing; students with learning disabilities find it difficult to know what is adequate and what is not. Before a student can write well he or she must be conscious of what good writing is.

- Some students have difficulty organizing what they want to write. Help them learn different kinds of organizational schemes. Help them understand that outlines and other forms of organization are aids to good writing, not punishment.

- A student should try the following kind of organizational scheme instead of a linear outline. It may help.

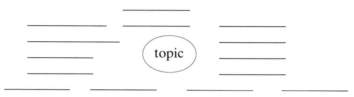

A topic is written in the center of a page. Words or phrases that tell about the topic are written around it. All words or phrases that belong together are circled with one color, other related ideas with another color. Each color will then form a basis for a paragraph or a section of the paper. This approach differs from some kinds of webbing, because the ideas come from the writer rather than from another person.

- When a student uses a linear outline, several lines should be left between topic headings so that ideas can be added as they occur. Forcing oneself to think of all ideas that belong under A before starting with B can be counter-productive.

- Permit students to dictate essays, reports, stories, etc. to another student or parent and then have it read back to them sentence by sentence so they are transcribing their own words. After students see the value of such an approach, they can then dictate into a tape recorder and transcribe their own words.

- Journals are used widely in schools. They are used differently in different areas, however. At times, students are to write in them every day on any subject they wish. At times the teacher assigns a topic. Sometimes teachers read them and sometimes they do not. It needs to be made clear to the students whether their journals are private or will be shared with others.

Samples of writing from children experiencing difficulty.

go
rgt
in
wilh m
sq
cut

The Sin is Hot
and the Bollb is Hot

The People
People Wher working oneday
and They saw dinosoz the Tires
to kill 'om but They coldent
the dinasors killd thm and They
rold the wold.

Use of Computers for Written Formulation

The use of computers/word processors can help learning disabled students be more successful with writing. Some parents who are unfamiliar with computers may have unreasonable expectations about how much computers will help their son or daughter with writing. Computer instruction should be presented carefully. Each new task should be mastered before moving on. Avoid making demands beyond what can be handled comfortably. If children resist using computers, because they cannot use them effectively, they may be without a useful tool for a long time.

Presented well, students can appreciate how word processors assist in formulating ideas. Relieved from the tedium of recopying, they move words and phrases and can improve formulation of ideas. However, students cannot be expected to use the computer for written assignments until they have some skill with the keyboard. Until they have some sense of mastery over the keys, the computer is not really a tool.

- As mentioned before, spelling problems can be so severe that spell checkers are not much help, but the use of spell checkers should be taught and their use encouraged if effective for individual students. Students must understand that not all errors will be identified. They are not finished with proofreading work just because it has been submitted to a spell check.
- Teach use of grammar checkers if they seem to help. They may confuse students, and they need to learn limitations of the grammar check programs.

SUMMARY

Students with learning disabilities in written expression can be helped to write better. They need to see value in writing, use it for practical purposes, and be willing to practice. In order to practice, they must have a mechanical instrument of expression, whether pencil, pen, or keyboard. They need to have enough of a sense of spelling that they are willing to use words that are in their vocabularies. And they need to formulate ideas with a sense of purpose and a knowledge that what they write will be appreciated for the amount of effort invested.

CHAPTER 6

OTHER THAN WORDS
Learning and Related Social, Emotional, and Nonverbal Functioning

Words are important to our lives and to our learning. However, important elements of getting along with others, solving problems, and appreciating the world around us occur without words. Robert Ornstein indicated the significance of nonverbal function when he wrote, "Consider describing a spiral staircase. Most would begin using words and quickly begin to gesture in the air. Or consider attempting to ride a bicycle purely from verbal instruction." [1]

Interpretation of, and reactions to, nonverbal information affects social interaction or the ability to get along with others. How others view us influences what they think of us, which in turn contributes to our self-image. Both verbal and nonverbal cues are essential for learning and for getting along with others, and they facilitate learning about ourselves.

Multiple nonverbal cues that help us decide our actions are processed constantly. We notice if a child feels unwell and should stay home from school. We determine whether it is a good time to make a request or a complaint depending on the nonverbal mannerisms of another. By looking at the sky, we decide if we will need to carry an umbrella. The amount of cereal at home or computer paper at work causes us to make a list or inform the person in charge what is needed before a shortage occurs. We make judgments about how fast we have to walk or drive before a traffic light changes. Most of us process nonverbal cues constantly, many of them simultaneously, nearly automatically with little conscious awareness. Most children react this way as well; however, some do not. These children have problems with those parts of messages and the environment that do not involve words.

Children and adolescents with trouble in nonverbal areas may have emotional difficulties. They may experience problems relating to a peer or to a group, and they may have a specific disability with nonverbal learning. Often these areas become intertwined in complex ways and are difficult to tease apart. Because of the overlap among the areas of emotional functioning, social interaction, and nonverbal learning, these somewhat disparate areas are included in this chapter.

Children do not show us their learning. They show the products of learning through their words, a block construction, a drawing, or a written report. They often do not tell us about their feelings, but inform us directly or indirectly by actions and words. When they behave in ways that are outside what is expected for their age, education, and social group some explanation for the behavior difference is sought.

Social, emotional, and cognitive development interact with verbal and nonverbal learning. Children with speech and language disorders have an increased risk of psychiatric problems, and children with psychiatric disorders are at higher risk for speech and language disorders. Those with speech and language problems in the preschool years are at risk for learning failure in first grade. There is some evidence that those with nonverbal learning disabilities are at greater risk for social–emotional difficulties than those with verbal learning disabilities, although children with verbal learning disabilities may also have difficulties in social–emotional areas.[2,3,4]

As we learn increasing amounts about human behavior as related to brain function, we discover that there are relationships between our thinking and our feeling that would not have been expected in times past. Conditions previously regarded as emotional are now seen as caused by biological factors. The expression "It's all in your head" is not as insulting as has been generally suggested. Our heads, after all, refer to the function of our brains. It is not always possible or even desirable to separate physiologic functions from emotional states. In everyday life, when we experience common anxiety or extreme fear, we are aware of physical reactions including rapid heart rate or breathing problems. There are changes in brain chemistry as well when these events occur. Attention deficit disorders, depression, and schizophrenia are conditions related to and affected by brain anatomy and physiology—the structure, function, and chemistry of the brain. Altering the function of neurotransmitters with medication allows some individuals with emotional difficulties to function better. (However, these individuals may make even greater gains by understanding and changing behaviors and self-concept issues through psychotherapy in combination with effective medication.)

We must resist the tendency to make a quick diagnosis of behavior and/or emotional disorders without consideration of a learning disability. Some behavioral and emotional problems may result from basic deficits in learning. For instance, lack of perception of social cues can result in rudeness on the part of children, and the resulting rejection from those around them cause them to feel bad about themselves. Social–emotional–behavioral troubles in children and adolescents with learning disabilities may be subtle or may be masked in ways that are difficult to understand. The more problems that exist in learning and emotional areas, even if each one by itself is mild, the greater the complications faced by children or adolescents with these problems. Untangling these complexities challenges those who seek to teach or otherwise help them.

The severity of a symptom does not necessarily represent the extent of any problem. A mild problem with decoding words does not necessarily have a mild impact on the life of a college student. A speech problem regarded as mild may not be mild to the individual who has it. Significant disorders in nonverbal learning—nonverbal problem solving or visual spatial perceptions—may be overlooked in the early grades because of adequate functioning in reading and spelling. In the same way, it may be difficult for parents and teachers to tell from surface behaviors, the nature of a child or adolescent's emotional difficulty. Often, observed behavior covers emotional anguish. Sometimes difficulties will only show when there is an increase in the complexity and the amount of material that needs to be mastered, or when an individual is feeling personal stress for any one of myriad reasons. Children and adolescents may appear to be functioning adequately while suffering without complaint. Class clowns may use buffoonery to cover feelings of inadequacy in learning. A display of bravado can mask worries about academic functioning. I have seldom seen a child with an "I don't care" attitude about school who, in fact, did not care about school performance. We must ask questions in a way that allows children and teenagers to express their worries and concerns as related to school. Some who feel particularly threatened do not believe an adult could be interested in their ideas and concerns. They regard any attempt to question as criticism.

COMMON BEHAVIORS THAT SUGGEST NEED FOR REFERRAL.

There are common behaviors of children and adolescents that, when they persist, suggest additional questions may need to be asked of parents and, possibly, some further referral considered. These behaviors include:

- a generalized lack of energy;

- an air of dejection;
- little or no sense of pleasure in accomplishments;
- no response to praise;
- refusal to try;
- fear to risk being wrong;
- repeatedly saying "I don't know;"
- constant comments such as "How did I do?" or "Did I get any right?";
- sense of isolation; and
- problems making and keeping friends

Children are generally curious, with a sense of energy and enthusiasm. If they show an ongoing sense of dejection, with lack of energy toward school and school work in spite of adequate sleep and with no drug use or major crisis, there is reason for concern. Often when teenagers are asked if they complete their homework, they say, "No," and when asked why say, "I just don't feel like it." Often they mean just that. It is not that they do not care about school or are being purposefully oppositional, rather, they have no energy to pick up a book and a pencil to begin. Some will tell of lying in their rooms doing nothing. Music or the television may be playing, but they say they do not really listen to it; it is just there. These same youngsters may take no pleasure in their accomplishments and show no response to praise when they have performed well.

Another concern is when children refuse to try because they fear being wrong. They are difficult to test and to teach. It takes a long time to know what they know, because they will not offer responses that can be evaluated. They may hesitate to write the first sentence on a page or the first line on a computer screen until they regard it as being perfect. With such an attitude they can wait for minutes, weeks, and months with no production, as they await perfection.

When children say "I don't know" before a task is presented or before instructions and "How did I do?" or "Did I get any right?" as soon as they provide a response, they are showing a sense of anxiety and a fear of failure. They have begun to develop a sense of "Why try when I am sure to be wrong." Such an attitude that continues into middle school can be seen in a refusal to perform any writing task; in-class assignments and homework are most often incomplete. Failing a test or a class does not seem to provide motivation to complete assigned work.

Other concerns are children or adolescents who are isolated or keep to themselves. If they prefer solitary occupations such as computer games or listening to music alone, they may not be regarded as having problems. They are not getting into trouble. But some with these isolating behaviors may be depressed, while others may not know how to initiate or maintain social contact with peers. An 11-year-old boy said, "I don't know what the problem is.

The kids can't seem to like me. That happened in my other school, too." Such children and teens may not know how to initiate and reciprocate with "kid talk" and "kid actions."

These observed behaviors may lead an educator to request further evaluation by a mental-health consultant. We should not "wait and see." When children experience continuing school failure or are feeling bad, waiting can sometimes cause them to lose a whole school year. Intervention becomes increasingly important in high school because a learning-disabled student with or without emotional difficulties, who is not receiving appropriate assistance may fail the year, further reinforcing a poor self-image.

EMOTIONAL DIFFICULTIES

Even with increasing research and greater sophistication about learning and attention, there is far from universal agreement about learning and emotional conditions in children and adolescents and how they should be classified and managed. Clinicians and teachers, on one hand, and researchers, on the other, often seem to be talking about different entities as they discuss the same child.

Attention Deficit and Disruptive Behavior Disorders

Some children and adolescents with learning disabilities also have psychiatric problems. Some disorders that may accompany learning disabilities are *Attention-Deficit and Disruptive Behavior Disorders*. These include *Attention-Deficit Hyperactivity Disorder* (ADHD), *Oppositional Defiant Disorder*, and *Conduct Disorder*.

The main psychiatric disorders diagnosed in those with learning disabilities are attentional problems. Reports of how much overlap there is between learning disabilities and attentional difficulties vary. From a large study of school children in a northeastern state, 11 percent of children with attention disorders were classified as having learning disabilities in either reading or arithmetic, and 33 percent of children with learning disabilities met criteria for having attention deficit disorder.[5] Another estimate is that of children and adolescents with learning disabilities, between 20 and 25 percent will also have ADHD, and of children and adolescents with ADHD, 50 to 80 percent will also have learning disabilities.[6] Learning disabilities and attention deficit hyperactivity disorders are two separate conditions even though they may occur in the same individual; each need different kinds of intervention.

Anyone who has seen, lived with, or tried to teach a child with ADHD remembers the experience. Here is how I described the behavior of a 9-year-old boy I saw for evaluation of his language and learning.

Sam was cooperative with a friendly and engaging manner. He wanted to please. He was comfortable verbally and spontaneous in asking questions and making comments about the testing. He was in almost constant motion, sitting on his heels, curling his arms around his knees, flinging his arm over the back of the chair. He was not still for more than seconds at a time unless he was engaged in a motor activity such as using a pencil for drawing or writing words. Unlike most children who develop a consistent way of responding to tasks where they must indicate the answer, by pointing, for example, Sam was inconsistent. Sometimes he would point with his index finger, but he would also use his elbow, move his finger in a circular motion above the page before pointing, walk his fingers across the desk surface, and tap his fingers toward the stimulus like playing the piano. He picked up and fingered objects on the desk including pencils, paper clips, and stapler. He pulled erasers off pencils and twisted paper clips out of shape. He had difficulty with memory during the testing. Instructions frequently needed to be repeated. He seemed to forget in the middle of a task what he was expected to do. He had trouble staying with a task for longer than a half-minute. His inattention seemed beyond his voluntary control. He could always be redirected to complete tasks and was pleased when he was successful.

As described in DSM-IV[7] ADHD can be specified as

1. *Attention-Deficit/Hyperactivity Disorder, Combined Type*
2. *Attention-Deficit/Hyperactivity Disorder, Predominantly Inattentive Type*
3. *Attention-Deficit/Hyperactivity Disorder, Predominantly Hyperactive-Impulsive Type*

ADHD usually begins before the age of seven and includes some of the following characteristics: fidgeting or squirming, or in adolescents, a sense of restlessness; difficulty remaining seated; easily distracted by noises and events in the environment; difficulty waiting to take turns; blurting out answers to questions; trouble following through on instructions even though there is a desire to do so; and problems sustaining and shifting attention. Children may talk excessively, interrupt others, seem not to listen, lose things necessary for activities at school or at home, and fail to consider consequences of their actions. Parents recognize these children immediately when described, and teachers know them in their classrooms.

Rating scales that are completed by parents and teachers regarding students' behaviors are in common use. They are valuable clinically and may help lead to effective management. But the range of factors relating to attention, or even how to best describe what attention is or is not, remain unclear.

It is easier to conduct research to study the motor and restlessness components of ADHD than the part of the problem involving attention.[8] Researchers have studied and documented the motor overactivity of ADHD more than the attentional component. Teachers and clinicians often see children who cannot pay attention or concentrate, yet show no motor restlessness or overactivity. Precise delineation of attentional disorders remains elusive.

Attention-Deficit Hyperactivity Disorder (ADHD) is a diagnosis that is defined in psychiatric terminology, although the labeling is commonly offered by psychologists, social workers, teachers, and parents, as well as primary care physicians. ADHD can exist without hyperactivity and overactivity does not have to be present 24 hours a day. Sometimes children can focus and sustain attention on tasks at which they are being successful. Unfortunately, ADHD has been the topic of much coverage in the popular press. Extreme cases are often presented and descriptions of perfectly normal behaviors are offered as examples of ADHD, with medication prescribed for children who do not need it. These articles are misleading and can prevent children and adolescents from receiving helpful treatment. Not all very active behavior is appropriately classified as ADHD. Severe hyperactivity can signal other physical and/or emotional conditions. Children and teenagers with receptive language disorders may also have problems paying attention.

Parents with concerns about attentional disorders need to seek out competent physicians and trust their diagnoses and recommendations. Generalized comments from newspapers, magazines, or television do not refer to a specific child. There are many references available for parents and others interested in ADHD. In them, attentional problems are discussed in some detail and various management plans are described that can serve as supplements to what professionals tell parents about their children.

Oppositional Defiant Disorder is characterized by such actions on the part of individuals as losing one's temper, arguing, defying requests or rules, deliberately annoying others, and blaming others for his or her own behavior. In addition, the individual may be easily annoyed and spiteful. Oppositional defiant disorder is more serious than attention-deficit hyperactivity disorder and sometimes accompanies it.

Most serious of the disruptive behavior disorders is *Conduct Disorder*. Conduct disorder may involve aggression to people and animals, destruction of property, deceitfulness or theft, and serious violations of rules. Such activities as stealing, running away overnight, lying, deliberate fire-setting, cruelty to animals, truancy, destroying property, using a weapon, and forcing sexual activity on another may be included. Some children diagnosed early with ADHD may later be diagnosed as having conduct disorders. Researchers and practitioners are developing rating scales and profiles that may predict which youngsters with ADHD may later have conduct disorders.

Other Emotional Difficulties

Other emotional difficulties may accompany learning disabilities. When we classify any human behavior, including emotional behavior, those classified often will not fit into rigid categories. A thing can be a cat or not a cat, a vehicle or not a vehicle. But it is more complicated when we wish to say a person is or is not dyslexic or does or does not have emotional difficulties, for example.

The major classifying system for emotional problems is called *The Diagnostic and Statistical Manual of Mental Disorders-Fourth Edition* (DSM-IV), published by the American Psychiatric Association and revised in 1994. This is a system used to categorize emotional difficulties in adults and developmental and emotional problems in children. This system has meaning to those in mental health fields and those in clinical practice including physicians, psychologists, social workers, and clinical teachers. It is not the only set of codes that exist, and it is not the one used by most school systems, so it may have limited communicative value between mental health professionals and school personnel. Any categorizing system represents a current state of knowledge and agreement of some committee of professionals. It may not be the best or the most useful, but using such a system helps those who use it communicate more easily.

Some of the emotional problems identified in children and adolescents (in addition to ADHD, which is discussed above) and included in DSM-IV are listed here, because parents and teachers need to know the labels that are used in reports about their children.

Anxiety Disorders are another set of emotional difficulties that can occur in children. Some of the conditions are *Phobias*, *Post Traumatic Stress Disorder*, and *Obsessive Compulsive Disorder*. Obsessive compulsive disorders are being diagnosed more frequently in children and are responsive to treatment.[9] Anxiety may be characterized in some children by overactive behavior. Anxiety and ADHD may be difficult to tease apart; although sometimes ADHD and anxiety are both present in a child or adolescent who has learning disabilities.

Mood Disorders include *Dysthymia* and *Depression*. Dysthymia is a type of depression in which there is depressed mood over a period of a year with less severe symptoms than major depression. Mood disorders or depressive symptoms can be seen in young children and when present, need intervention. Depressed mood (or irritability in children and adolescents) can include such things as poor appetite or overeating, problems getting enough sleep or sleeping too much, low energy level, poor self-regard, problems with concentration and making decisions, and feelings of hopelessness. With such feelings, children and teenagers may find it hard to become involved in school. They may not have the energy available to profit from instruction. Clinically, many of the teenagers I see who have written-expressive language disorders, also carry the diagnosis of a mood disorder.

Of concern, as well, in children and adolescents with learning disabilities, as in others their age, are *Substance-Related Disorders* that include use and abuse of drugs and/or alcohol. Impulsive adolescents with learning disabilities may have poor judgment and perhaps be more vulnerable to substance abuse than others, and the desire to be accepted as one of the group may be even stronger in those who feel themselves inadequate because of their learning disabilities.

Eating disorders including *Anorexia Nervosa* and *Bulimia Nervosa* also need to receive attention, particularly in teenage girls. With increasing opportunities for girls to become involved with competitive athletics, emphasis on perfection and control of body weight can lead to eating disorders. With the focus on physical appearance in our culture, young women as well as older ones, may experience a complex set of problems around eating. Seldom does an eating disorder exist in isolation; other problems are usually present.

Tic disorders, as listed in DSM-IV, include *Tourette's Disorder*, *Chronic Motor or Vocal Tic Disorder*, and *Transient Tic Disorder*. A tic is defined as "a sudden, rapid, recurrent, nonrhythmic, stereotyped motor movement or vocalization." Motor and vocal tics may be classified as simple or complex and boundaries between the two are not always clear. Some medications used for ADHD are believed by some professionals to increase or initiate a tic disorder.

Other Developmental Disorders

Included in the DSM-IV classification system are other disorders first observed in childhood. One is *Mental Retardation* with categories of mild, moderate, severe, profound, and unspecified. The basic problem is with cognitive functioning and the implication is that there are limits to what an individual can achieve.

Another category of developmental disorders is *Pervasive Developmental Disorder*, which now includes *Autistic Disorder*, *Rett's Disorder*, *Childhood Disintegrative Disorder*, *Asperger's Disorder*, and *Pervasive Developmental Disorder, Not Otherwise Specified*. These conditions are characterized by impairment in the development of give and take in social interaction, in developing appropriate verbal and nonverbal communication skills, and in engaging in imaginative activity. Autism has been referred to by some writers as a disorder of social cognition.[10]

Some of the emotional difficulties that may occur in children and adolescents with learning disabilities have been listed. There are other conditions in the emotional area that can co-exist with learning disabilities, but they are usually identified first because of serious worrisome behaviors, and consultation with a mental health professional is usually sought first. When the first contact about a troubling behavior is made with a mental health professional, if there is any relationship to school, consideration needs to be given to the possibility of a learning disability.

Learning Disorders in DSM-IV

Other developmental disorders in DSM-IV, and ones easily recognized at home and school, are listed as *Learning Disorders*. They reflect inadequate development in specific academic areas. These disorders are regarded as *Learning Disabilities* by educators. I do not believe that learning disorders are appropriately classified as mental disorders, even though there can be emotional difficulties in those with learning disabilities. However, I include these disorders here because the terms are used widely in medicine and psychology and are on conference programs at professional meetings attended by parents. Parents and teachers need to know that these conditions are so classified in a major reference work. They likely are included because of possible coverage by health insurance. The learning disorders remain disorders of a child's educational life and as such, are seldom regarded as health expenses to receive insurance coverage.

These conditions as listed in DSM-IV include:
- Learning Disorders
  —Reading Disorder (which includes disorders of word recognition or decoding and comprehension)
  —Mathematics Disorder
  —Disorder of Written Expression
  —Learning Disorder, Not Otherwise Specified
- Motor Skills Disorder
  —Developmental Coordination Disorder
- Communication Disorders
  —Expressive Language Disorder
  —Mixed Receptive-Expressive Language Disorder
  —Phonological Disorder (more commonly referred to as an articulation disorder)
  —Stuttering
  —Communication Disorder, Not Otherwise Specified

NONVERBAL LEARNING

A group of learning disorders omitted from DSM-IV, but that are likely to overlap various emotional difficulties, are disabilities in nonverbal learning. Most of what children are taught directly in school involves verbal learning. At one time, it was thought that if a person did not have words, one could not think. Now we regard that as a silly idea, and yet we see evidence of such beliefs—that without words there is no thought—by the way children are often judged in school. So much of what they are expected to learn is verbal. Reading and writing are verbal skills, and parts of math involve verbal learning as well. Failure in these areas is noticed; success is praised.

Accomplishment in nonverbal learning is not generally given the same attention as verbal learning. Yet in adult life those with nonverbal learning disabilities may find themselves in greater difficulty than those with verbal learning problems.[11,12,13] Clever people can hide reading and spelling problems, place themselves in positions where writing is not required, and make good use of spouses, secretaries, and computers to help with writing and poor spelling. It is not as easy to hide nonverbal problems. They are revealed in day-to-day activities and in person-to-person interactions.

Individuals with good nonverbal skills can turn their talents into such vocational choices as engineering, architecture, or visual arts, or they can use their good nonverbal skills for leisure time activities. Those with good oral verbal skills but poor nonverbal skills may find themselves in difficulty socially and in managing their time alone.

Neuroscientists have described language as organized in the left hemisphere of the brain, while many nonverbal activities have been assigned to the right hemisphere. As often happens with scientific findings that find their way into the popular press, we find descriptions of left-brain and right-brain learners. It is not uncommon for parents to speak of their left- or right-brained children. Much of this popular print and broadcast information is misleading or incorrect. We each need a whole brain to learn and to function.

As nonverbal functioning has received increasing attention, various conditions have been included. This discussion is in no way inclusive of all areas that are being investigated as nonverbal learning, but rather it is an attempt to encourage parents and others who deal with children to consider nonverbal as well as verbal learning.

Nonverbal learning can include, in the broadest sense, what we think and do that is not verbal, that does not involve words as symbols in some form. Nonverbal communication with its nuances for social interactions—awareness of the body and moving the body in space; visual-spatial interpretation and management of two-dimensional materials on a flat table as well as three-dimensional objects in space; parts of mathematical reasoning based on how space is conceptualized and how numbers relate to space; the visual arts; and how one organizes time and space—can all be considered as being in the nonverbal realm.

We consider the same mechanisms in nonverbal as in verbal learning. We ask how individuals perceive or understand nonverbal objects and events and how they express themselves nonverbally—again a look at both receptive and expressive parts of functioning. Before an event can be acted upon, it must be noticed or perceived and have some meaning for an individual. People with no learning disabilities vary in what they notice and how they make decisions about things that are nonverbal. For nonverbal functioning to be regarded as outside the range of normal, the behaviors must trouble the individuals or interfere with their getting along at home, school, or with peers to such a degree that they or others express concern.

Nonverbal Parts of Verbal Messages

Although speech receives most attention when considering communication, nonverbal parts of the speaking act convey information as well. *Prosody* refers to the nonverbal part of verbal messages—the stresses, inflectional patterns, and melody that gives speech its emotional tone (discussed in Chapter 3). A person's voice is given individual qualities by intensity or volume, pitch, resonance, rate, and rhythm. We can purposefully or by chance convey meaning with variations in these qualities. Those who use their voices professionally (actors, singers, or public speakers) control and manipulate these attributes in using their voices. Otherwise, these qualities are determined by speakers' physical and psychological conditions and can become the basis for social categorization. A person's voice can cause judgments about whether he or she is ill or well, for instance, or whether brash, a bore, or a loud mouth. Other vocalizations that communicate are laughing, sobbing, moaning, whining, or yawning audibly while another person is speaking. We need to evaluate children to see if they interpret these nonverbal cues and if they show appropriate variations in their own speech.

Gestures and Signs

The use of gestures and signs are parts of nonverbal communication. They can be used for emphasis to accompany speech and/or as substitution for words or numbers. Signs are used by referees for athletic events, policemen for directing traffic, and floor managers in television studios. Examples of common signs in everyday use include using the forefinger and thumb arranged in a circle to mean *okay* or job well done, or holding a finger to the lips to indicate a person should be quiet in place of saying "Sh!" Signs or gestures vary within cultures to convey positive or negative messages.

Facial Expression

We judge the mood of others and show our own feelings through facial expression and changes in those expressions. Changes in facial expression can signal joy, surprise, anger, fear, sadness, loathing, shock, approval, and many other states. Such variations can accompany speech or be independent from what is being said. Sometimes a facial expression contradicts what we are saying and can be more powerful in conveying meaning than words. Or some individuals show little change in facial expression but do show variations in tone of speaking. Emotion that is reflected primarily by nonverbal demeanor and facial expression is referred to as *affect*. We need to know if children perceive differences in affect and if they use appropriate affect to convey what they wish to say. If there is dissonance between the words used and the affect shown, this needs to be explained.

Actions

Actions individuals use, including walking, eating, drinking, and driving a car, communicate about the person doing the action. The way a person walks suggests how he or she feels. A brisk stride with head held high and arms swinging is different from a walk with head down, shoulders slumped, and slow gait. The way individuals drive cars can communicate impatience, rudeness, or danger. The manner in which we consume food at a table suggests to some the importance of certain social behaviors learned in the home.

Proxemics

Another way to communicate nonverbally is relating one's body in space to the space of others. This is learned by children from a young age, although it seldom seems to be taught directly. The spatial relationship between an individual and another person is referred to as *proxemics* and is culturally determined. Generally distance is referred to as intimate, personal, social, and public distance. Intimate distance is touching another in protection, comfort, and lovemaking. Personal distance represents the informal contact between family members and some friends and is about one to one and one-half feet. Social distance is that used with acquaintances and is about 4 to 12 feet. Finally, public distance is about 12 feet.[14] (Public space is violated in elevators which results in some unusual studying of the ceiling, the lights that indicates floors, or the back of another's head. It is understandable that elevator behaviors occur so often in comedy routines.) In cultures other than that of the United States, individuals may stand closer to others than we may find acceptable. Diplomats and their families must quickly make adjustments to these conventions of space so that they do not insult their hosts. When our personal space is invaded, we feel threatened, and have negative or hostile feelings.

Bodies Related to Objects in Space

We seem to know automatically where our bodies are in space. We generally do not go around bumping into things. There are variations of awareness of the body in space, however. For example, some people seem to enjoy having discussions while standing in doorways with little recognition that others need that space to go in and out. Shopping for groceries is another time when we may confront those who move as though they and their carts are alone in the aisles, however, for the most part we are aware of where our bodies are in space and in relation to others sharing the same general space.

Display of Possessions

The display of material things, intentionally or unintentionally, is another part of nonverbal communication. Included are such things as personal dress and selection and arrangement of furniture in our homes. Individuals' clothing and jewelry can tell how they regard fashion, how they show a professional manner, or what kind of image they wish to exhibit. A messy or tidy house when no one is expected to drop by can inform us about standards of housekeeping. The casual placement of rustic furniture in a room with magazines tossed about signals a different expected behavior from a formal room with precious antiques.

Nonverbal Problem Solving

Effectively interpreting and acting upon social cues is a kind of nonverbal problem solving. In daily activity, nonverbal cues are constantly acted upon. Mothers know in an instant if a child is not feeling well, and they juggle dozens of nonverbal cues as they prepare their families for the day. Store owners make nonverbal judgments about those entering their workplaces. Sometimes they overgeneralize and are fearful of the wrong people, while at other times, they trust a well-dressed person who has mischief or crime in mind.

Architects, automobile designers, carpenters, and other craftsmen spend their lives solving nonverbal problems through manipulation of materials. They must all understand how parts of objects and materials fit together. Rather than use words, they must conceptualize, nonverbally, how an object will look and how it will function.

Visual–Spatial Functioning

Judging size and space, building with blocks, and managing puzzles all require some facility with visual-spatial perception and organization as does estimating distance when crossing a street or participating in games. Using a pencil to draw and to write also requires a sense of visual-spatial organization combined with motor movements.

Other Nonverbal Communication

Pragmatics—the use of language in a social context—is discussed in Chapter 3. Using language for social interaction requires attention to these nonverbal cues. Failure to interpret such cues correctly, or failure to even know such cues exist, can interfere with children and adults getting along with others.

Nonverbal communicative behaviors are culturally determined. As such, they change from time to time. Politeness, how respect for elders or authority figures is shown, how formality and informality is expressed, all change. The differences and changes can cause problems between generations and between those of different cultures. For the most part, these behaviors are learned easily as children grow up, but those with difficulty in nonverbal areas may not pay attention to the cues.

Problems in Nonverbal Behavior

Some of these difficulties interfere with interpretation of cues about the social-emotional environment. Individuals with such problems may not "read" nonverbal cues that are nearly automatic for most people; they may experience difficulty in perceiving and using appropriate social cues. They may not notice when others are disgusted by their behaviors. They fail to see that another child is about to cry or is ready to strike out in rage or is so annoyed he or she is about to go home. They may also fail to interpret nonverbal looks that precede disciplinary action.

These children can be hypersensitive, become slighted easily, and misunderstand teasing so they react to words rather than a playful tone of voice. Just as they misinterpret negative cues they may fail to notice that another is happy or is giving positive nonverbal cues that say "I like you."

They may not respect personal space, getting much too close to strangers or to playmates. They may not recognize formal situations. They may show inappropriate physical and verbal distance from strangers, and may unwittingly display rudeness to authority figures.

Such failures to interpret nonverbal social communicative cues can cause difficulties with peers and also with adults, including teachers. Some of these children and adolescents really do not care at all about others and regard themselves as the center of the universe, but most of them suffer enormously because they do not know how to make friends, how to sustain relationships, or simply how to be liked by others.

Social skills deficits are now being regarded as one kind of learning disability. But such students need careful evaluation to determine why they have such difficulties—if they do not perceive cues, if they have not been taught, or if for some reason they are rejecting common rules of social behavior.

Motor Coordination

Babies learn early to coordinate their bodies by first crawling and then walking. This early awareness of the body and moving it in space develops toward flexibility and grace to an amazing level in athletes—basketball players, dancers, gymnasts, and skaters, for instance. But ordinary people who do not have great talents also can execute motor skills easily for locomotion and leisure athletic activity.

Problems with gross motor function are identified in the first hours or days of life. Motor dysfunctions grouped under the general term of cerebral palsy are among those diagnosed early. More subtle problems are observed later in development. When children or adolescents do not move their bodies easily in a coordinated way, they may trip or stumble easily. The are often referred to as clumsy or as klutzes. These conditions are classified in DSM-IV under *Motor Skills Disorders* as a *Developmental Coordination Disorder*. This disorder is characterized by poor performance or delays in reaching motor developmental milestones, clumsiness, poor performance in sports, and poor handwriting. Motor milestones include turning over, sitting, crawling, and walking. Children, as they grow, are expected to become adept at buttoning, tying shoes, using scissors, and manipulating crayons, pencils, and eating utensils. Playing with puzzles, small blocks, and later building models involve motor skills for which some level of success is expected. Although mastery of these skills is expected in childhood, some adults with nonverbal learning disabilities cannot tie shoes, button shirts, use hooks and eyes, or fold letters to fit in envelopes.

Learning to type or to use a keyboard for a computer is commonly recommended for students who have coordination problems for handwriting. Although this can be a wonderful compensatory device, students with fine motor coordination problems may have a difficult time learning the motor patterns that relate the fingers to the keys. With knowledgeable and caring teachers they can learn, and it is an important skill to acquire, even though learning may take some additional effort for them. Parents need to be careful that skill is taught by a person who understands problems of motor coordination rather than by someone who has taught only those who move their fingers easily. General typing teachers often fail to understand motor skill disorders.

Weaknesses in the area of motor coordination can be accepted and smiled upon fondly in adults we care about but can be devastating for children who are taunted by their peers. Jokes are often made about children failing blocks and coloring and yet we should be alert to the notion that such children may be giving early clues to potential problems with coordination that will affect in-school and out-of-school activities. Early attention is focused on children picking up finger foods and then shifting to use of a spoon. However, later coordinated use of eating utensils may not be taught and school-age children, and older ones, can be annoying at the dinner table, embarrassing to others, and humiliating to themselves if they cannot manipulate a knife and fork. Children need to learn the coordinated use of objects in their hands in addition to using a pencil for writing. They also need to learn to tie shoes and not depend completely on shoes that fasten in alternative ways. Being unable to tie shoes can cause embarrassment.

Sports

Some facility with sports is expected of children as they grow. Boys with severe academic problems are accepted as part of the group if they are good athletes. Successful athletes are admired by both children and adults. Boys with minimally acceptable athletic skills, able to participate in groups without calling undue attention to themselves by poor functioning, also fare well. Increasingly, girls are participating in sports so this has become a domain of acceptance or rejection for them also. Athletic participation along with a focus on physical fitness makes it important that parents and teachers help children develop skills in these areas. If parents stay away from these activities themselves, they can call upon friends or other adults to help their children. Some schools and communities have recreational programs for children who find physical activities difficult. Some physical education teachers have had educational preparation to teach children who have difficulty with motor activities.

Youngsters with learning disabilities and problems with athletics may not look different from anyone else. They would not qualify for the Special Olympics, for instance. But they need to have the activities broken into small components so they can master each part of the motor activity. It may be a good idea to teach them activities that they can practice independently such as swimming, tether ball, or skiing until they become more comfortable. Once they have some sense of motor mastery, they may be more able to participate in team sports. Adults need patience and creativity in developing ways to teach such children.

Some children cannot manage team sports, because rules are confusing, or because of short-term auditory memory weaknesses, problems with motor sequential memory, or attentional problems, but they need a different kind of management than those who have difficulty with basic motor coordination.

Related Problems

Learning-disabled children and adolescents may show some behaviors that are not measured by standardized tests. Nevertheless, it is important to consider such behaviors. They may be part of deficits in specific areas of learning, including nonverbal learning, or they may relate to attentional difficulties. They include:

* slow rate of response;
* lack of alternative plans;

- lack of monitoring of responses;
- poor organization and planning;
- hypersensitivity to questioning; and
- lack of sense of possible mastery

Slow Rate of Response

Some children are slow in responding whether giving a verbal response, writing, dressing, getting to the dinner table, going from locker to class on time, or completing a test. There is a delay from the time of any input to the time an individual responds. Some of these children seem slow in processing information, or manipulating information mentally, as well as responding. This behavior is different from the dawdling child who is able with effort to "hurry up." Slow moving children need more time to process information and/or express it in an appropriate form. It is essential that extended time be provided for such students without penalty. They think and move as fast as they can. I have never been successful in helping such children respond faster, but some do seem to pick up some speed of response as they grow. Unless we are running a race, engaged in a dangerous occupation, managing medical emergencies, or confronting a most unusual circumstance, it is seldom necessary for us to move or think as fast as possible. Yet we demand speed from developing students all along their educational paths. Having extended time may be the only accommodation many learning-disabled students need, but it can be a salvation for them to demonstrate what they know.

Rigidity

Some students commonly lack any alternative plan; show a rigidity in responding. If they learn one way to reach an answer, they do not accept that there can be other ways to achieve an answer. Middle-school-age youngsters and teenagers often tell me, "I really studied hard. I knew the material. But then she changed the question. So I couldn't get it." Other examples include: If an ingredient is missing from a recipe, he gives no consideration to what could be used as a substitute; if the bridge is out, she would not find another way to get to the other side of the stream; if lunch money is in one pocket, and money for an after-school snack is in another pocket, and lunch money is lost, he might not reach into the other pocket for money that is there. For such children, as long as an answer comes to them easily, all is well. If they are unsure, however, they do not seem to be able to call on alternative ways to solve a problem. This can result in immediate frustration and fury if they cannot spell a word, solve a problem, find a puzzle piece, or locate the correct cable for connecting two pieces of computer equipment.

Some students with learning disabilities believe that they should know an answer or acquire a skill without investing any effort. As soon as the slightest difficulty is encountered they are ready to give up. They become impatient and disgusted with themselves. They think they should be able to play baseball like a professional the first time they touch a ball or that they should play a guitar as well as their favorite star with only a few lessons. Attics and basements are filled with projects barely begun because children (and their parents at times) did not understand the amount of work necessary to learn a new skill or complete a project. It is important to help children understand the steps that are necessary, while always assisting them to remember the goal.

Automatic Monitoring

Some children with learning disabilities may not be able to monitor their language and actions the way most other children do. For effective language use and for other learning, monitoring is constant and automatic. There are continual shifts from foreground (what is right in front of us such as reading, typing, preparing dinner) to background (sounds of heating system, lights flickering, music playing). We are alert to changes, making constant adjustments. We react to fluctuations in background sounds of radio or television or to children at play when a change in sound or a level of quiet can mean trouble. We modify how we speak with a child, peer, significant other, or authority figure. We judge whether an answer is right or wrong. Some learning-disabled children have trouble with this kind of monitoring. They appear to have a generalized lack of awareness—awareness that can be observed in a first grader forming a single letter or a high-school student writing an essay. They have little sense of realistic self-evaluation. If asked for an opinion, they will often think that what they have done is wrong or poor; although some will believe they are always right. We must help these students monitor and evaluate what they have said or produced. Part of monitoring and regulation includes an awareness that there are some steps that must be taken every time a specific task is performed. Each sentence written must start with a capital letter and end with a punctuation mark. Every sentence or report must be proofread for errors and checked for spelling. Every arithmetic problem must be scanned for the sign that tells what operation must be done.

Organization

Many learning-disabled students have problems with organization and planning. They do not know if they have enough space to finish writing a word on a line, cannot judge how long it will take to complete homework, or how much time must be allotted to get to an appointment on time. They get in trouble with peers who are meeting to attend a party, with family members who are sick of waiting for them, and as adults, with co-workers who become impatient with what they regard as rude behaviors. They must be helped to appreciate time and to relate activities to a specified period of time.

Hypersensitivity to Questions

Some people with learning disabilities are hypersensitive to questioning. They seem unable to believe that an adult would want to know how they generate an answer or what they are thinking while they are attempting to solve a problem. Confident children love to talk about themselves; many children with learning problems regard any kind of query as criticism. We must help them understand that we are interested not only in what they do, but how they think. By sharing their ideas, thoughts, and information processing they may clarify their own thoughts and ideas and allow adults to understand where they need assistance.

A Sense of the Merely Possible

Finally, many learning disabled individuals seem to lack a sense of what is possible. For any of us to try something new we have to feel, at some level, that we will succeed. Those with learning disabilities have often experienced so much school failure that they may have forgotten that success is possible. They will require assistance to recognize that with structured teaching, reinforcement, and practice, they can achieve. Often they need proof that learning is possible for them. Proof may need to be provided for them—seeing additions to lists of words that can be read, the number of pages, chapters, or books that have been read, or time it takes to complete a task. Record keeping becomes important as proof that such individuals are, indeed, learning, that they know more today than they did yesterday, and a lot more than they did last month.

ADDITIONAL SOCIAL-EMOTIONAL PROBLEMS

In addition, there are other conditions that affect how children and adolescents feel about themselves. There is no yardstick to measure behavioral reaction to failure and to tasks that are too hard. We have no gauge of how many hours of school failure typical children and adolescents must experience before they give up and no longer invest themselves in learning. They will say "I pay attention if I like it" but have very little to like in school, because success is rare. Having to struggle a little to reach a new level of understanding is a challenge, but when there is little opportunity to master a skill, discouragement and hopelessness result. Many students with learning disabilities are constantly expected to perform in ways they cannot possibly manage. They must spell words they cannot read or are required to read texts in science and social studies that contain words they cannot decode.

They are asked to complete math problems while being totally lost about what is being presented in class.

Constantly being given the message that one does not measure up has to have a major impact on an individual's self-concept. Some will regard failure as a call to try harder, but most are so discouraged by failure that they give up. They begin regarding themselves as failing students and soon thereafter as failed people.

Understimulation

On the other hand, some bright children and adolescents with learning disabilities are understimulated. They may not be presented with complex comprehension questions in remedial reading classes, so their thinking is not challenged. The levels of concepts they are expected to master are reduced, and they have little preparation to think in an abstract way. With related spelling and writing problems, they may not learn to expose their knowledge through writing. Such students may be placed in the lowest classes in high school when their minds function at a level far in advance of their basic reading and writing skills.

Being Average in a High-Achieving Family

Another problem that faces some young people is not a learning disability at all but the fact of being average in a high-achieving family. They are achieving as fast and as well as they can. No amount of specialized tutoring will permit them to catch up academically with their more intellectually talented parents and brothers and sisters. Different families comprise different kinds of achievers. Parents who have always been academically successful may have great difficulty in understanding a child who is not equally talented. Families of musicians may find it hard to accept a child with little or only average musical talent. Engineers may find it hard to appreciate a child whose interests and talents are in the humanities, and athletes can be frustrated by klutzy offspring. Being average does not doom us to failure. It does not mean that such individuals will not be highly successful, productive adults. They will simply choose different paths from other family members. Understanding and supportive parents and teachers must help them along the way.

IDENTIFYING PROBLEMS

Times of change—moving to a new house, having a parent leave the home because of divorce, or change related to school in moving from kindergarten into first grade, from elementary to middle school, from middle school to high school, and from high school to college—may be times to identify both learning and emotional problems. While taking a history, we may learn that the problems have existed for a long time, but it is the burden imposed by change and greater amounts of material to be managed, decreased time in which to complete work, and increased expectations for independence that call attention to persistent, even if mild, difficulties.

When school personnel test children for learning and behavioral issues, they most often use a child's performance in school as a measure. A child may be functioning adequately in school but far below the level of his or her intelligence. A child's behavior may not bother the teachers or other students, but some learning disabled students may become quiet, withdrawn, and possibly depressed. If such problems do not interfere with school work in a noticeable way, they may not be regarded as being significant at school. Emotional problems must be severe enough to interfere with learning before special help is provided in schools, thus depriving some children of treatment that could serve them well. Children with emotional difficulties are often evaluated because of behavioral interference in the classroom rather than for emotional difficulties that affect their lives in a broader sense. This is not to fault schools. Contrary to popular thinking and writing in some newspaper columns and letters to editors, schools really cannot do everything. But when emotional difficulties are noticed in children, even if they do not interfere with learning or with others in the classroom, parents need to be informed.

MANAGEMENT OF COMBINED LEARNING AND EMOTIONAL PROBLEMS

Children with combined learning disabilities and emotional problems need a multifaceted approach. They are likely to require one or more of the following and perhaps all of them:
- good models at home;
- modified or special teaching;
- a behavioral approach;
- counseling or psychotherapy; and/or
- medication.

Models at Home

Models for many behaviors are learned at home. From an early age, children imitate what they see. Children with learning disabilities and emotional problems often need more structure than their peers require. Often children and adolescents with learning and/or emotional difficulties are disorganized. Disorganized children will never learn to be organized if their homes are in chaos. They may need help to organize time and space. Time organization includes knowing what can be accomplished in specified periods of time—10 minutes, a half-hour, and an hour. Space includes their rooms, trash cans, desks in school, or a glass into which juice is to be poured.

Children are more likely to complete homework if other family members are also working. It is hard to concentrate on difficult work when everyone else is watching television. Children will not know that books have value if there are no books in the home and no adult is seen reading. They need to see evidence that their struggle in school has usefulness to adults. Seeing adults read suggests that reading is important. Some children, even with good models of verbal and nonverbal behaviors at home, may not learn from the models unless they are specifically directed to pay attention to them. They do not seem to notice or profit from what occurs around them.

All children also need to know that they have value to their parents just for being who they are, that there is more to life than school performance. Often in busy families with both parents working, the only private time learning-disabled children have with a parent is while struggling with homework every night or studying for tests. Making time for pleasurable activities that child and family can do together is essential.

Modified or Special Teaching

All children need educational programs that teach them to acquire new knowledge, practice what is learned, and achieve mastery, with the instruction beginning at a stage at which the child is successful. Some of them will need special help with academic subjects. They may need additional support from classroom teachers, special education teachers, or private tutors. Many classroom teachers are willing to give some extra help to students who experience difficulty. They simply do not have time to provide very much extra in large-group situations. But sometimes, just encouraging words, spoken aloud or written on papers, in recognition that students have invested a lot of work and that they have some special quality that stands out, will go a long way to keep the student encouraged.

Some students will require pull-out programs, that is, being removed from class for special teaching. They will need to spend time with a resource teacher. They may be in resource classes for a specified period each day or for a certain number of hours per week. During the resource time, they will have help with their areas of weakness. Some children will be in resource rooms all day, because they have learning and emotional problems that are so pervasive that they cannot manage in large classrooms.

Private tutoring to supplement what is provided in the classroom will be needed by some students who do not receive enough special education time for them to learn. The need for private services is likely to increase as public school special education programs are changed so that children cannot have individualized instruction. Commonly, special services stop too soon. Children are not provided with enough time to practice and apply what they have learned in order to use it independently. When such is the case, parents may choose to provide private tutoring so their children will learn as much as they are capable of learning. At times, students of any age may need tutoring to learn underlying basic skills, to learn to decode words for independent reading at their level of ability, for example, or to fill in gaps in basic arithmetic knowledge. At other times, particularly older students will require subject tutoring, or tutoring in the area in which they are confronting difficulty. A science course or an extremely difficult unit in English may be better managed with some supportive tutoring. A student experiencing depression may not learn much during a depressive episode and may need some tutoring to fill in what was missed.

Archie Silver and Rosa Hagin[15] make important observations about the differences in approach between psychotherapy and remedial teaching. For therapy, they say, the child's strengths are used. If the child is good verbally, verbal therapy may be used. If the child is poor verbally with strengths in the nonverbal realm, then more of the session would involve nonverbal materials, drawing, use of toys, and nonverbal games. For remedial education the child is taught to improve his or her deficient areas as strengths are used for teaching and to offer support.

Katrina De Hirsch[16] wrote that the goal of individual teaching, tutoring, or remediation for those with learning problems involves teaching specific skills but also promoting enjoyment of mastery for its own sake rather than for some external reward. Appropriate teaching or tutoring can serve to help a child's emotional development as well as his or her learning.

Behavioral Approach

A behavioral approach reinforces accepted behaviors and helps children learn consequences of their actions. Such a program may be set up by a psychologist or sometimes by a school guidance counselor. Usually one behavior is targeted at a time. At home, this behavior might be setting the table every night, putting dishes in the dishwasher, taking out the trash, starting homework at a specified time, getting dressed in the morning with only one reminder, or having the backpack prepared at night, before going to sleep. At school, the targeted behavior might be refraining from talking out of turn, ceasing hitting others on the playground, turning in assignments every day— at first for one class and later for every class, or getting to class on time. Rewards are given when tasks are completed as expected. Immediate rewards can be check marks, stars, smiley faces, stickers, or some other method of points. These points can then be traded for a larger reward, but one that is not too large to be achieved in a reasonable time considering the individual's age. Points can be taken away for failing to complete the agreed upon act or task.

A behavioral approach allows children to appreciate consequences of their own actions in a concrete way. It also helps them make judgments about available choices and can help inhibit impulsivity. Some additional suggestions follow.

- Help children with attentional problems recognize that they are having a problem paying attention. Help them to see when the lack of attention interferes with time at home and in school. Often they are not aware that paying attention is difficult for them. They feel they get yelled at "for no reason." Some level of self-awareness is necessary for them to try to make changes.
- It is important that a child is paying attention when directions are given or questions asked.
- It is essential to determine that an instruction is understood and remembered. A problem with language comprehension or auditory memory can interfere with this process.
- Distractions need to be reduced. At home, this can mean studying should be done in an area free from toys, a television set, or appealing activities. (Some children and adolescents say they study better when music is playing, however.) At school being away from a window or from children who are likely to contribute to distractions can be helpful.
- Reduce the length of an assignment or break it into shorter, visually more manageable parts. Fold paper to show just one row of math problems or to see just three spelling words instead of a list of ten. As children get older, they should be able to reduce assignments into shorter segments by themselves.
- Plan frequent breaks as part of study or work time.
- Make positive comments concerning efforts to pay attention to complete tasks.
- Establish reasonable incentives for success. Set short-term goals. However, earning privileges or special treats will take a longer period of time.
- Establish what are unacceptable behaviors and those that will not be tolerated. Hurting another physically or verbally and destroying one's own possessions or those of another should not be permitted. Conversely, others, including siblings and classmates, should not be permitted to torment a child with emotional and/or learning problems, physically or verbally, or to damage or destroy his or her possessions. Sometimes we seem to make greater demands on the child with attentional problems than we do on those without such problems.
- Children or adolescents can be helped if, during a quiet time, behaviors that presented a problem during the day are discussed. Offer alternative ways, or develop with the youngster different ways, of handing difficult issues.

- Help students learn to monitor their own behaviors, to tell themselves (subvocally) rules or learned phrases to circumvent difficulties. Only a few of these statements should be developed at one time so the mind is not cluttered. Some of these can be: "Slow down." "Think." "Wait a second." "Take your time." "It's all right."

Counseling or Psychotherapy

Counseling or psychotherapy is not used by as many adults as could benefit from it and certainly is not provided for many children who could be helped immeasurably. Research is mixed on the results of counseling of any kind. Believing that we should not deprive children of anything that will help them grow, I believe therapy does help many of them. Children learn better ways of coping and their parents learn to understand and manage problems better. Older children learn to understand the nature of their combined emotional and learning problems and to establish realistic goals for themselves. In therapy they often learn, just as some adults do, that they have far better abilities than they ever believed. They may become more open to instruction provided in school. Many begin to develop hope, and hope grows as they untangle emotional difficulties and cope with their learning disabilities.

I have known a group of children with severe emotional and learning problems, of the pervasive developmental disability type, who were in long-term psychotherapy combined with special education and some private tutoring from time to time. Their parents were willing to support the therapy and also fight for maximum services for their children at school. These young people are now successful young adults pursuing college. Without long-term therapy, they would not have been successful.

Medication

Often children with combined learning disabilities and emotional difficulties do well with medication. Many children with ADHD show positive responses to medication. To deprive a child of medication when he or she can benefit from it can be compared with depriving a diabetic of insulin. To appreciate how medication can help, we merely have to observe a child with severe overactive behavior and almost no concentration, able to function comfortably for the first time at school and home, or a depressed person who is finally able to get out of bed in the morning and put one foot in front of the other to begin the day.

News magazines, television talk shows, and pseudo-news programs from time to time offer programs that are highly critical of medications. Public and independent schools in their attempts to establish strong antidrug campaigns often fail to inform students about the difference between doctor-prescribed medicine and street or recreational drugs. This results in some children of middle school age or older refusing to take medication that can help them.

With it becoming increasingly difficult to have psychotherapy covered by health insurance plans, it is more common for children to be prescribed medication with no other support. I believe this is a mistake that can have serious consequences. Children need to know what medication will and will not do. A skillful child and adolescent psychiatrist whom I have worked with over a long period of time tells children and adolescents that the medication (for ADHD) "will help you pay attention better if you want to pay attention."[17] This prevents them from thinking that the pill is controlling their behavior; they are controlling their own behavior. Counseling or psychotherapy, in addition to relieving psychological pain, helps children understand what to expect if they are taking medication, to learn possible reasons they feel and act as they do, and also to realize why other children may have rejected them because of their annoying or withdrawing behaviors.

SPECIAL CONSIDERATIONS FOR CHILDREN WITH LANGUAGE AND LEARNING DISABILITIES

When professionals see children and adolescents with learning disabilities, it is essential that they understand the nature of the learning. Children with poor language skills may have difficulty making an association between feelings and the words used to express the feelings of anger, fear, disappointment, dismay, joy, and so on. They may not understand the language a professional uses. They have trouble understanding questions asked. Sometimes a seeming shyness or reluctance to respond results from a receptive language deficit. Overactivity can also result from lack of comprehension. Inappropriate use of language in a social context troubles many youngsters who have learning and emotional problems, so they may not know how to interact, even though they have been exposed to suitable models. Parents and teachers, along with physicians and other mental health professionals, must be aware of language, language disorders, and learning disabilities when working with children and adolescents. The children will only be successful when learning is attended to along with other needs.

TO TREAT OR NOT TO TREAT

I know there are many who say that special education (or psychotherapy) is not effective over the long term. It is said by critics, not always facetiously, that fifty percent of those with problems get better with therapy and fifty percent do not, while fifty percent untreated get better and fifty percent do not. We do not have good prospective studies that show matched groups of treated and untreated (or appropriately taught or untaught) subjects followed to adulthood. There are some follow-up studies, though. Moreover, we do see, through natural occurrences, adults, referred by social workers, psychologists, and psychiatrists for assessment of their learning who have never had previous help. Some have graduated from high school and attended some college. Many present an appearance of being successful. They have jobs, stable family relationships, and contribute to the community. Some in long marriages have never "confessed" to a spouse that they have limited education or significant problems with reading. They expend inordinate amounts of energy on trying to hide their learning disabilities. They feel absolutely worthless and nearly without exception regard themselves as stupid.

Others are in low-paying jobs or jobs that they regard as unimportant. Some have skills to manage better jobs but are reluctant to apply for them. They are afraid to initiate a telephone call to learn about requirements for certain jobs or whether a written examination is required. (Parenthetically, the more education required for a job, the less rigid are the requirements. It is possible to take the bar examination to practice as an attorney or to take board exams to practice medicine with more special circumstances being acceptable than it is to take a written examination to qualify as a plumber, electrician, or hairdresser.)

Would these adults have a better sense of emotional well being if they had had earlier special help with learning or early counseling? We do not know. But every individual who grows up with a learning disability develops with the learning disability as part of his or her self-image. Based on what we know of emotionally troubled adults with learning disabilities, I believe we should provide any services possible that can prevent children from suffering despair as they grow up.

Some self-help and parents' groups may be available in a community, but caution must be exercised. One parent's child may not have the same kind of problem as another child. Groups involving troubled parents should have a professional at the group meetings or as a consultant. Sensitive issues and serious problems may emerge that require professional management. An empathic, but unskilled, listener may not be enough.

Any time there is a question about child behavior, there can be unscrupulous people taking advantage of a parent's worry. Parents must be careful about any product or treatment that promises a cure or quick results or that advertises being 100 percent successful. Nothing in dealing with human behavior is effective with every individual. Too many variables influence results. This means that highly priced and advertised products and programs may not be effective.

Looking into the future can be dangerous, and we are not really good at making predictions about human behavior, because multiple events can occur to impede or facilitate learning. But we need to help children understand their particular kinds of learning disabilities and/or emotional difficulties, what they mean, and what possible impact they will have on life at home and at school.

Students with learning disabilities have to work harder to master what may come easily to their peers. If dyslexic, they may always be slow readers and need to plan for extra time. If they have ADHD, they will need to make adjustments to cope in various situations. If they have special education and tutors throughout school, they need to understand why. If they have had counseling, they need to know why. Without knowing why they needed these special services, they advance into young adulthood confused about why they experience difficulty and anger that they must exert more effort than others. To tell them they have a learning disability may come as a surprise to them. It can be valuable to give a label rather than a generalized statement. Statements such as "We all learn differently—just do your best" contribute little to their understanding of their unique selves. I have seen numbers of college students, failing courses and about to flunk out, who are surprised to learn that they have a learning disability. They say they went to tutoring or for therapy because their parents said they had to go. Sometimes this may be denial on their parts, but often parents never wanted the children to think they were different or that they had a problem. Students, as they grow, need to understand that they are capable of achieving but that they must work harder than their peers who never have had to deal with learning disabilities.

The emotional problems mentioned in this chapter are mild to moderate. I believe, however, that they are common in children and adolescents with learning disabilities and can have a severe impact when combined with their learning patterns. What happens to children's learning while they are experiencing severe attentional difficulties or any one of an array of emotional difficulties is something we do not know. They may attend to only partial signals and information may be distorted. They may not take newly learned facts and ideas and relate them to their own experiences to help the new information stay in memory. Just as children who do not play with blocks have no practice in building with them, and children who never play with rhyming words have a gap in phonological development, so older children with learning and attentional disorders may need assistance to fill in what may have been missed.

SUMMARY

Silver and Hagin[18] include a quotation from Lauretta Bender when she was writing about the design copying from her *Visual Motor Gestalt Test*, that can serve as a summary when we interact with children. She wrote, "A child cannot make an error on reproduction. However a child produces the gestalt test, it is a perfect, complete, and correct projection of that child's experience at that time and at the level of his total maturation, including whatever personality, maturation, and organismic problems he may have...." I believe that those children and adolescents we work with do what they can do during the time we spend with them. Understanding that, we can make contributions to both their learning and their emotional well being.

CHAPTER 7

ESPECIALLY FOR . . .

The most frequent requests from parents and teachers are for specific suggestions to help children and adults with learning disabilities. Older students ask what they can do to help themselves. The following suggestions are for them.

ESPECIALLY FOR PARENTS
Working with the School

- Understand what is expected of your child each year in school. When there is a learning disability present, you need to know if he or she is required to complete the same work as others in that grade or if special accommodations are made.
- Be sure you and your child understand how learning will be evaluated. Are report card grades awarded according to ability, as a reflection of what can be expected of a child in view of problems, or do grades reflect the same scale for everyone?
- Check that you and your child's teachers are in agreement about expectations. Hard work is acceptable and necessary, but requirements need to make sense and to be at a level that allows your child to learn successfully.
- Be sure your child is not understimulated, that he or she is constantly learning new material. Review is good and helps what is newly learned stay in memory. Being presented with exactly the same materials month after month seldom facilitates learning.

- Know the kind of assistance the teachers expect you to provide at home.
- Ask teachers what you can do to help. Request specific suggestions. Would a family trip to a museum or science center contribute to your child's learning in a particular unit? Are there books that should be read aloud as a family?
- If the student cannot read the required science and social studies texts, should you read them aloud to him or her?
- Is it expected that your child either read, or have read to him or her, the textbooks used for class?
- Discuss issues of homework so that your child, the teacher, and you agree what work is reasonable for the child to do after school hours. Hours of battles about homework between the child and parent are harmful and will not serve the purpose of learning.
- If there are behavioral issues, be sure your child's teacher knows when you want to be informed. At times, teachers want to work out a problem with the student without the parent being informed. At other times, parents need to know, particularly if there is a serious violation of a school rule or a safety issue.
- If homework is not completed by your young child, you should be informed early, perhaps after your child misses homework twice in a two-week period. If a plan is necessary to get the assignments home, get them completed, and get them returned to school, you need to be involved in its development and implementation.
- Many students with learning disabilities cannot manage on their own until they are older. Age alone cannot determine independence. Some will need supportive help far longer than others. Your involvement may need to be more than supervision alone. Teenagers need to be part of the decision about how much help is needed or wanted.
- If a teenager is having excessive difficulty with a course and it is time to study for final exams, he or she might be best served by spending time studying for the classes in which there is a chance of success. Spending most of the time on what is hard can result in failure in those subjects in which he or she could do well.
- For some students who can decode but cannot handle the volume of material to be read, it is helpful to use tapes and records produced for the blind. In some communities, a professional, often a physician or psychologist, must write a statement about the reading problem in order for the person to qualify.
- Complete books on tape with accompanying texts are available.[1]
- Modification of assignments, such as reducing the number of problems to be solved or producing the final product in a different way, may be necessary so that the student can function successfully and as indepen-

dently as possible. Completing a project on his or her own with modifications is better than meeting the requirement with excessive parental involvement. It should be the child's project, not a parent's.

- While your child is receiving special help, the teacher in the regular class may be willing to accept oral or taped reports rather than written ones. This should be done only until the student can handle writing independently.

- Those who can profit from listening to material a second time might be permitted to use tape recorders for class. This may not, however, be of help if your child has severe auditory memory problems.

- Your child must be willing to accept modifications, if teachers permit, and understand the risk of being regarded as different.

- A decision will need to be made when students think about taking standardized examinations such as the SATs, LSATs, MCATs, GREs, and GMATs about whether or not they choose to be identified as being handicapped. They may benefit from modifications in test procedures by having extended time or having the tests read orally. Such requests can only be made if the same modifications have been made in high school. If students wish to participate in special programs at the college level they must identify themselves as having learning disabilities in order to be considered. They cannot decide that they would like to receive help from the special center or program right before final exams when they are in danger of failing. Options about identifying themselves as having a learning disability should be explained to them, and then they should make the decision.

- High school students who are planning for college should understand that they do not need to stay at the same school for four years. They may make decisions one year, or even one semester, at a time. Anxiety is high in all students as they are leaving home, often for the first time. Learning disabled students not only have the normal anxiety, but fear they may fail academically.

Supervising Homework

- Homework is your child's responsibility, not yours. He or she needs to complete it as independently as possible. However, students with learning disabilities may need help for longer periods of time than their peers. Some will need help organizing their time, deciding how much time should be spent on each paper or subject. Others will need drill for spelling. Some need help to prepare materials for study, and some will want to be quizzed before tests.

- You *can* help with work from school. You can have your child read words lists or other materials suggested by the teacher or tutor. Such practice should be with material that has already been taught. Review and reinforcement at home are important.

- As you help with homework, provide drill, and supervise studying for tests, teach your child the principles of how to do the tasks on his or her own.
- If your child is reading text for meaning and does not know a word, do not encourage him or her to "sound out" the word. Taking time to do this interferes with the train of thought. Tell the child the word. (Reading text—phrases, sentences, or longer units—is different from reading new words that have just been taught and that are presented on cards or lists. For reading new single words, have the child try to read each word.)
- If your child is engaged in writing a sentence or paragraph and asks for help spelling a word, tell him or her how to spell the word. The goal here is to encourage the flow of writing to convey ideas.
- Consider providing a small spelling device that can be carried in a notebook so spelling can be checked when needed. (There are a number of electronic spelling aids on the market.)

Helping with Organization

- If your child has problems with organization of papers, notebooks, backpacks, desks, or rooms, provide step-by-step instructions for organization. Many children and teenagers may not know where to start. A plan for young children can use pictures, and for older children, printed directions.
- The last thing before preparing for bed, have your child place all clothes and supplies needed for the next day in a specific place, the same place each time, to aid in remembering. Materials needed for school can be put right in front of the door the child will be using in the morning, so that unless they are picked up they will cause him or her to fall over them.
- After a period of reminding your child, write a list that he or she can check off each night. This will help toward independent remembering and is not such a big jump from being reminded by the parents to accomplishing the task totally alone.
- Hold regular clean-out sessions for backpacks and notebooks.
- Help organize notebooks, and periodically check them with your child. Buying them and providing covers, paper, and stickers are not enough. Provide assistance so that notebooks are organized, useful, and contain current and appropriate material.
- Consider the use of color-coded dividers in notebooks or different colored notebooks. One color could be used for reading/language, another color for math, etc.

- You may need to work out a plan with your child and his or her teacher to be sure assignments reach home, are completed, and returned to school on time.
- Help plan long-term assignments. Use a large wall calendar with due dates of projects starred in color. Then help your child plan what must be accomplished each week. Write on the calendar what will be completed by the end of each week or even each day. This kind of organizational assistance may be needed for a long time.
- If you as a parent are disorganized, try to change just one thing you do, and let your child see you are trying to change. Use a grocery list, keep a list of what is needed from the market, or list chores you hope to accomplish. Place the materials you need to take to work with you or need to complete first thing in the morning in a certain place, so you can be reminded as well. If you are disorganized, you cannot expect your child to be different.
- Give your child choices about time to do homework and what homework should be done first. List what has to be done, but allow the order of the tasks to be decided. Everyone needs a break. Immediately on returning home from school may not be the best time to do homework for some students, while others prefer this time so it will be finished and they will have time for play or television.

Stimulating Language and Learning

- Talk with your child. Use time in the car for conversation. Try to have dinner together and use this time for talk. Discuss issues. Exchange ideas. Ask for opinions. Conversation is a way to share information, to question, to expand ideas, to summarize, to clarify, and to know what other family members are thinking and doing.
- As enriching experiences are provided, talk about them—what will be seen, what is being seen, what was seen. Expect responses that can be words or actions or just a nod that they are attending to what you are saying.
- Television will not go away. Make it an active time. Talk about the program you are watching. During commercials, ask what will happen next. Ask how the child or adolescent would feel in the same situation. Would he or she have solved the problem differently? Any humor, apart from slapstick, is likely to have some idea or lesson, even if it is only why an action or event is regarded as funny.
- It is important to monitor television programs your child watches. Young children should not be exposed to horror stories or programs with an emphasis on violence. Such exposure can cause bad dreams or frighten them in ways they are reluctant to reveal.

- Read aloud to both young and older children. Such reading develops their concepts and vocabulary until they can read independently. Reading aloud keeps alive the notion that books have value and that it is worth struggling to learn to read, because the rewards are great. Reading aloud as a family can create lasting memories and may develop a life-long interest in literature.

- If your child can read at all, encourage him or her to read—cereal boxes, labels on cans, captions under pictures, logos, street signs, comic books, magazines, or easy books. Any reading reinforces and makes reading better.

- Be aware of your child's knowing, or not knowing words in oral vocabulary. Encourage learning and using words appropriate to your home and culture. Often, learning disabled children are not able to profit from incidental learning in the same way as children free from learning problems. What is to be learned needs to be made explicit. Talk about new, unusual, or hard words.

- Read to your dyslexic child whatever his or her age, not only textbooks and school assignments but also literature or popular fiction. This teaches the magic of the printed word, keeps interest high, and can encourage your child to stay with the difficult task of learning to read. Adults with reading disabilities may have weak vocabularies, because they are not learning new words from print. Word meanings can be acquired by hearing material read aloud. There is no magic time when students can handle lengthy reading assignments alone. Your child may need to have readers throughout his or her school career to cover the required volume of material.

- If given money and encouraged to see if change is correct when buying comic books or school clothes, your child can learn in a practical way about money. He or she needs to understand that money is necessary, that credit cards must be paid.

- Different kinds of studying are necessary for different kinds of tests. Provide help in studying for tests in the way they will be tested. This also prepares him or her in multiple ways to study independently.

- If your child's spelling tests are in written form, home practice should be writing from dictation.

- If your child has word retrieval problems, then or she must practice learning specific single words—new vocabulary for science, social studies, or English (parts of plants, generals who led troops, dates of particular historical events, authors, titles of books). Have the child write the word to be learned on one side of an index card and the definition (phrase or sentence) on the other. He or she should read the single word and try to say the definition on the other side of the card, then reverse the process—read the definition and practice recalling the single word. Instead of using separate index cards for each word, the student could fold a piece of paper and list the single words on one column (one side of the fold) with the definitions on the other.

- If your child is to take an essay test, have him or her plan how responses to various topics could be organized and written.

Chores

- Have your child help with chores. Talk while doing them. Classification and categorization can be learned by sorting and putting away groceries or separating laundry. Engaging in such activities with your child can promote communication.
- Helping with chores at home is a way to practice math. Young children can practice beginning addition and subtraction while setting the table. Cooking teaches fractions. The idea of different shapes containing equal amounts can be demonstrated with liquid and dry-ingredient measures.
- Expect your children or adolescent with learning disabilities to help with household chores. This allows him or her to develop a sense of confidence as contributing members of the household.

Fostering a Positive Self-Image.

- Encourage your child to be independent and to assume responsibility for his or her actions and the consequences of those actions. Such expectations can be regarded as measures of competence.[2] You are showing respect for your child by requiring him or her to make contributions to the household. For toddlers, this can mean putting toys away, for slightly older children, setting the table for dinner, for school-age children, making beds, emptying trash cans, filling the dishwasher and/or sorting items for recycling, and for teenagers, running errands in the family car and following the rules of driving.
- Help your child learn to make judgments and develop a sense of responsibility at an early age. Then responsibility assumed during adolescence will be greater. He or she will have had practice in making decisions and respecting family rules. Age 16 is not the time to begin setting standards for behavior and safety.
- Discuss problem solving with your child at a young age. If you need a new appliance, talk about it. If you are buying a new car, discuss types. If a home improvement project is being considered, discuss steps of deciding how to solve it, what materials will be needed, what materials you already have, what stores have the materials needed, who should be hired to accomplish the job, or how much time will be required if you are doing the job yourself. As soon as you feel it is appropriate, talk

about the cost of home items including groceries, utilities, and so forth. Many teenagers and college students have no idea about the cost of daily living.

- Stress that contributions can be made in ways other than being successful in school. Doing chores and having family responsibilities on a regular basis as a contributing and valued family member are important.

- Your adult friends and co-workers provide examples of the value of activities and successes apart from schoolwork. From a young age and continuing through adolescence, youngsters should have an opportunity to know what is involved in various work experiences, what is required on a day-to-day basis. Often college students decide to major in areas about which they know nothing.

- Successes in leisure activities are important and can relate to life goals. Trying out many different leisure activities can open worlds that your child or adolescent may never have considered.

- Reinforce, or search for, things your child or adolescent is good at—sports, art, dramatics, cooking, being a good friend, helping in important ways at home, recycling, serving as a community volunteer, working with elderly people—so that he or she can know he or she is making a contribution. What you praise must be real even for the youngest child. Children are savvy and know when adults are being phony.

- Everyone needs to have pleasurable leisure time activities—some to be carried out with others and some to be enjoyed alone. Each individual has some area in which he or she is interested or can develop an interest. Every child should be good, and can be good, at something.

- Recognize that children and adolescents may feel bad about themselves as learners. They may feel bad even if they deny it.

- Do not be afraid that your child or adolescent will find out that he or she has a learning disability or a learning difference. They already know it. They have the direct experience of not measuring up in school or in the family. Sometimes knowing that there is a problem that has a name can relieve long-term unexplained anxiety.

- Parents teach all the time—by example in the work they do, in activities they choose for leisure time, how they acquire information, how they treat family members and those outside the family.

Helping Children Understand

- Children and adolescents must understand the nature of their learning disability. Your child needs to know that some of us are naturally adept in some areas, while others have to work hard to accomplish the same things. Provide comparisons for him or her regarding different talents that people have. Point out that adults contribute to society in different ways. We need professionals in education, medicine, and law, but our lives are also enriched enormously by artists, musicians, poets, and athletes. We need builders, but we also need dreamers. We need those who help us think, but also those who help us play.

- Help your child or adolescent understand his or her learning problem. Be descriptive as in "You have a specific problem with remembering how words look, making it difficult to remember how to spell them."
- Do not talk about brain function or dysfunction until your child is ready to fully understand how the brain is responsible for many things in human behavior, including talents, what we do well, and what we do poorly. Many children and adolescents hold on to images of "a defective brain" or "a hole in the head."
- Assure your child that there are other people with similar problems. Share appropriate books or literature.
- Read to them, or encourage them to read fiction about children and teens with learning disabilities. (A list of such books is included in the references.)
- Be consistent with rules and follow through with consequences. Do not make rules you do not intend to have followed.
- At every age foster curiosity.
- Help children and adolescents "notice" perceptual attributes, concepts, ideas, others' feelings, how things fit together, how seemingly unusual customs, behaviors, ideas relate to their own lives.
- Help your child understand that success in anything, including learning, when one is learning disabled, requires commitment and hard work. In early school years, parents can prod children to try, to do homework, to participate in tutoring sessions. However, as students reach middle school age or a bit older, they need to be willing to be an active part of the learning situation. As young adults, they may decide they have had enough schooling, tutoring, or help from home. They may seek independence, and this is admirable. The push toward independence in a child means that the parents have raised them well. But as older teens or young adults, they need to know that they can return to school later, that they can have tutoring later, and that they can seek help from parents or other adults when they are adults themselves.
- Community college is often a good choice for struggling students. Students will have role models in other young and older adults who are serious about school. At the same time they may take a reduced case load. They can learn that they are in control of their learning and their

studying. Many community colleges also have learning centers to assist students who need some support.

- Set reasonable goals and expectations. Just because you may have reached personal goals, do not expect your child will have the same goals for education or work.
- If you have had similar learning problems, discuss them with your child. Let your child know you understand the struggle and discouragement he or she feels. If you do not understand, think of a task that is impossible for you (climbing a mountain, designing a building, becoming an expert at tennis, preparing an exquisite dinner) and visualize yourself learning to do that task.
- From an early age, let your child see how you use reading for information, pleasure, and entertainment—instructions to program a VCR, a recipe for a favorite food, information about a new interest or world event.
- Help your child gain a realistic understanding about finances. A job in a fast-food restaurant is adequate for a teenager's spending money, but it is not adequate for rent, food, clothes, or caring for another. The pay is inadequate for independent living.
- Help your child or adolescent understand that the better his or her skills, the greater are his or her options for the future.

Family Leisure Time

- Spend time alone with each child engaging in an activity of mutual enjoyment. Busy work schedules make this difficult, but it is worth it for your child's development. Such interactions also provide joy to parents. This time needs to be apart from time spent on homework. So often children and adolescents with learning disabilities have the idea that the only things that matter to their parents are related to school.
- Do not overschedule your children. Allow free time and help him or her plan its use. Organization of free time requires practice.
- Games can help with tasks related to school. It is not necessary to spend a lot of money on "educational games." Games should be fun and children learn from ordinary games. Board games and card games teach children to learn to wait, to learn rules, to take turns, to ask questions, to make predictions, to develop strategies, to accept losing, to manage winning, and generally to develop mastery.
- Expose children to a wide variety of games and activities so that they can choose those at which they would like to excel. Physical activity, sports, board games, and books need to be emphasized, as well as computer games.

- It is particularly important for bright children with learning disabilities to learn games and activities at which they can interact with other children in age-appropriate ways. There can be a tendency for some children to become overly involved with computer games or fantasy activities that result in an isolation from others that is unhealthy for social-emotional growth.

Developing Interpersonal Communication

- Help children and adolescents learn social rules of the household, of games, of school, of peers, and of the community in the same way that they have learned rules of phonics, grammar, or math. Children may not pick up incidental social cues and may need help with the proper way to act with friends and strangers. If necessary, practice what to say or use role playing. This makes some children uncomfortable but is welcomed by others.
- Teach good manners and the reasons for such rules. This helps children learn to interact appropriately with peers and adults. It also helps them begin to understand how what they do and say has an impact on others. It may encourage them to think consciously about how their actions can affect others, often in ways they do not intend.

Additional Professional Consultations

- If your child has problems with attention or concentration, medical assessment is often necessary. It is helpful for the physician to have documentation of the times and circumstances of difficulty with attention. If the attentional problems occur when the task is difficult, then a change in task expectation may be necessary. If attention cannot be focused, even when the child is engaged in something that is enjoyed, a different kind of intervention may be used. Some physicians will send checklists to the parents and school to aid in observation of attention, concentration, and activity level. Contrary to popular belief, children and adolescents who have attention deficit disorder do not have attentional difficulties all the time. Those who have attention deficit hyperactivity disorder are not hyperactive all the time.
- At the time of an initial evaluation and throughout the intervention process, ask questions so that you understand the nature of your child's learning disability. Parents have a right to know how the problem will affect their child in the classroom, at home, and in the community.
- From the time of the initial evaluation, it is essential that both parents are involved. Both parents need to understand the problem and support intervention efforts. Supervising homework and helping study for tests should be shared by the parents.

- Many separated and divorced families are able to be jointly involved in diagnostic and treatment processes. Both parents, if at all involved in their child's life, need to understand the nature of the learning problems, reasons for tutoring, and the necessity to help with studying.
- In single-parent families, others in the support network may need to be included, such as another adult living in the home, a grandparent who provides care, or a baby-sitter.
- If parents work, they should request that professionals provide interpretation of test results during evening hours.
- Translations of professional jargon may be necessary. It is a sign of intelligence and sophistication to say you do not understand. Terms are used differently by different professionals. For a term or word to have communicative value, it must have shared meaning.
- Remember that each professional has a value system, just as does each parent. Find out what these values (attitudes or prejudices) are when they might influence your child. Values include, for example, attitudes toward private versus public education, commitment to one kind of intervention approach, and belief or total opposition to use of medication.

Records and Memorabilia

- Keep records. Do not ever give your only copy of a report to a professional. You should keep a file with your own copies.
- Keep samples of your child's work, at least one sample from each year, maybe one to show the best and one to show the poorest performance. Such samples show schoolwork over a period of time. They can also document long-term strengths and weaknesses when your child is an adult. As I see adults who were never identified as having learning disabilities and even those who were diagnosed early, it is helpful to have these early documentations of problems. Memory of events is subjective.

Selecting a Tutor

- Be clear about what you expect from a tutor. Tutorials represent a way of teaching and do not necessarily mean that the student has any trouble with learning.
- Some tutoring means a one-to-one interaction between a teacher and a student in study of any subject.
- Another kind of tutoring is to help a student pass a course—foreign language, algebra, or English, for instance. The qualifications of tutors vary and the tutor can be a professional, a peer, or an advanced student a bit older than the one being tutored. Such tutors generally know the subject matter but may not know how to teach basic skills. Learning disabled

students may require such tutoring from time to time throughout their education, even while receiving remedial services designed to improve the underlying reading or other disability.

- It is helpful to have a child tested before selecting a tutor or a remedial program. School years for children pass quickly. It is not unusual to see teenagers whose parents report concerns from the student's first grade, but help was never sought because the parents thought each year might be better. Instead, a crisis is reached when the student refuses to go to school or fails all classes. Learning disabilities, including reading failure, seldom disappear without specific help.

- The kind of tutoring that I refer to throughout this book is the teaching of basic skills, such as how to decode words or understand text. This is done by highly skilled and specially educated persons. Such tutoring is often lengthy and must be provided until skills are learned. If 6-year-old children have tutoring to learn to read, they do not have a lot of time or material to make up. They are also less likely to carry the emotional baggage that comes with being a reading failure. In contrast, teenagers with limited decoding or comprehension skills not only have to learn systematically about how print represents speech, but they are likely to have missed out on both vocabulary and general information, because they have not added to their knowledge base through reading. Many learning disabled students need tutoring for basic skills and general tutoring to help them through the school years.

- Rather than using time from the specialized tutor to work on homework, studying for tests, and getting through the year's coursework, a homework helper can be used. Such a helper can be an advanced and sensitive high school or college student.

- Individual specialized private tutoring is not inexpensive. If you plan for your child to attend college and have a fund established, you may want to use these funds to have specialized, high-quality special tutoring or remediation. Without good basic skills, the student is unlikely to attend college. Appropriate special teaching for decoding so the reader can read almost any word in print is economical in the long term. I find older teenagers, who never had the precise, intense work with decoding long words, discouraging. Their ability to manage long words remains deficient so they cannot handle texts they need or wish to read. Even if such specialized tutoring or special teaching is more expensive than the nice lady down the street helping after school, it may be worth a financial sacrifice.

- When selecting a private tutor, look for flexibility and sensitivity as well as good professional qualifications.

- Ask a prospective tutor if the diagnostic report and recommendations make sense and if he or she is comfortable with implementing the recommendations.

- Parents and students both need to have some sense of how the tutor plans to work. The tutor should be able to provide a plan.
- The goals of tutoring or remediation must be explicit for the parents and student. They should be stated clearly and at the level of maturity and understanding of the student.
- The tutor or teacher needs to provide some indication of how progress will be judged.
- Qualifications of a tutor or teacher need to be clear. Special teachers need education to qualify for specialized tutoring. A consumer will wish to know if a tutor has been taught to use a special approach. If a tutor has training, it must be clear what the training is—attending a lecture, taking a one-day course, or taking a course in undergraduate or graduate school, with some teaching practice done under supervision.
- Private tutors may be willing to provide names of students who have been tutored or give other sources of reference.
- Characteristics such as confidence, warmth, professionalism, and organization are important in special teachers. There is a chemistry in all human relationships that involves subjective reactions and judgments. Those that work include a mutual respect between tutor and learner. A tutor or special teacher also needs to display qualities that mesh with parent's values and desires.
- Next to professional qualifications, the most important quality of a tutor or special teacher is that he or she relates well to the student being tutored. Several sessions may be necessary to know if the relationship is satisfactory. If the child expresses discomfort and does not wish to attend most of the time, parents need to speak with the tutor. If children of any age complain about a tutor, ask them to be specific. "I just don't want to go" or "It's not helping" are not good reasons for discontinuing.
- When students are in public school programs, parents cannot choose the special teacher. Some children and adolescents strongly object to being pulled out of classrooms for special assistance. If children are bothered by this, the issue needs to be dealt with at school. All students need to respect others who differ in learning. (Having special teachers work with students in the classroom as opposed to pull-out programs will not provide the best services to students with significant learning disabilities, in my opinion.)
- Breaks from special education or tutoring are sometimes necessary. The early identified learning disabled child may need time off from tutoring or summer school.

- Some students, at certain stages of skill development, may profit enormously from summer school or intensive tutoring over a summer.

How to Judge Progress

- Parents of children with problems may find it helpful to think in 2-month chunks of time. For example, if a child hates reading and refuses to do the work and a program of support from school or outside school is offered, in about 2 months there should be something positive noted, such as the child's being more willing to try or having some sense of accomplishment. Changes in reading in the classroom will not necessarily be seen quickly. Older students will have more to make up, not only in learning to read but also in acquiring vocabulary, reading to learn and retain information, and becoming familiar with vocabulary and literature that their peers with good reading have mastered.
- Monitor your child's progress. With special help there should be improvement. If not, the teacher or tutor should be questioned. An alternative approach may be necessary. Discuss goals and approximate times they will be accomplished with the teacher or tutor.
- Serve as your child's advocates. This means that you must be clear about the nature of the problem. All terminology used to discuss learning disabilities can be understood by parents. You should not feel that you do not or cannot understand because learning disabilities is not your field or that you are not educated enough to understand. The most competent and caring professional does not have the interest of your child or adolescent at heart as much as you do.
- Conversely, any intervention must be in place long enough to determine if it is making a difference. This is why the selection of competent individuals is so important. Parents often seem to grasp at straws, trying anything that is suggested by other parents or people they meet at parties or at work, see on television talk shows, or who appear in commercials. This often ends up being very costly with limited results. Changing patterns of learning or behavior does not happen quickly. It is often slow and steady rather than quick and dramatic.
- It is important that special services are not discontinued too soon. Any new skill we learn must be practiced under supervision until it becomes a part of us and can be put into use automatically.

Consideration of Other Family Members

- Consider the rest of the family when making decisions about the learning disabled member as far as financial issues, choice of schools, and parental time spent with each child are concerned. The nonlearning disabled child or children can develop quite serious problems in an attempt to gain some of the attention focused on the child with the learning problem.

- Evaluate and plan for time available if both parents are working. Spend time with the child with a learning problem and also with your children who may not have learning disabilities.
- Plan for time alone, without the children.
- Learn the nature of the teaching approach being used so questions from the child can be answered appropriately and so that supervision of homework can be meaningful.
- Establish a family goal of learning new words or trying new tasks. Children of various ages can participate in categorizing or classifying (clean laundry, contents of grocery bags to freezer or shelf, flatware container from dishwasher into drawers). Name new or familiar vegetables or other foods being served.
- Encourage children and teenagers to keep diaries or journals that are not to be corrected. Young children can draw a picture and write one word or one sentence. Older children can write ideas, thoughts, and feelings. The whole family may take 5 or 10 minutes a day writing in their personal journals. Before the writing is begun, decide if the journals are personal or if they are to be shared with others (family members, grandparents, a teacher).
- Some learning disabled children and adolescents are willing to keep summer journals or diaries. Free from demands of school, they can write for 10 minutes each day. Again decide if the journals are personal or communal.

ESPECIALLY FOR TEACHERS

- Do not scold a child with attention deficit hyperactivity disorder for moving around a lot or for not paying attention.
- Do help the child develop ways to wait, to increase the time of sitting still, and do provide frequent breaks to walk around if needed.
- Help students become advocates for themselves and to develop ways to ask questions and to stand up for themselves without being rude to adults or peers.
- Understand the impact of the learning disability. An auditory memory problem affects everything that is presented orally. An oral language comprehension problem affects learning new vocabulary in any subject as well as for reading comprehension. A reading problem affects reading in reading class but also printed instructions, word problems in math, texts in science, social studies, and novels.
- Consider making allowances for the learning disability in requirements for extracurricular activities during middle and secondary school. Sometimes

this is the only place the teenager can shine. However, realistic time limits must be respected. If school teams take too much time, community recreation teams or coaching younger children may be alternatives.

- Try to establish a school program that is likely to allow the student to meet with some success.
- Provide opportunities within the school setting for students to show areas of strength. If they or the family have unusual interests or travels, permit oral reporting to the class. Children and adolescents must be able to see that their strengths have value for education and for later life.
- Help them develop skills of self-appraisal to recognize successes as well as disappointing outcomes.
- Help students appreciate that much of what must be done can be tedious. Everything cannot be fun.
- Help relate new learning to what is already known.
- Within tutoring hour or special education time, let the student choose the order of tasks. A certain number of things must be done, but the student can decide what to do first.
- Allow extended time, without penalty, for in-class assignments and for tests, if needed.
- Offer help when students are observed to need it. Learning disabled or troubled students are embarrassed or shy about saying they need help.
- Consider students' feelings when they ask questions. They may feel that teachers belittle them in responding to what they ask. They may misinterpret what is said as insulting because of a language comprehension difficulty.
- If they do ask questions, or have missed a concept, it is helpful to have it explained in a different way.
- Use visual aids for teaching.
- Avoid pale purple dittos or light gray photocopies. Visual materials must be clear and easily interpreted for all students, but especially for those with learning disabilities.
- If assignments and tests are handwritten, care must be taken that the material is legible. Students with reading disabilities may take a long time to learn to read the cursive writing of others. Printing is better. Typed copy is best.
- Assignments must be clear when given. Presenting them in writing is best.
- Overview statements and summary statements are helpful.
- Teach for mastery.
- Do not assume that because it has been presented, it has been learned. Many more repetitions and much more practice may be necessary for the student with a learning disability to achieve mastery.

- Do not assume readiness. Age alone does not make a student ready to begin to read, to write an essay, to manage an abstract idea.
- Provide encouragement and support for efforts made even if the product does not meet your expectations.
- Reduce length of assignments to manageable portions—a row of addition problems, five spelling words, only one sentence read aloud with a parent reading the rest of a page. These reductions should be made only as long as they are needed.
- Provide a structure or plan for long-term assignments.
- Some of the time, accept projects rather than always requiring written work.
- If performance on a test is very poor, consider giving the test orally and averaging the grades.
- With learning disabilities, ADHD, and/or emotional difficulties there is no specific age when we can expect the student's memory and organizational skills to be good. They need assistance until they can function independently.
- A contract among school, student, and parents, so that all are in agreement about what has to be done, is often useful.
- The learning disabled student should take notes to improve note-taking skills but should have access to good notes for studying. A good student could be asked to take notes on carbon or NCR paper.
- Assign a homework buddy. This person can help with homework if needed or just be available to check with about what the assignment is.
- It is important that peer assistants be chosen by a teacher or other adult authority and that they agree to this important and confidential job.
- The use of a homework sheet can be helpful to some students. The student writes the assignment on a sheet, and it is initialed by the teacher, taken home, and then initialed by the parent before and after the assignment is completed.
- Learning disabled students should always have a special place to write assignments (separate notebook, section of one notebook).
- Encourage students to use one notebook.
- Students must realize that late assignments are not acceptable.
- Be willing to consider giving separate grades for content and style in written work.
- When students have a learning disability in spelling, points should not be taken off on tests in subjects such as social studies and science. If you feel that correct spelling is essential, perhaps you could give separate grades for correct answers and for spelling.
- Permit use of a calculator for math.
- Give students permission to take formulas to math class. They can then be tested on application rather than memory.

- Help students understand that questions can have multiple answers.
- Help them develop alternative ways to approach problems.
- Help them understand that there are no dumb questions.
- Foster curiosity.
- Encourage them to notice things, to become good observers of things in nature, feelings of others, etc.
- Help them appreciate the purpose of rules.
- Allow opportunities for extra credit, if possible. This can make up for a lower test grade.
- Encourage students to keep up with review of notes from class and with chapters to be read, dividing long-term assignments into smaller segments.
- Help them plan realistically for how much time it will take to read a chapter, a short story, a novel and how much time it will take at the library, and to write.
- Everyone needs scheduled breaks during study time. Some need frequent short breaks. Others would rather work for an hour or longer and then take a longer break.
- Discourage the practice of waiting until the last minute to study for a test or write a paper. Good students may get away with this. Students with even mild learning disabilities need to plan.
- Teach the concept of rewriting, but to make it better not because the original is wrong. Suggest that the student put a paper aside and edit it the following day.
- If you are writing a letter or report that can be shared with students, have them help you. Let them see you make small word changes, select a stronger verb, a different adjective, move around a sentence part.
- If students want to use tape recorders, be sure their auditory memory is good enough to support this effort. It will take as much time to listen to the tape as the class takes. Is this efficient?
- It is invaluable when you understand the impact of learning problems on the subject you teach. This becomes particularly important in the middle and secondary levels when the student has a number of teachers.
- Consider giving separate grades for content, style of writing, spelling, grammar usage, capitalization, and punctuation on written assignments.
- Visual aids, such as writing on the board or presenting transparencies or handouts, are useful. Students beyond the high school level may be able to choose courses taught by instructors who use visual aids.
- Be careful in demanding rewriting for neatness. This may be too great a burden if there was a struggle for the first copy. Rewriting could be done on another day.
- Children or adolescents may need help with proofreading. They may not be able to detect errors on their own. Do not correct mistakes, but

point out the paragraph or line with the error, and see if the student can find the error on his or her own.

- It is important to reinforce activities that the student does well so that even the poorest student can experience getting "high marks" in some school class or activity.

ESPECIALLY FOR OLDER STUDENTS

The following are recommendations that can help during college years and also in graduate school. They may also be used by middle and secondary students with some supervision.

General

- Request services from the school learning center
  —for assistance in getting extended time for tests and in-class assignments,
  —for assistance with selection of instructors who
    —are empathic with students who have learning disabilities;
    —provide detailed course outlines;
    —use visual aids or write on the board; and
    —would consider alternative test procedures.
  —for direct tutoring that may be available.
  —for assistance in acquiring Books on Tape to help with courses having a lot of reading.
- Plan your class schedule so that you do not take a heavy load of courses requiring a lot of reading in one semester.
- Request extended time for tests and in-class assignments when needed.
- Always go to class. Do not miss class.
- Always turn in assignments on time. This is one way of letting teachers know you care about the class.
- Always do extra credit work if it is possible. This can help make up for a lower test grade.
- Keep up with reviewing notes from class, reading chapters, dividing long-term assignments into smaller segments. Do not let yourself get far behind, or you may feel overwhelmed and become immobilized.
- Remember, If you have difficulty with any part of the learning process you cannot cram for a test or write a paper at the last minute. Good students may get away with this. Students with even mild learning disabilities need to plan ahead.
- Because you take a longer time to formulate ideas it will be helpful for you to write a draft of a paper and come back to it the following day to edit it.

- If you take a tape recorder to class, remember that it will take as much time to listen to it as the class takes. You may be better off taping the class but taking notes at the same time. You can use the tape if you need to check something.
- If you are doing poorly in a course and starting to feel overwhelmed and if you have been getting help from the school learning center and have asked for clarification from the instructor, but continue to feel that a course is too burdensome and is interfering with studying for other courses, drop the course.
  —Be sure to determine before you make such a decision if, when you drop the course, you will still be a full-time student and can live in campus housing.
  —Make the decision about dropping the course when you can still get a refund rather than waiting until late in the quarter or semester when you have failed several tests.
  —Dropping a course early will not reflect a failure on your transcript and will not lower your grade point average.
  —Be sure to read your college catalogue carefully and be sure you understand your school's regulations about dropping courses and maintaining full-time student status.

Word Retrieval

- If you have a word retrieval problem, you will need to study differently for objective tests than for essay tests. For example, in studying definitions, a word should be put on one side of an index card and the definition on the other. The word should be read and the definition retrieved from memory, but you should also practice reading the definition and retrieving the specific word. The same procedure applies for studying battles and their dates, persons and their contributions, etc. Such studying, both from specific to broad concept and from broad concept to specific is essential for students with word-finding problems.
- If you cannot recall an answer to a homework or test item, skip over it and come back to it later. Mark the item in such a way that it is not forgotten so it can be worked on later.

Taking Notes

- Read the chapter or section to be discussed in class, before class. In that way you will have an idea of what to anticipate and will be able to take better, more useful notes.
- Take notes on one side of the paper only. For example, take notes on the left-hand page. Summarize notes after class on the right-hand page. The rewriting can help organize thinking and aid memory. During class, mark

a place in your notes if you do not understand a concept that has been presented. After class, check with another student or with the instructor.

- Underline or highlight important points in your notes.
- Organize notes in the way that questions might be asked on tests.
- Develop and organize notes as possible responses to test questions.
- Integrate readings from text with notes from class.
- Pay attention to the kinds of questions the teacher uses to stimulate discussion in class. If such questions are asked in one instance, they are likely to be asked in another, for example, on a test.
- Have a clear understanding of how study must differ for an essay test from an objective one.
- Try to choose instructors who make liberal use of such visual aids as writing on the board or using transparencies.

Reading Texts

- Regard reading as an active process. Think about what has just been read, reformulate it, and write notes on it. Just "reading" without regarding it as an active process results in reaching he bottom of a page and not having really read anything.
- We study (read) a short story or novel differently from a chapter in social studies. In both areas, there needs to be some grounding in what you expect from what is to be read. Active participation while reading is essential. This is something that able students seem to do automatically without even being aware of their own organizational plans, but students who do less well need assistance. Some preparation must be done before we begin to read. In reading a short story or novel, for example, it can be helpful to know:
  —about the author;
  —what kinds of works he or she usually writes;
  —the period in which the story was written;
  —if the story or book is being read by itself or as part of a unit with similar themes;
  —if it is being read because it is regarded as a classic; and
  —if it has relevance for the reader today.
- Develop a structure for reading fiction. You can make a form for an organizational framework with such headings as:
  —setting, including time and place;
  —characters;
  —main plot;
  —sub-plot;
  —conflict;
  —resolution of conflict.

- There is no one right way to prepare material for study. Different preparation is needed for different subjects and for different instructors.
- In social sciences and most other courses, texts are written (usually) in a straightforward way.
  —The beginning of the book has an introductory chapter.
  —The beginning of the chapter has an introductory paragraph.
  —The beginning of a paragraph has an introductory sentence.
- Look at the table of contents to see how a book is organized. Having an idea of the overall plan is helpful.
- Look at the index at the end of the book. Is it by author or subject or both?
- It is important to own the book, not borrow it from a friend or use one from the library.
- Look at study questions at the ends of chapters to guide understanding while reading.
- Pay attention to headings and italics. They suggest important points.
- Some students find it helpful to read aloud. (Choose a place where you will not disturb others.)
- Highlight or underline important points only.
- Write notes in the margins.
- Write summary statements
- When you take notes during reading, often the first sentence in a paragraph is the main idea of the paragraph.
- Sometimes it is best to skim the section first to see what it is about. Then reread it more carefully, taking notes while you read.
- Integrate information from text with information from class.
- Early in a course, determine how long it takes you to read a chapter with full concentration and adequate breaks so you can plan your time wisely.

Essay Tests and Essay Assignments

- Spend time to understand the question fully. Some questions have more than one part.
- Make brief notes of words and phrases you want to include in your answer.
- Questions must be read carefully for such words as: *list, discuss, compare-contrast.*
- The word *who* requires a name of a person in the answer, *why*, a reason.
- Underline key words in the questions.
- Practice with such questions as How did *X* affect *Y*?, What was the influence of *X* on *Y*? How is *X* used?
- Restate the question as part of the answer.
- Take care to stay on the point.

- Answer only the question asked, and take care that the specific question is answered.
- Provide several specific supporting points for every generalization or topic presented.
- Outside information or personal experience should be brought into a question only when asked for.

Other Written Assignments

- Every paragraph, essay question, or paper needs to start with a beginning or opening statement. You cannot merely start writing. Do not worry about being boring. Have the introductory statement say, for example, "I will discuss three reasons why___," "During recent times___," "During the 1970s___" "At the time of the Reformation___," "A lesson learned from___"
- Use transition words between each paragraph and each section. Some transition words can be of help to you. These are referred to as Signal Words and are listed in *The New Reading Teacher's Book of Lists*.[3] Attend to these words when you see them in print. They may help with comprehension. Use them in your writing. They include:
  —continuation signals such as *and, also, another, likewise*;
  —change-of-direction signals such as *although, but, conversely, however*;
  —sequence signals such as *first, second, third*; *A, B, C*; *in the first place, for one thing*;
  —illustration signals such as *for example, specifically, to illustrate*;
  —emphasis signals such as *a major development, it all boils down to, a significant factor*;
  —Cause, condition, or result signals such as *because, so, consequently*;
  —Spatial signals such as *between, on, by, adjacent*;
  —Comparison-contrast signals such as *best, less than, different from, although*;
  —Conclusion signals such as *consequently, finally, in conclusion*;
  —Fuzz signals such as *almost, it looks like, seems like, was reported, probably*; and
  —Nonword emphasis signals that can include: the exclamation point (!), underlining, use of italics or bold type, subheads, paragraph indentations, illustrations, and numbered points.
- For every paragraph, remember to include: a topic sentence, two or three or more supporting sentences, and a concluding statement.
- Think about what you are writing. Are you trying to describe, request, inform, complain, persuade, or amuse?
- Be aware if you are providing facts or expressing your own opinion.
- Once you can write good paragraphs, you can see how a paragraph can

be expanded into an essay by writing a topic paragraph, two or three supporting paragraphs, and a concluding one.

- Creative writing and report writing are different. You have more latitude when writing a story or creative essay. A report follows more rigid rules.
- Some students are helped if they dictate written assignments such as essays, reports, or stories into a tape recorder and transcribe their own words.
- Read aloud what you have written:
  —Does it make sense?
  —Does it say what you want it to say?
  —Is the style maintained? Colloquial language, slang, and street talk should be used only to make a specific point or in dialogue. Otherwise, essays and papers should be written with a more formal style. Formal and colloquial style should not be mixed unless there is a specific purpose for doing so. If in doubt about what is expected for papers for a course, it is best to stay with the more formal.
- Keep a checklist for every writing assignment. Include such items as:
  —Are complete sentences used?
  —Are capital letters present and used correctly?
  —Is punctuation present and used correctly?
  —Is the beginning of the paragraph indented?
  —After indenting the beginning of the paragraph, do the rest of the lines go to the margin?
  —Has the passage been read aloud for errors?
  —Are subjects and verbs in agreement?
  —Are pronoun referents clear?
  —Is there a topic sentence?
  —Are supporting sentences used?
  —Are you sure you do not use the same word or form of a word in the same sentence or paragraph? (It is incorrect to write "As an explanation, I will explain..." or "In this discussion, I will discuss...")
  —Is there a concluding sentence?
  —If what is written is longer than a paragraph, are correct transitions made and transition words used between paragraphs and ideas?
  —If footnotes are required, are they inserted correctly?
  —If a bibliography is required, is it attached?
  —Are all names spelled correctly in the text and in the bibliography?
  —Is the piece free of errors of word usage, misspelling, and run-on sentences ?
  —Is the piece free of other errors noted by instructors in your previous writing?

- Some students have difficulty organizing what they want to write. There are different ways to organize materials. See Chapter 5 for suggestions about organizing material for writing.

ESPECIALLY FOR ADULTS WITH LEARNING DISABILITIES

- Beware of any educational treatment or procedure that promises a cure or states it is always successful.
- Be careful about spending money on any technique, procedure, book, or device that says it will teach or cure.
- Be sure you understand test results. Ask questions until you do understand. If necessary, make another appointment. Part of the consultation about your learning should be that you understand the opinion of the consultant, the terms used, and recommendations made.
- Get a written report from the educational consultant or diagnostician.
- Keep a copy of all reports about your learning disability. Keep them all together in a place where you can easily find them. Banks, post offices, or copy businesses have photocopy machines that you can use to make copies for a small fee.
- Do not be afraid of a label. A label is a name. We name things so we are able to talk about them. Saying someone has a problem of a specific kind should allow everyone involved to discuss the individual and the condition more easily. Labels themselves are not harmful; they are just words. How they are used may be harmful.
- Know that there are others with similar problems. Share appropriate books, literature, or programs as you discover them.
- If you have oral language problems, be aware of the impact on your learning and daily living.
- Do not regard computer spell checkers as solutions to spelling problems. A fair sense of spelling is needed to choose from the array of choices provided. You may need to have someone proofread for errors after you have used the spell checker to assure accuracy.

Organization

Busy people with demanding schedules could not function without their calendars or appointment books. They need organizational plans and some way to aid their memory. There is nothing wrong with individuals whose plans and schedules cannot be kept in their heads. Learning problems should not be used as an excuse for disorganization with the expectation that others should accept it. It is possible to become better organized, if you choose.

- Everyone forgets things when they are concentrating on something else. A person who sews loses scissors in the middle of cutting paper or fabric; a cook misplaces a cap off a spice bottle in the middle of making an elaborate dish; a busy person wanders into a room and forgets why he or she is there. This is normal and is not characteristic of those with learning disabilities alone.

- Always have a special place—a calendar or book—to write assignments, appointments, etc., and use it regularly.
- Keep lists to help remember. Carry around an appointment book with each day marked and lists of what must be remembered for that day. Write things that must be accomplished on a big wall calendar. Or keep lists of things to be done on different colored pads of paper—one color for work and another color for home.
- Organization of time is also important. It is insulting to keep others waiting because you have not judged time well. Wear a watch. Write down how long it takes to get to places you often go. Be on time for social, business, and professional appointments. (You then have a right to expect others to be on time as well.)
- Before retiring, place briefcase, backpack, or supplies needed for the next day in the same place each night. In front of the door is a good place, because you will trip over it on the way out.
- If you have trouble following directions to an office or to someone's house, try using a map or have someone give very specific directions. Many people think they cannot use a map, because they have never tried. If they try, they can use it well. Do not immediately blame yourself if you don't follow directions well. Often people give bad directions.
- When you write the directions to get to a place, write them also for how you return.
- Write thank-you notes to acknowledge nice things people do for you—birthday gifts, condolences, special favors. Having a learning disability is no excuse for rudeness or bad manners.

Problems on the Job

- Get a written report about your learning disability to be shared with a supervisor or boss. Be sure to read it first (or have it read to you) so you know what it says.
- All jobs have requirements that must be met.
- Do you have the skills to meet the requirements for the job? A person with poor auditory memory may not be able to take phone messages. A person with poor reading may not be able to handle a job where reading is required. A person with poor skills in written expressive language cannot write reports.
- Everyone has a right to know why he or she is laid off or fired.

—Was it because of a learning disability or for other reasons?

—If you think you have been discriminated against, there are legal or grievance procedures in most companies or agencies.

Licensing Exams

Be sure you understand the requirements before considering or studying for a job. What are the requirements for entrance into the program of study and what are requirements to practice the job or skill? The following could be considered:

- What skills are necessary as entrance into the program?
- Is a written test required?
- If so, are there modifications possible such as taking the test untimed, with extended time, or having the test read to you?
- If accepted into a training program, how is testing for mastery of the material evaluated?
- Are written exams required?
- Are oral exams permitted?
- Are you tested to get the job or to keep it? Is the test on practical hands-on knowledge, or is it a written test?
- Once the course of study is completed, are written exams necessary for certification or to be licensed to practice? If so, are modifications permitted in taking these exams?
- It is better to know requirements before entering into an endeavor rather than to be disappointed. Certain levels of skills are necessary for anything you choose to do. If you don't have the necessary skills, can you acquire them, or should you consider another area of study? A certain level of reading is needed for some jobs, less for others.
- If a written exam does not relate to the practice of the skill, you can question it. Different states license differently. Some unions for skilled workers are more rigid in the test requirements than are professional schools of law, medicine, or social work. If you regard a test as unfair, it may help to fight to change rules and regulations, but this often takes many years.
- You need to find out in writing what the rules are. There are precedents in many fields where exceptions have been made. Talk to the person in charge. The person who answers the phone in large agencies (such as licensing boards for state government) may be quite rigid in responding, while the supervisor or the person in charge of a program might show some flexibility.

ESPECIALLY FOR THOSE HELPING ADULTS WITH LEARNING DISABILITIES

- Suggest that these adults "notice" perceptual attributes, concepts, ideas, others' feelings, how things fit together, how seemingly unusual cus-

toms, behaviors, ideas relate to their own lives.
- Encourage reading aloud. This can be a family activity of value to all members to gain new information and improve vocabulary.
- Help adults understand that the better the skills, the greater the future options.
- Ask adults' opinions about what they think is wrong with their learning. "Can you tell me why this is hard for you?" They are often astute in describing why they think they are experiencing difficulty.
- Read reports of the assessments.
- Be sure you understand terminology used in reports. New terms are included in reports all the time. They often mean something different from what we would expect.
- Help adults understand areas of strength. Nearly everyone does something at which he or she can excel.
- Help them develop skills of self-appraisal to recognize successes.
- Encourage adults to share some of their concerns with friends or colleagues. They will find many of these people have similar quirks even if they are not learning disabled. If they feel they have no one to talk with, they may need to consider counseling to help them learn to find peers for socialization.

SUMMARY

Children, adolescents, and adults with learning disabilities are special people. They have a full range of learning competencies and flaws, winning ways and annoying quirks. They are infinitely fascinating, often exasperating, and always challenging to teachers and other professionals, to parents, and to others who live with them.

Whatever the financial constraints, we must continue to find ways to teach individuals with learning disabilities. To educate them, we cannot allow only compensations and accommodations for their learning weaknesses. To be kind to them, whatever their handicapping condition, but to refrain from teaching them, is a terrible cruelty. We must help them open the windows of their minds to reveal their intellects—to use their strengths to cope with their deficits. They will reward us beyond measure for our efforts. Thousands of them already have.

NOTES

Chapter 1
1. Gardner 1980, p. 93
2. Piaget 1973
3. Myklebust 1954
4. Erickson 1950/1963
5. Fraiburg 1959
6. Eisenberg, cited in Northern and Downs
7. Eimas, Siqueland, Jusczyk, and Vigorito 1971, pp. 303–06
8. N. Chomsky 1957
9. Pinker 1994
10. Rymer 1993
11. Burka 1983, p. 196
12. de Hirsch, Jansky, and Langford 1966
13. Adams 1990
14. Kavanagh 1986
15. Thomas and Chess 1977
16. Gail Haley in Trelease 1985, p. 14

Chapter 2
1. Kavanagh and Truss, 1988, pp. 550–51
2. See Gardner 1979, and Sacks 1985 for descriptions of individuals after stroke or other neurological problems.
3. Johnson and Myklebust 1967
4. See Geschwind 1984 for a discussion of lack of musical talent in a society where music is a requirement.
5. Wechsler 1989
6. Wechsler 1991
7. Wechsler 1991
8. Gardner 1983
9. W. Johnson 1965

Chapter 3
1. Parker 1962. "My language is me" was the response of an emotionally disturbed young man as he reached the end of his psychotherapy. His therapist had asked him if he would mind if she wrote about their hours together as she learned his own self-developed language so she could communicate with him.
2. Pinker 1994
3. Liberman and Liberman 1990

4. Blachman 1987, 1991
5. Lundberg 1987
6. Brady and Shankweiler 1991
7. Vygotsky 1962, p. 120
8. Maria 1989, describes how to relate unfamiliar experiences to the lives of children.
9. Calfee 1984, also provides teaching suggestions for making seemingly foreign environments and concepts relevant to difficult-to-reach populations.
10. Fry, Fountoukidis, and Polk 1985
11. Pinker 1994, provides a discussion of William's Syndrome where children speak clearly, with good vocabulary and syntax but understand in limited ways.
12. DSM-IV 1994
13. Baratz and Shuy 1969
14. Labov 1972

Chapter 4
1. See Balmuth 1992; Mathews 1966; and Richardson 1990 for historical descriptions of writing systems.
2. Gibson and Levin 1975, p. 557
3. Chall 1983
4. Hall 1993, p. 3
5. Chall 1967
6. Balmuth 1992
7. See Stanovich 1993, who questions using discrepancy formulas with IQ as a measure of writing systems.
8. Liberman 1973
9. Liberman and Liberman 1990
10. Blachman 1987, 1991
11. Lundberg 1987
12. Bell 1986
13. Maria 1990, p. 43
14. Zigmond and Cicci 1968
15. Lindamood 1993
16. Blachman 1990
17. Perspectives 1993

18. Clark 1988
19. Clark and Uhry 1995
20. Rawson 1989
21. Moats 1991, 1995
22. Henry 1990
23. Cicci 1983
24. Mathews 1966, p. 208
25. Carlisle 1989, 1991
26. Maria 1989
27. Fry, Fountoukidis, and Polk 1985

Chapter 5
1. Campbell 1991, p. 90
2. Luria 1975, p. 69
3. Gardner 1980
4. Kellogg and O'Dell 1967
5. Lowenfeld 1957
6. Gesell 1940
7. Beery 1989
8. Bender 1938
9. cited in Gibson and Levin 1975
10. King 1985
11. Molloy 1961
12. King 1985, p. 3
13. Thurber 1988
14. Bryant and Bradley 1980
15. Read 1981, p. 112
16. Bisssex 1980
17. Carlisle 1987
18. Moats 1991; Moats and Smith 1992; Moats 1995
19 Henry 1990
20. Frith 1983
21. Anderson 1992
22. Shaughnessy 1977
23. Rosenthal 1993, p. 12
24. Abeel and Murphy 1994
25. Myklebust 1965
26. Hamill and Larsen 1978
27. Woodcock and Johnson 1989
28. Newcomer and Barenbaum 1993, p. 583
29. King 1985

Chapter 6
1. Ornstein 1972

2. Cantwell and Baker 1987, 1992
3. Beitchman, Hood, Rochon, and Peterson 1989
4. Scahill, Jekel, and Schilling 1991
5. Shaywitz and Shaywitz 1992
6. Silver 1992
7. DSM-IV 1995
8. Barkley 1994
9. Rapoport 1989
10. Pennington 1991
11. Johnson and Myklebust 1967
12. Myklebust 1975
13. Rourke 1994, 1995

14. Benthall and Polhemus
15. Silver and Hagin 1990
16. de Hirsch 1977
17. Kaiser, personal communication
18. Silver and Hagin 1990, p. 253

Chapter 7
1. Recorded Books, Inc., 270 Skipjack Road, Prince Frederick, Maryland 20678
2. Kaiser, personal communication
3. Fry, Fountoukidis, and Polk 1985

BIBLIOGRAPHY

Abeel, S. with watercolors by C. R. Murphy. 1994. *Reach for the Moon*. Duluth MN: Pfeifer-Hamilton Publishers.

Ackerman, P., and Kappelman, M. 1978. *Signals: What Your Child Is Really Telling You*. New York: New American Library, Inc.

Adams, M. J. *Beginning to Read: Thinking and Learning about Print*. 1990. Cambridge MA: MIT Press.

Alley, G., and Deshler, D. 1979. *Teaching the Learning Disabled Adolescent: Strategies and Methods*. Denver, CO: Love Publishing.

American Psychiatric Association: *Diagnostic and Statistical Manual of Mental Disorders*, Fourth Edition. 1994. Washington, DC: American Psychiatric Association

Anderson, C. W. 1992. The Underlining Option. *Their World* 58–59.

Apgar, V., and Beck, J. 1974. *Is My Baby All Right*? New York: Pocket Books.

Badian, N. A. 1994. Preschool prediction: Orthographic and phonologic skills, and reading. *Annals of Dyslexia*. 44:3–25.

Bain, A. M., Bailet, L. L., and Moats, L. C. 1991. *Written Language Disorders: Theory into Practice*. Austin TX: PRO-ED.

Balmuth, M. 1992. *Roots of Phonics*. Timonium MD: York Press.

Baratz, J. C., and Shuy, R. W., eds. 1969. *Teaching Black Children to Read*. Washington, DC: Center for Applied Linguistics.

Barkley, R. A. 1994. The assessment of attention in children. In *Frames of Reference for the Assessment of Learning Disabilities: New Views on Measurement Issues*, ed. G. R. Lyon. Baltimore: Paul H. Brookes Publishing Co.

Barrie, B. 1994. *Adam Zigzag*. New York: Delacorte Press.

Beery, K. E. 1989. The VMI: *The Developmental Test of Visual-Motor Integration*, 3rd Revision. Cleveland: Modern Curriculum Press.

Beitchman, J. H., Hood, J., Rochon, J., and Peterson, M. 1989. Empirical classification of speech/language impairment in children. *Journal of the American Academy of Child and Adolescent Psychiatry*. 28,1:118–23.

Bell, N. 1986. *Visualizing and Verbalizing: For Langauge Comprehension and Thinking*. Paso Robles CA: Academy of Reading Publications.

Bellugi, U. 1971. Some language comprehension tests. In *Training in Early Childhood Education*, ed. C. S. Lavatelli. Published for the ERIC Clearinghouse on Early Childhood Education. University of Illinois Press.

Bender, L. 1938. *A Visual Motor Gestalt Test and Its Clinical Use*. Research Monograph No. 3. New York: The American Orthopsychiatric Association.

Benthall, J., and Polhemus, T. 1975. *The Body as a Medium of Expression*. New York: E. P. Dutton & Co., Inc.

Benton, A. L. 1964. Developmental aphasia and brain damage. *Cortex*. 1:40–52.

Benton, A. L. 1980. Dyslexia: Evolution of a concept. *Bulletin of The Orton Dyslexia Society*. 30:10–26.

Berniger, V.W. 1994. Future directions for research on writing disabilities: Integrating endogenous and exogenous variables. In *Frames of Reference for the Assessment of Learning Disabilities: New Views on Measurement Issues*, ed. G. R.Lyon. Baltimore: Paul H. Brookes Publishing Co.

Betancourt, J. 1993. *My Name is ~~Brain~~ Brian*. New York: Scholastic Inc.

Bissex, G.L. 1980. *GNYS AT WRK: A Child Learns to Write and Read*. Cambridge, MA: Harvard University Press.

Blachman, B. A. 1987. An alternative classroom reading program for learning disabled and other low-achieving children. In *Intimacy with Language*. Baltimore: The Orton Dyslexia Society.

Blachman, B. A. 1991. Getting ready to read: Learning how print maps to speech. In *The Language Continuum: From Infancy to Literacy*, ed. J. F. Kavanagh. Parkton MD: York Press.

Bloom, L., and Lahey, M. 1978. *Language Development and Language Disorders*. New York: John Wiley & Sons.

Boehm, A. E. 1986. *Boehm Test of Basic Concepts-Revised*. (Manual) San Antonio: The Psychological Corporation.

Bos, C. S., and Vaughn, S. 1991. *Strategies for Teaching Students with Learning and Behavior Problems*. Boston: Allyn and Bacon.

Brady, S. A., and Shankweiler, D. P., eds. 1991. *Phonological Processes in Literacy: A Tribute to Isabelle Y. Liberman*. Hillsdale, N.J.: Lawrence Erlbaum Associates.

Brutten, M., Richardson, S. O., and Mangel, C. 1973. *Something's Wrong with My Child: A Parents' Book about Children with Learning Disabilities*. New York: Harcourt Brace Jovanovich, Inc.

Bryant, P. E., and Bradley, L. 1980. Why children sometimes write words which they do not read. In *Cognitive Processes in Spelling*, ed. U. Frith. New York: Academic Press.

Burka, A. 1983. The emotional reality of a learning disability. *Annals of Dyslexia*. 33:289–301.

Calfee, R. 1984. Apply cognitive psychology to educational practice: The mind of the reading teacher. *Annals of Dyslexia.* 34:219–40

Calfee, R. 1988. Beyond decoding: Pictures of expository prose. *Annals of Dyslexia.* 38:243–57.

Campbell, J. with Moyers, B. 1991. The *Power of Myth.* New York: Doubleday, Anchor Books.

Cantwell, D. P., and Baker, L. 1987. *Developmental Speech and Language Disorders.* New York: The Guilford Press

Cantwell, D. P., and Baker, L. 1992. Association between attention deficit-hyperactivity disorder and learning disorders. In *Attention Deficit Disorder Comes of Age: Toward the Twenty-First Century,* eds. S. E. Shaywitz and B. A. Shaywitz. Austin TX: PRO-ED.

Capute, A. J., Accardo, P.J., and Shapiro, B.K. 1994. *Learning Disabilities Spectrum: ADD, ADHD, & LD.* Baltimore: York Press.

Carlisle, J. F. 1987. The use of morphological knowledge in spelling derived forms by learning-disabled and normal students. *Annals of Dyslexia.* 37:90–108.

Carlisle, J. F. 1989. Diagnosing comprehension deficits through listening and reading. *Annals of Dyslexia.* 34:159–76.

Carlisle, J. F. 1991. Language comprehension and text structure. In *The Language Continuum: From Infancy to Literacy,* ed. J. Kavanagh. Parkton, MD: York Press.

Carroll, J. 1976. The nature of the reading process. In *Theoretical Models and Processes of Reading,* eds. H. Singer and R. B. Ruddell. Newark, DE: International Reading Association.

Chall, J. S. 1967. *Learning to Read: The Great Debate.* New York: McGraw Hill

Chall, J. S. 1983. *Stages of Reading Development.* New York: Mc Graw-Hill.

Chomsky, C. 1969. *The Acquisition of Language from Five to Ten.* Cambridge, MA: MIT Press.

Chomsky, N. 1957. *Syntactic Structures.* The Hague: Mouton.

Chomsky, N. 1965. *Aspects of the Theory of Syntax.* Cambridge MA: MIT Press.

Church, J. 1966. *Language and the Discovery of Reality.* New York. Vintage Books. A Division of Random House.

Cicci, R. 1979. Evaluation and treatment of oral language disorders. *Communicative Disorders: An Audio Journal for Continuing Education.* 3,8.

Cicci, R. 1980. Written language disorders. *Bulletin of The Orton Society,* 30:240–51.

Cicci, R. 1983. Disorders of written language. In *Progress in Learning Disabilities, Vol 5,* ed. H. R. Myklebust. New York: Grune & Stratton.

Cicci, R. 1991. Teaching language handicapped children. In *The Language Continuum: From Infancy to Literacy,* ed. J. F. Kavanagh. Parkton, MD: York Press

Claiborne, R. 1983. *Our Marvelous Native Tongue: The Life and Times of the English Language.* New York: Times Books/Random House.

Clark, D. B. 1988. *Dyslexia: Theory & Practice of Remedial Instruction.* Parkton MD: York Press.

Clark, D. B., and Uhry, J. K. 1995. *Dyslexia: Theory & Practice of Remedial Instruction,* 2nd ed. Baltimore: York Press.

Cross, E., Stoner, J., and Anderson, W. 1990. *Essential Roots.* Cambridge MA: Educators Publishing Service.

Damasio, A. R. 1994. *Descartes' Error: Emotion, Reason and the Human Brain*. New York: G. P. Putnam's Sons.

Davis, 1994. *Mother Tongue: How Humans Create Language*. New York: A Birch Lane Press Book/Carol Publishing Group.

de Hirsch, K. 1977. Interaction between the educational therapist and child. *Bulletin of The Orton Society*. 27. (Reprint No. 53) (Also in *Language and the Developing Child*).

de Hirsch, K. 1984. *Language and the Developing Child*. Monograph No. 4. Baltimore: The Orton Dyslexia Society.

de Hirsch, K., Jansky, J., and Langford, W. S. 1966. *Predicting Reading Failure*. New York: Harper and Row.

Denckla, M. B. 1994. Measurement of executive function. *In Frames of Reference for the Assessment of Learning Disabilities: New Views on Measurement Issues*, ed. G. R. Lyon. Baltimore: Paul H. Brookes Publishing Co.

Dickinson, D., and McCabe, A. 1991. The acquisition and development of language: A social interactionist account of language and literacy development. In *The Language Continuum: From Infancy to Literacy*, ed. J. F. Kavanagh. Parkton MD: York Press.

Duane, D. D., and Gray D. B. 1991. *The Reading Brain: The Biological Basis of Dyslexia*. Parkton MD: York Press.

Dwyer, K. M. with photographs by Beirne, B. 1991. *What do You Mean I Have a Learning Disability*. New York NY: Walker and Company.

Eimas, P. D., Siqueland, E. R., Jusczyk, K. P., and Vigorito, J. 1971. Speech Perception in Infants. *Science*. 171: 303–06.

Eisenberg, A. M., and Smith R. R. *Nonverbal Communication*. Indianapolis: The Bobbs-Merrill Company, Inc.

Eisenson, J. 1972. *Aphasia in Children*. New York: Harper and Row.

Erikson, E. 1950/1963. *Childhood and Society*. New York: Norton.

Ferguson, C. A., Menn, L., and Stoel-Gammon, C. 1992. *Phonological Development: Models, Research, Implications*. Timonium MD: York Press.

Fraiburg, S. H. 1959. *The Magic Years: Understanding and Handling the Problems of Early Childhood*. New York: Charles Scribner's Sons.

Frith, U. 1980. *Cognitive Processes in Spelling*. London: Academic Press.

Frith, U. 1983. The similarities and differences between reading and spelling problems. In *Developmental Neuropsychiatry*, ed. M. Rutter. New York: The Guilford Press.

Fry, B. F., Fountoukidis, D. L., and Polk, J. K. 1985. *The New Reading Teacher's Book of Lists*. Englewood Cliffs, NJ: Prentice-Hall.

Galaburda, A. M., ed. 1989. *From Reading to Neurons*. Cambridge MA: A Bradford Book/MIT Press.

Gardner, H. 1979. *The Shattered Mind*. New York: Basic Books.

Gardner, H. 1980. *Artful Scribbles: The Significance of Children's Drawings*. New York: Basic Books.

Gardner, H. 1983. *Frames of Mind: The Theory of Multiple Intelligences*. New York: Basic Books.

Gardner, H. 1993. *Creating Minds: An Anatomy of Creativity Seen Through the Lives of Freud, Picasso, Stravinsky, Eliot, Graham, and Gandhi.* New York: Basic Books.

Gazzaniga, M. S. 1985. *The Social Brain: Discovering the Networks of the Mind.* New York: Basic Books, Inc.

Gehret, J. A with illustrations and design by DePauw, S. A. 1990. *The Don't Give Up Kid and Learning Differences.* Fairport NY: Verbal Images Press

Gelb, I. J. 1963. *A Study of Writing.* Chicago: University of Chicago Press.

Gerber, P. J., and Reiff, H. B. 1991. *Speaking for Themselves: Ethnographic Interviews with Adults with Learning Disabilities.* Ann Arbor: University of Michigan Press.

Geschwind, N. 1984. The brain of a learning-disabled individual. *Annals of Dyslexia.* 34: 319–27.

Gesell, A. 1940. *The First Five Years of Life: A Guide to the Study of the Preschool Child.* New York: Harper & Brothers.

Gibson, E. J., and Levin, H. 1975. *The Psychology of Reading.* Cambridge MA: MIT Press.

Gillingham, A., and Stillman, B.W. 1966. *Remedial Training for Children with Specific Disability in Reading, Spelling, and Penmanship* (7th Edition). Cambridge MA: Educators Publishing Service.

Goldstein, K. 1948. *Language and Language Disturbances.* New York: Grune & Stratton.

Graves, D. H. 1983. *Writing: Teachers & Children at Work.* Portsmouth NH: Heinemann.

Greg, N. 1986. Cohesion: Inter and intra sentence errors. *Journal of Learning Disabilities.* 19,6:338–41.

Greg, N. 1991. Disorders of written expression. In *Written Language Disorders*, eds. A. M. Bain, L. L. Bailet, and L. C. Moats. Austin TX: PRO-ED.

Gundlach, R. A. 1981. On the nature and development of children's writing. In *Writing: The Nature of Development and Teaching of Written Communication.* Vol. 2., *Process, Development and Communication*, eds. C. H. Frederiksen and J. F. Dominic. Hillsdale NJ: Lawrence Erlbaum Associates.

Hall, D. August 1, 1993. The books not read, the lines not written: A poet confronts his mortality. *The New York Times Book Review.*

Hammill, D. D., and Larsen, S.C. 1978. *The Test of Written Language.* Austin: PRO-ED.

Hanna, P. R., Hodges, R. E., and Hanna, J. S. 1971. *Spelling: Structure and Strategies.* Boston: Houghton Mifflin.

Hazel, J. S., and Schumaker, J. B. 1988. Social skills and learning disabilities: Current issues and recommendations for future research. In *Learning Disabilities: Proceedings of the National Conference*, eds. J. F. Kavanagh and T. J. Truss. Parkton MD: York Press.

Heath, S. B. 1983. *Ways with Words: Language, Life, and Work in Communities and Classrooms.* Cambridge: Cambridge University Press.

Hennings, D. G., and Grant, B. M. 1981 *Written Expression in the Language Arts: Ideas and Skills*, 2nd edition New York: Teachers College Press.

Henry, M. K. 1988. Beyond phonics: Integrated decoding and spelling based on word organization and structure. *Annals of Dyslexia.* 38:258–75.

Henry, M. K. 1990. *Words*. Los Gatos, CA: Lex Press.

Henry, M.K., and Redding, N. C. 1990. *Tutor 1, Tutor 2, Tutor 3*. Los Gatos, CA: Lex Press.

Hooper, S. R., Montgomery, J., Swartz, C., Reed, M. S., Sandler, A. D., Levine, M. D., Watson, T. E., and Wasileski, T. 1994. Measurement of Written Language Expression. In *Frames of Reference for the Assessment of Learning Disabilities: New Views on Measurement Issues*, ed. G. R. Lyon. Baltimore: Paul H. Brookes Publishing Co.

Ingersoll, B. 1988. *Your Hyperactive Child: A Parent's Guide to Coping with Attention Deficit Disorder*. New York: Doubleday.

Janover, C. with illustrations by Epstein, E. 1988. *Josh: A Boy with Dyslexia*. Burlington VT: Waterfront Books.

Janover, C. 1995. *The Worst Speller in Jr. High*. Edited by Rosemary Wallner. Minneapolis: Free Spirit Publishing, Inc.

Jansky, J. J. 1975. The marginally ready child. *Bulletin of The Orton Society*. 25:69–85.

Jansky, J. J. 1981. Developmental reading disorders (alexia and dyslexia). In *Comprehensive Textbook of Psychiatry*, 3rd Edition. Vol. 3, eds. H. Kaplan, A. Freedman, and B. Sadock. Baltimore: Williams and Wilkins.

Jansky, J., and de Hirsch, K. 1972. *Preventing Reading Failure*. New York: Harper and Row.

Johnson, D. J. 1985. Using reading and writing to improve oral language skills. *Topics in Language Disorders*. 5,3:55–69.

Johnson, D. J. 1988. Specific developmental disabilities of reading, writing, and mathematics. In *Learning Disabilities: Proceedings of the National Conference*, eds. J. F. Kavanagh and T. J. Truss. Parkton MD: York Press.

Johnson, D. J. 1991. Written language. In *The Language Continuum: From Infancy to Literacy*, ed. J. F. Kavanagh. Parkton, MD: York Press.

Johnson, D. J. 1993. Measurement of listening and speaking. In *Frames of Reference for the Assessment of Learning Disabilities: New Views on Measurement Issues*, ed. G. R. Lyon. Baltimore: Paul H. Brookes Publishing Co.

Johnson, D. J., and Myklebust, H. R. 1967. *Learning Disabilities: Educational Principles and Practices*. New York: Grune & Stratton.

Johnson, D. J., and Blalock, J. W. 1987. *Learning Disabilities: Clinical Studies*. Orlando FL: Grune & Stratton.

Johnson, W. 1965. You can't write writing. In *The Use and Misuse of Language*, ed. S. I. Hayakawa. New York: Premier Books. World Library. 4th Printing.

Kaiser, T. (personal communication)

Katz, J., and Wilde, L. 1985. Auditory perceptual disorders in children. In *Handbook of Clinical Audiology*, third edition, ed. J Katz. Baltimore: Williams and Wilkins.

Kavanagh, J. F., ed. 1986. *Otitis Media and Child Development*. Parkton, MD: York Press.

Kavanagh, J. F., ed. 1991. *The Language Continuum: From Infancy to Literacy*. Parkton MD: York Press.

Kavanagh, J. F., and Truss, T. J. 1988. *Learning Disabilities: Proceedings of the National Conference*. Parkton, MD: York Press.

Kellogg, R. with O'Dell, S. 1967. *The Psychology of Children's Art*. New York: CRM-Random House Publication.

King, D. H. 1985. *Writing Skills for the Adolescent*. Cambridge MA: Educators Publishing Service.

Labov, W. 1972. *Language in the Inner City: Studies in the Black English Vernacular*. Philadelphia: University of Pennsylvania Press.

Larson, V. L., and McKinley, N. L. 1985. General intervention principles with language impaired adolescents. *Topics in Language Disorders*. 5,3:70–77.

Lennenberg, E. H. 1967. *Biological Foundations of Language*. New York: John Wiley & Sons, Inc.

Leong, C. K. 1986. What does accessing a morphemic script tell us about reading and reading disorders in an alphabetic script? *Annals of Dyslexia*. 36:82–102

Leong, C. K. 1987. *Children with Specific Reading Disabilities*. Lisse, The Netherlands: Swets and Zeitlinger.

Levine, M. 1990. *Keeping A Head in School: A Student's Book about Learning Abilities and Learning Disorders*. Cambridge MA: Educators Publishing Service, Inc.

Levine, M. 1993. *All Kinds of Minds: A Young Student's Book about Learning Abilities and Learning Disorders*. 1993. Cambridge MA: Educators Publishing Service, Inc.

Liberman, I. Y. 1973. Segmentation of the spoken word and reading acquisition. *Bulletin of The Orton Society*. 23:65–77.

Liberman, I. Y., and Liberman, A. M. 1990. Whole language vs. code emphasis: Underlying assumptions and their implications for reading instruction. *Annals of Dyslexia*. 40:51–76.

Lindamood, P. C. 1993. Issues in researching the link between phonological awareness, learning disabilities, and spelling. In *Frames of Reference for the Assessment of Learning Disabilities: New Views on Measurement Issues*, ed. G. R. Lyon. Baltimore: Paul H. Brookes Publishing Co.

Litowitz, B. E. 1981. Developmental issues in written language. *Topics in Language Disorders*. 1:73–89.

Little, S. S. 1993. Nonverbal learning disabilities and socioemotional functioning: A review of recent literature. *Journal of Learning Disabilities*. 26,10:653–65.

Lundberg, I. 1987. Phonological awareness facilitates reading and spelling acquisition. In *Intimacy with Language*. Baltimore: The Orton Dyslexia Society.

Luria, A. R. 1975. *The Man with a Shattered World*. Harmondswoth, Middlesex, England: Penguin Books Ltd.

Lyon, G. R., Gray, D. B., Kavanagh, J. F., and Krasnegor, N. A. 1993. *Better Understanding Learning Disabilities: New Views from Research and Their Implications for Education and Public Policies*. Baltimore: Paul H. Brookes Publishing Co.

Lyon, G. R., ed. 1994. *Frames of Reference for the Assessment of Learning Disabilities: New Views on Measurement Issues*. Baltimore: Paul H. Brookes Publishing Co.

McGinnis, M. A. 1963. *Aphasic Children: Identification and Education by the Association Method*. Washington, DC: Alexander Graham Bell Association for the Deaf.

McNeill, D. 1970. The development of language. In *Carmichael's Manual of Child Psychology*, ed. P. H. Mussen. 3rd Edition. New York: John Wiley & Sons, Inc.

Maria, K. 1990. *Reading Comprehension Instructon: Issues & Strategies*. Parkton MD: York Press.

Mather, N. 1991. Computer-assisted instruction. In *Strategies for Teaching Students with Learning and Behavior Problems*, eds. C. S. Bos, and S. Vaughn, Boston: Allyn and Bacon.

Mathews, M. M. 1966. *Teaching to Read: Historically Considered*. Chicago: University of Chicago Press.

Meyer, A., Pisha, B., and Rose, D. 1991. Process and product in writing: Computer as Enabler. In *Written Language Disorders: Theory into Practice*, eds. A. M. Bain, L. L. Bailet, and L. C. Moats. Austin TX: PRO-ED.

Moats, L. C. 1991. Principles of English spelling. In *Written Language Disorders*, eds. A. M. Bain, L. L. Bailet, and L. C. Moats. Austin TX: PRO-ED.

Moats, L. C. 1994. The missing foundation in teacher education: Knowledge of the structure of spoken and written language. *Annals of Dyslexia*. 44:81–102.

Moats, L. C. 1995. *Spelling: Development, Disability, and Instruction*. Baltimore: York Press.

Moats, L. C., and Smith, C. 1992. Derivational morphology: Why it should be included in language assessment and instruction. *Language, Speech, and Hearing Services in Schools*. 23:312–19.

Molloy, J. S. 1961. *Teaching the Retarded Child to Talk*. New York: the John Day Company.

Monroe, M. 1932. *Children Who Cannot Read*. Chicago: University of Chicago Press.

Moss, R. A., with Dunlap, H. D. 1990. *Why Johnny Can't Concentrate: Coping with Attention Deficit Problems*. New York: Bantam Books.

Myklebust, H. R. 1954. *Auditory Disorders*. New York: Grune & Stratton

Myklebust, H. R. 1960. *The Psychology of Deafness*. New York: Grune & Stratton.

Myklebust, H. R. 1965. *Development and Disorders of Written Language, Vol. I. Picture Story Language Test*. New York: Grune & Stratton.

Myklebust, H. R. 1971. Childhood aphasia: An evolving concept. In *Handbook of Speech Pathology and Audiology*, ed. L. Travis. New York: Appleton-Century-Crofts.

Myklebust, H. R. 1975. Nonverbal learning disabilities. Assessment and intervention. In *Progress in Learning Disabilities*, Vol.3., ed. H. R. Myklebust. New York: Grune & Stratton.

Newcomer, P. L., and Barenbaum, E. M. 1991. The written composing ability of children with learning disabilities: A review of the literature from 1980 to 1990. *Journal of Learning Disabilities*. 24,10:578–639.

Northern, J. L., and Downs, M. P. 1991. *Hearing in Children*. Fourth Edition. Baltimore: Williams & Wilkins.

Ornstein, R. E. 1972. *The Psychology of Consciousness*. New York: Viking Press.

Orton, S. T. 1937. *Reading, Writing and Speech Problems in Children*. New York: Norton.

Osman, B. B. 1979. *Learning Disabilities: A Family Affair*. New York: Random House.

Osman, B. B. in association with Blinder, H. 1982. *No One to Play With: The Social Side of Learning Disabilities.* New York: Random House.

Paley, V. G. 1995. *Kwanzaa and Me: A Teacher's Story.* Cambridge MA: Harvard University Press.

Parker, B. 1962. *My Language is Me.* New York: Ballantine Books.

Parnell, M. M. 1995. Characteristics of language-disordered children. In *Human Communication and its Disorders: A Review,* Vol. 4, ed. H. Winitz. Baltimore: York Press.

Pennington, B. F. 1991. *Diagnosing Learning Disorders: A Neuropsychological Framework.* New York: The Guilford Press.

Perspectives. 1993. Through the barricades: Multisensory approaches. 19, 2:7–12.

Phelps-Gunn, R., and Phelps-Terasaki, D. 1982. *Written Language Instruction.* Rockville MD: Aspen.

Phelps-Terasaki, Phelps-Gunn, R., and Stetson, E.G. 1983. *Remediation and Instruction in Language.* Rockville MD: Aspen.

Piaget, J. 1973. *The Child and Reality: Problems of Genetic Psychology.* New York: Grossman Publishers.

Piaget, J., and Inhelder, B. 1969. *The Psychology of the Child.* New York. Basic Books

Pinker, S. 1994. *The Language Instinct: How the Mind Creates Language.* New York: William Morrow and Company, Inc.

Rak, E. T. 1970. *The Spell of Words.* Cambridge MA: Educators Publishing Service.

Rapoport, J. L. 1989. *The Boy Who Couldn't Stop Washing: The Experience and Treatment of Obsessive-Compulsive Disorder.* New York: E. P. Dutton.

Rawson, M. B. 1968. *Developmental Language Disability: Adult Accomplishments of Dyslexic Boys.* Baltimore: Johns Hopkins University Press.

Rawson, M.B. 1989. *The Many Faces of Dyslexia.* Baltimore: The Orton Dyslexia Society.

Rawson, M. B. 1995. *Dyslexia over the Lifespan: A Fifty-Five Year Longitudinal Study.* Cambridge MA: Educators Publishing Service.

Read, C. 1981. Spelling is not the inverse of reading. In *Writing: The Nature of Development and Teaching of Written Communication.* Vol. 2. *Process, Development and Communication,* eds. C. H. Frederiksen, and J. F. Dominic. Hillsdale NJ: Lawrence Erlbaum Associates.

Richardson, E., and DiBenedetto, B. 1991. Acquiring the linguistic code for reading: A model for teaching and learning. In *The Language Continuum: From Infancy to Literacy,* ed. J. F. Kavanagh. Parkton, MD: York Press.

Richardson, S. O. 1989. Specific developmental dyslexia: Retrospective and prospective views. *Annals of Dyslexia.* 34. (Also reprint 115 of The Orton Dyslexia Society.)

Richardson, S. O. 1991. Evolution of approaches to beginning reading and the need for diversification in education. In *All Language and the Creation of Literacy.* Baltimore: The Orton Dyslexia Society.

Rief, S. F. 1993. *How to Reach and Teach ADD/ADHD Children.* West Nyack NY: Center for Applied Research in Education.

Roswell, F. G., and Chall, J. S. 1994. *Creating Successful Readers: A Practical Guide to Testing and Teaching at All Levels.* Chicago: The Riverside Publishing Company.

Rourke, B. P. 1994. Neuropsychological assessment of children with learning disabilities: Measurement issues. In *Frames of Reference for the Assessment of Learning Disabilities: New Views on Measurement Issues*, ed. G. R. Lyon, Baltimore:
Paul H. Brookes Publishing Co.

Rourke, B. P. 1995. Identifying features of the syndrome of nonverbal learning disabilities in children. *Perspectives*. (Newsletter of The Orton Dyslexia Society).
21, 1:10–13.

Ruesch, J., and Kees, W. 1972 (Orig. 1956). *Nonverbal Communication: Notes on the
Visual Perception of Human Relations*. Berkely: University of California Press.

Rymer, R. 1993. *Genie: A Scientific Tragedy*. New York: HarperCollins.

Sacks, O. 1985. *The Man Who Mistook His Wife for a Hat*. New York: Summit
Books/Simon Schuster.

Scahill, L., Jekel, J. F., and Schilling, L. S. 1991. Screening child psychiatric inpatients
for communication disorder: A pilot study. *Archives of Psychiatric Nursing*.
5,1:31–37.

Shaughnessy, M. P. 1977. Errors and expectations: *A Guide for the Teacher of Basic
Writing*. New York: Oxford University Press.

Shaywitz, S. E., and Shaywitz, B. A. 1988. Attention deficit disorder: Current perspectives. In *Learning Disabilities: Proceedings of the National Conference,* eds.
J. F. Kavanagh and T. J. Truss. Parkton MD: York Press.

Shaywitz, S. E., and Shaywitz, B. A., eds. 1992. *Attention Deficit Disorder Comes of
Age: Toward the Twenty-First Century*. Austin TX: PRO-ED.

Sheffield, B. B. 1991. The structured flexibility of Orton-Gillingham. *Annals of
Dyslexia*. 41:41–54.

Silver, A. A., and Hagin, R. A. 1990. *Disorders of Learning in Childhood*. New York:
John Wiley & Sons.

Silver, L. B. 1992. Diagnosis of attention-deficit hyperactivity disorder in adult life.
Child and Adolescent Psychiatric Clinics of North America. 1:2.

Silver, L. B. 1993. *Dr. Larry Silver's Advice to Parents on Attention-Deficit Hyperactivity Disorder*. Washington, DC: American Psychiatric Press.

Slingerland, B.H. 1971. *A Multi-sensory Approach to Language Arts for Specific
Language Disability Children: A Guide for Primary Teachers*. Cambridge MA:
Educators Publishing Service.

Smith, S. L. 1979. *No Easy Answers: Teaching the Learning Disabled Child*.
Cambridge, MA: Winthrop Publishers, Inc.

Smith, S. L. 1991. *Succeeding against the Odds: How the Learning Disabled Can
Realize Their Promise*. New York: Jeremy P. Archer/Perigee Books/The
Putnam Publishing Group.

Smith, S. L., and illustrated by Booz, B. 1994. *Different is not Bad. Different is the
World: A Book about Disabilities*. Longmont CO: Sopris West.

Spreen, O. 1989. The relationship between learning disability, emotional disorders,
and neuropsychology: Some results and observations. *Journal of Clinical
Experimental Neuropsychology*. 11,1:117–40.

Stanovich, K. E. 1993. The construct validity of discrepancy definitions of reading disability. In *Better Understanding of Learning Disabilities: New Views from
Research and Their Implications for Education and Public Policies*, eds. G. R.

Lyon, D. B. Gray, J. F. Kavanagh, and N. A. Krasegnor. Baltimore: Paul H. Brookes Publishing Co.

Steere, A., Peck, C. Z., and Kahn, L. 1971. *Solving Language Difficulties: Remedial Routines.* Cambridge MA: Educators Publishing Service.

Strauss, A. A., and Lehtinen, L. E. 1947. *Psychopathology and Education of the Brain Injured Child.* Vol. I. New York: Grune & Stratton.

Strauss, A. A., and Kephart, N. C. 1955. *Psychopathology and Education of the Brain Injured Child: Progress in Theory and Clinic.* Vol. II. New York: Grune & Stratton.

Swanson, H. L., ed. 1991. *Handbook on the Assessment of Learning Disabilities: Theory, Research, and Practice.* Austin TX: PRO-ED.

Tallal, P. 1988. Developmental language disorders. In *Learning Disabilities: Proceedings of the National Conference,* eds. J. F. Kavanagh and T. J. Truss. Parkton MD: York Press.

Thomas, A., and Chess, S. 1977. *Temperament and Development.* New York: Brunner/Mazel.

Thorndike, R. L., Hagen, E. P., and Sattler, J. M. 1986. *The Stanford-Binet Intelligence Scale: Fourth Edition.* Guide for Administration and Scoring. Chicago: The Riverside Publishing Company.

Thurber, D. N. 1988. The D'Nealian Pencil Grip. *Communication Outlook, 9,* 4.

Topics in Language Disorders. 1992. Word Finding Problems in Children and Adolescents: Intervention Issues. 13, 1. Butler, K. G. ed. and German, D. J., Issue ed.

Topics in Language Disorders. 1994. From Phonology to Metaphonology: Issues, Assessment, and Intervention. 14,2. Butler, K. G. ed. and Hodson, B. W. Issue ed.

Topics in Language Disorders. 1994. ADD and Its Relationships to Spoken and Written Language. 14, 4. Butler, K. G. ed. and Kavanagh, J. F. and Lyon, G. R., Issue eds.

Trelease, J. 1985. *The Read Aloud Handbook.* New York: Penguin Books.

Vail, P. L. 1981. *Clear and Lively Writing: Language Games and Activities for Everyone.* New York: Walker & Co.

Vail, P. L. 1994. *Emotion: The On Off Switch for Learning.* New York: Walker & Co. Modern Learning Press.

Valletutti, P. 1983. The social and emotional problems of children with learning disabilities. *Learning Disabilities.* II:2. New York: Grune and Stratton.

Voeller, K. K. S. 1994. Techniques for measuring social competence in children. In *Frames of Reference for the Assessment of Learning Disabilities: New Views on Measurement Issues,* ed. G. R. Lyon. Baltimore: Paul H. Brookes Publishing Co.

Vygotsky, L. S. 1962. *Thought and Language.* Cambridge MA: MIT Press.

Wallach, G. P., and Butler, K. G. 1994. *Language Learning Disabilities in School-Age Children and Adolescents: Some Principles and Application.* Riverside NJ: Macmillan Publishing Co.

Wechsler, D. 1991. Manual for the *Wechsler Intelligence Scale for Children—Third Edition* (WISC—III). New York: Psychological Corporation. Harcourt Brace Jovanovich.

Wechsler, D. 1989. Manual for the *Wechsler Preschool and Primary Scale of Intelligence—Revised* (WPPSI-R). New York: Psychological Corporation. Harcourt Brace Jovanovich

Wechsler, D. 1981. Manual for the *Wechsler Adult Intelligence Scale—Revised* (WAIS-R). New York: Psychological Corporation. Harcourt Brace Jovanovich

Weiner, E. S. 1980. Diagnostic evaluation of writing skills. *Journal of Learning Disabilities*, 13,1:48–53.

Wender, P. H. 1987. *The Hyperactive Child, Adolescent, and Adult: Attention Deficit Disorder through the Lifespan.* New York: Oxford University Press.

Werner, H., and Kaplan, B. 1964. *Symbol Formation: An Organismic-Developmental Approach to Language and the Expression of Thought.* New York: John Wiley & Sons.

West, T. G. *In the Mind's Eye: Visual Thinkers, Gifted People with Learning Difficulties, Computer Images, and the Ironies of Creativity.* Buffalo NY: Prometheus Books.

Whiteman, M. F., ed. 1981. *Writing: The Nature, Development, and Teaching of Written Communication.* Vol.1. *Variation in Writing: Functional and Linguistic-Cultural Differences.* Hillsdale NJ: Lawrence Erlbaum Associates.

Wiig, E. H., and Semel, E. M. 1976. *Language Disabilities in Children and Adolescents.* Columbus OH: Charles E. Merrill Publishing Company. A Bell & Howell Company.

Wiig, E. H., and Semel, E. M. 1980. *Learning Assessment and Intervention for the Learning Disabled.* Columbus OH: Charles E. Merrill Publishing Company. A Bell & Howell Company.

Wodrich, D. L. 1994. *Attention Deficit Hyperactivity Disorder: What Every Parent Wants to Know.* Baltimore: Paul H. Brookes Publishing Co.

Zigmond, N. and Cicci, R. 1968. *Auditory Learning.* San Rafael CA: Dimensions in Early Learning.

APPENDIX A
Some Tests to Evaluate Spoken Language

Listed are some tests to evaluate spoken language understanding and production. Each person who assesses language, has tests that are useful to him or her. This list is not meant to be inclusive but rather to suggest some tests that I find useful. No evaluation of a child's or adolescent's language can be made with tests alone. We must always consider the language an individual must have to function at the communicative level he or she needs or wants. Every response made, either to show understanding or to express thoughts and ideas, is considered as part of a spoken language assessment.

Receptive-Expressive Emergent Language Scale. (REEL) Ages birth to 3 years. Bzoch, K. R., and League, R. 1971. Austin TX: PRO-ED. Interview with mother or caregiver regarding specific developmental milestones. See also Manual that accompanies the test: "Assessing Language Skills in Infancy."

Peabody Picture Vocabulary Test-Revised-(PPVT-R) Ages 2-6 to adult. Dunn, L. M., and Dunn, L. M. 1981. Circle Pines MN: American Guidance Service. A measure of receptive single word vocabulary. The person hears a word and is required to select from four pictures the one to represent the word that he or she hears.

Receptive One-Word Picture Vocabulary Test (ROWPVT). Ages 2-9 to 9-11 years. Gardner, M. F. 1985. Novato CA: Academic Therapy Publications. Child selects a picture to represent a word that he or she hears. (Spanish version available.)

Boehm Test of Basic Concepts-Preschool Version. Ages 3 to 5 years. Boehm, A. E. 1986. The Psychological Corporation/Harcourt Brace Jovanovich, Inc. Child hears a spoken word or sentence and points to one of three pictures to show understanding.

Boehm Test of Basic Concepts-Revised. Kindergarten, first, and second grades. Boehm, A. E. 1986. The Psychological Corporation/Harcourt Brace Jovanovich, Inc. Measures concepts and vocabulary typically used by teachers for instruction. The child hears an oral direction and must mark the correct drawing.

Test of Auditory Comprehension of Language-Revised (TACL-R). Ages 2 to 9-11. Carrow-Woolfolk, E. 1985. Chicago: Riverside Publishing Co. Measures single words and syntax understanding. The child hears a word or sentence and points to one of three pictures to represent the word or sentence. (Spanish version available.)

Expressive One-Word Picture Vocabulary Test-Revised. (EOWPVT-R)- Ages 2 to 12. Gardner, M. F. 1990. Novato CA: Academic Therapy Publications. Child sees a picture and names it.

Expressive One-Word Picture Vocabulary Test-Extended. (EOWPVT-UE) Ages 12 through 15 years. Gardner, M.F. 1990. Novato CA: Academic Therapy Publications. Individual names pictures.

Test of Word Finding. (TWF) German, D. J. 1986. Ages 6-6 to 12-11. Chicago: Riverside Publishing Company. Measures child's facility with word finding under various conditions including:
1. Picture Naming: Nouns
2. Sentence Completion Naming
3. Description Naming
4. Picture Naming: Verbs
5. Picture Naming Categories

Carrow Elicited Language Inventory (CELI). Carrow-Woolfolk, E. 1974. Ages 3-0 to 7-11. Chicago: Riverside Publishing Co. Child imitates sentences he or she hears.

Test of Language Development-Primary-(TOLD-P:2) Ages 4-0 to 8-11. Newcomer, P. L. and Hammill, D. D. 1985. Austin TX: PRO-ED. Subtests include:
1. Picture Vocabulary. Child hears a word and selects from four pictures one to represent the word.
2. Vocabulary. Child hears a word and must give two definitions of the word.
3. Grammatic Understanding. Child hears sentence and selects a picture.

4. Sentence Imitation. Child hears a sentence and must repeat it.
5. Grammatic Completion. Child hears a sentence and must complete it using acceptable morphological forms.
6. Word Discrimination. Child hears two words and must tell if they are the same or not.
7. Articulation. Child sees pictures which are used to stimulate him or her to say words containing target sounds

Test of Language Development-Intermediate-2. (TOLD-2:2) Ages 8-6 to 12-11. Newcomer, P. L. and Hammill, D. D. 1985. Austin TX: PRO-ED. Subtests include:
1. Sentence Combining. Child hears two or more sentences and must combine them into a single sentence
2. Generals. Child hears words and must provide a category word that tells how the words are alike.
3. Vocabulary. Child hears two words and must tell if the two words mean the same, are opposite, or have no relationship to each other
4. Word Ordering. Child hears words and must arrange them in order to form a sentence.
5. Grammatic Comprehension. Child hears sentences and must tell if they are correct or if they contain an error.
6. Malapropisms. Child hears a sentence and must identify incorrect word usage.

Test of Adolescent and Adult Language-Third Edition. (TOAL-3) Ages 12 to 25 years. Hammill, D. D.; Brown, V. L.; Larsen, S. C. & Wiederholt, J.L. 1981, 1987. Austin TX: Pro-ED. Subtests measure:
1. Listening—understanding of speech.
2. Speaking—oral expression of ideas.
3. Reading—understanding printed language.
4. Writing—ability to express thoughts through writing.
5. Spoken Language—ability to listen and speak
6. Written Language—ability to read and write
7. Vocabulary—ability to understand use of words for communication.
8. Grammar—ability to understand and generate syntactic and morphological structures.
9. Receptive Language—ability to understand both spoken and written language
10. Expressive Language—ability to produce written and spoken language.

Clinical Evaluation of Language Fundamentals-Preschool (CELF-Preschool)—Ages 3-0 to 6-11. Wiig, E. H, Secord, W., and Semel, E. 1992. The Psychological Corporation/Harcourt Brace Jovanovich. Includes receptive and expressive measures:

Receptive Language Subtests:
1. Linguistic Concepts. Child points to animals as they are named and with verbal concepts (for example *either, next to, after*) presented
2. Sentence Structure. Child hears sentences and must select a picture from an array of pictures to represent each sentence.
3. Basic Concepts. The child sees pictures and must select the one that represents what is heard (such as *This boy is happy. This one is sad.*)

Expressive Language Subtests
1. Recalling Sentences in Context. A story, accompanied by pictures and with the story characters making comments, is read to the child who must repeat what a character just has said.
2. Formulating Labels. The child is shown pictures and must provide a noun or verb to tell about the picture.
3. Word Structure. The child must complete sentences using structures such as plurals and correct verb tense.

*Clinical Evaluation of Language Fundamentals-Revised (CELF-R)— Ages 5-7 to 16-11. Semel, E., Wiig, E. H., and Secord, W. 1986. The Psychological Corporation. Includes subtests for measuring syntax, semantics, and memory.
1. Linguistic Concepts—assesses comprehension of concepts related to inclusion, exclusion, coordination, time, condition, and quantity; child must follow oral directions with various colored lines.
2. Word Structure—assesses knowledge of word structure rules in and expressive task; child sees pictures and must complete sentences—tests awareness of morphological endings.
3. Sentence Structure—assesses comprehension of structural rules at the sentence level; child selects picture to represent a sentence heard.
4. Oral Directions—assesses comprehension, recall, and execution of oral commands of increasing length and complexity; child carries out oral directions involving geometric shapes using color, size and shape.
5. Formulated Sentences—assesses formulation of simple compound, and complex sentences; child is given a word, or words to use in sentence. Picture is provided to be used if the child wishes.
6. Recalling Sentences—assesses recall and reproduction of surface structure as a function of syntactic complexity; child repeats sentences heard.
7. Word Classes—assesses the ability to categorize words that are related or words that are unrelated by semantic classes, opposites, spatial, or temporal features; child hears words and must tell the two that go together.

*CELF-Third Edition is scheduled for publication, fall 1995.

8. Sentence Assembly—assesses the ability to assemble syntactic structures into grammatically acceptable and semantically meaningful sentences; child sees phrase cards and arranges them in order to form two sentence
9. Semantic Relations—assesses interpretation of semantic relationships (temporal, spatial, passive, comparative) in spoken sentences;
10. Word Associations—assesses recall of labels for members of a semantic class within a time limit; child hears word and must tell words to fit in that category
11. Listening to Paragraphs—assesses comprehension, recall, and interpretation of factual data presented in spoken paragraphs; child listens to story and answers questions

Woodcock-Johnson Psychoeducational Battery-Revised (WJ-R)(selected subtests for spoken Language). Preschool through Adult. Woodcock, R. W. and Johnson, M. B. 1989. Chicago: Riverside Publishing Company.
From *WJ-R Tests of Cognitive Ability*
1. Picture Vocabulary—individual is shown pictures and asked to name them
2. Antonyms and Synonyms—word is given orally and individual provides antonym or synonym
3. Analogies—Individual completes the second pair in two two-word pairs
4. Listening Comprehension—a passage is heard and the final word must be supplied to indicate understanding of the passage.
5. Memory for Sentences—repeats sentences
From *WJ-R Tests of Achievement.*
General Knowledge: provides answers to general information questions about: Science, Social Studies, and Humanities
Mathematics:
1. Applied Problems—word problems that are read to the individual to be solved. The word problem is presented in print so that the child can read along with what is heard and for some problems the visual support of pictures is present. Auditory memory does not have to be relied on to solve the problems.
2. Quantitative Concepts—assesses knowledge of vocabulary and concepts related to math

The Test of Language Competence-Expanded Edition, Levels 1 and 2. Wiig. E. H. and Secord, W. 1989. Ages 5-0 to 18-11. Chicago: Riverside Publishing Company.
1. Ambiguous Sentences—the individual must tell two meanings of such sentences as "The elephant is ready to lift."

2. Listening Comprehension—Making Inferences: the person hears and reads two statements—an introductory one and concluding one—and must decide which two heard and read sentences could account for the outcome.
3. Oral Expression—Recreating Sentences: three words are presented and the person is shown a picture. He or she must make a sentence telling what one of the characters might have said about the situation
4. Figurative Language—requires both interpretation in one's own words of figurative statements (such as "He is crazy about that pet") and selecting from printed and heard statements what the statement means.

Lindamood Auditory Conceptualization Test (LAC). Lindamood, C. and Lindamood, P. 1971. Chicago: Riverside Publishing Company. Measures auditory perception of speech sounds (perception of speech phonemes) and can be used with any age individual.

Fisher-Logemann Test of Articulation Competence. Fisher, H. B. and Logemann, J. A. 1971. Chicago: Riverside Publishing Company. Assesses production of speech sounds by showing individual pictures to be named or sentences to be read.

APPENDIX B

Some Publishers of Language and Educational Tests
The Psychological Corporation. Harcourt Brace & Co. 555 Academic
   Court, San Antonio TX 78204-2498. 1-800-228-0752.
The Riverside Publishing Company. 8420 Bryn Mawr Avenue, Chicago IL
   60631. 1-800-323-9540.
PRO-Ed. 8700 Shoal Creek Boulevard, Austin Texas 78757-6897. 512-451-
   3246.

Some Publishers of Instructional Materials
Thinking Publications, 424 Galloway Street, P.O. Box 163, Eau Clair WI
   54702-0163. 1-800-225-GROW
Educators Publishing Service, Inc. 31 Smith Place, Cambridge MA 02138-
   1000. 1-800-225-5750.
Communications Skill Builders. 3830 East Bellevue., P.O. Box 42050-E93,
   Tucson AZ 85733. 602-323-7500.
LinguiSystems, 3100 4th Avenue, P.O. Box 747, East Moline IL 61244-0747.
   1-800-776-5332
Franklin Learning Resources. 122 Burrs Road, Mt. Holly NJ 08060. 1-800-
   525-9673

INDEX